I0044842

Rent Your Way To Freedom

Live Well Now While You Build Your Future

Second Edition

ERIC NIES

KEN Family Project Management
Cincinnati, Ohio

Cover

Picture: Eric Nies, February 2018

Citations:

"About half of Americans are not able to come up with $2,000 in 30 days."

Dubner, S. J. (November 22, 2017 @ 11:00pm). *Is America Ready for a "No-Lose Lottery"? (Update)*. Retrieved from http://freakonomics.com: http://freakonomics.com/podcast/say-no-no-lose-lottery-rebroadcast/

"American homeownership has fallen from a high of 68% to the current 63%. It is projected to hit 60.8% by 2025.

"Housing rental rates will surge over the long term: … 7.3 million of the 12.5 million net new households created over the next decade will rent. The sharing economy continues to deemphasize owning, so we expect more and more households to rent and current homeowners to become renters sooner than usual late in life…."

John Burns. (2016). Demographic Strategies for Real Estate. Washington, D.C: John Burns Real Estate Consulting.

Dedication

To my father, who taught me love of houses.

To my mother, who took care of houses.

To Jaybird, who inspired me to this write this book.

To my loved ones gaining freedom in their relationship with housing.

To my wife, for bringing me to the awareness that a mortgage is debt!

To all my landlords, who have been so good to me.

ISBN-13: 978-1-73210-571-3

Table of Contents

NOTES

When I talk about a house or renting or housing expense in general, I'm talking about the primary residence. Property, as a side investment, is a completely different story.

In many places, I use 9% or 9.5%as a market interest rate. That's because:
"The average annualized total return for the S&P 500 index over the past 90 years is 9.8 percent."

A 3.5% factor seemed to be a decent current long-term average of the mortgage interest price (even low). I used different rates, but never over 5% – which is not outlandish. The higher the mortgage interest, the less favorable ownership tends to be.

As a writing style I use the personal pronouns "you" and "I" very often. That does NOT *mean* YOU, *personally, as in the second person singular; rather, it is in the collective sense of you, in plural.*

My opinion is based on the housing situation, as I see it, in America. However, every situation, town and city, is different – down to the person and piece of property.

While this is based on my research, it is also based on my opinion and view. Though I am educated as an economist, I am not a financial adviser of any sort. I just present my conclusions and my views based on my perspective and research.

The research and perspective wades deeper than most would care to consider (it's certainly more than I ever considered when making my decisions to buy), but it is not exhaustive. There are many, many tax, accounting, and financial details of which I am not aware and have not researched. Those details can have significant impact to debunk my views and change the outcome.

Any information or ideas gained here are: USE AT YOUR OWN RISK.

Everyone's situation is different. Make your own decisions. Do your own research. If for nothing other than the location freedom and quality of life, my decision to be a "renter by choice" has worked out.

I hope this information renews your convictions, whatever they may be, or opens another perspective.

Foreword

Rent Your Way to Freedom was brought to my attention in the Fall of 2018 in connection with data showing that renting and reinvesting will "outperform owning and building equity in terms of wealth creation." This data was quoted in articles and released in association with my role as President of the American Real Estate Society, in collaboration with the Real Estate Initiative at the College of Business at Florida Atlantic University,

In 2018, emerging data began to show that "16 of the 23 cities covered in the Buy-vs-Rent index are in rent territory. "Across all of the data for the Index going back to 1982, only 49 times has a market in any given quarter been at this score or higher." This information bucked the trend and historic perception of homeownership and its role in personal asset and wealth development.

We've heard over and again: why rent when you can own? Or, don't throw your money away on rent. Don't rent property from someone else - you should always own. These and many other axioms have been offered up over the years as near absolute truths and have often gone unquestioned. The default belief is that all should own rather than rent. But, is this really true?

The national mania towards homeownership served the country well for years because property prices tended to rise steadily and typically at a faster rate than rents on comparable properties. In addition, alternative investments such as the stock market were, until recently out of reach for most individuals, thus leaving ownership an easy winner over renting. To be clear, as alternative investments have become more accessible, the debate is now between renting and reinvesting versus owning and building wealth through home equity accumulation.

While there have always been real estate cycles, national and local, they have (with exceptions for a few costal areas) been on the mild side…until the bursting of the residential real estate bubble in the latter part of the first decade of the 21st century. The ensuing decade produced another long cycle, which now appears to be peaking again in 2018, bringing the issue of timing clearly into the question.

The housing market has been strong. However, those who bought at the peak just before the bubble burst may still own a property that holds a current value less than its original purchase price; while those that bought in 2012 (which hindsight has shown was the clear bottom of the cycle) are reaping significant gains. All else equal and despite the strong housing market, renting and reinvesting was clearly the winning choice for those making a housing decision in (and just prior to) 2008. However, owning and accumulating equity was a better wealth creation strategy for those making a housing decision in 2012.

Thus, the choice of owning (and building equity) versus renting (and reinvesting elsewhere) is not so straight forward any longer in large part due to where you buy in the real estate cycle. Additionally, though less discussed and often overlooked in the quest toward ownership, there have always been issues of mobility, lifestyle preference, and savings discipline that throw the rent vs own decision into unclear waters. *Rent Your Way to Freedom* explores these issues in detail, encouraging deeper consideration of the rent vs buy alternative.

Due to increasingly high mobility rates and the persistent costs of selling/buying, it may clearly be more reasonable for those with shallower roots to rent rather than buy. For very disciplined savers, the performance of alternative investments might be outpacing property appreciation, making renting the optimal choice for wealth accumulation. For skilled and shrewd evaluators, well-bought and tightly managed home ownership investments can pay off in a rising market.

Of course, none of these things happen in isolation, making the decision to rent and reinvest versus own and build equity a very conditional question. That is, the answer could vary from one individual to another depending on circumstances. Clearly, we now face a not so straightforward decision matrix when it comes to housing choice and wealth accumulation.

A simple Rent-vs-Buy calculator doesn't always do the trick. Regardless, some celebrity "financial advisers" espouse a near de-facto recommendation towards the traditional "purchase and pay-off" approach. They prescribe home ownership, with a house paid off sooner than later, as the absolute best choice.

The power of *Rent Your Way to Freedom* is that it explores many different scenarios and asks that its readers simply consider some increasingly obvious alternatives, which are well laid out in a straight forward read.

Going forward, in America, we will all have to make better economic decisions as we become more responsible for our own investment choices. *Rent Your Way to Freedom* sets its readers on a path to making more informed investment housing choices. It is a highly recommended read.

Ken H. Johnson, Ph.D.

Real Estate Economist

American Real Estate Society -- President

Florida Atlantic University

Country Dream Realized

A friend, upon reading the first versions of this book, shared her story. She explained: "A house is a bad investment, and I know that. It's just that I lived through it and am still living it. And we do it anyway.

"We had great reasons to [buy]: more kids than average, homeschooling, happy to literally die in this house on 8 acres with a pool. But it's a bad investment and we'll be 76 and 81 when it's paid off – having paid a fortune in interest and being house poor these first few years in it. It's frightening…

"But seriously, even with the economic situations in 2001 and 2008 eating up our 401(k), we would have been better off NOT *buying our last house and investing that money instead.*

"We lived in our previous home 17 years, paid $130K for it and sold for $200K. So, in 17 years, we profited *something like $40K – after all the expenses (lawn service, lawn mower, putting on a deck, putting on a roof, so much more) not to mention fees of owning, buying, selling, refinancing twice, realtor fees, taxes, etc.*

"And this is with my husband being a DIY guy. The fees would easily be double on many things if he had not been able to fix our sinks and toilets, put on our roof himself with the help of the kids, etc.

"So we used that $40K to buy 4 acres of land (honestly, just so someone would not build a house right on top of us in the country). But wouldn't that have been better in the long run if it had been invested?

"That land will increase in value, a tiny bit, but that's all, and it's going to take a long time, then, just to find a buyer. When I think of the interest paid on our other house and what we will pay on new house, it drives me batty.

"So yes, we are a special case with our country dream realized. But people in their 20s and 30s REALLY *need to check out your book. It makes a lot of sense, and I'll be handing each of my five children (who might have had college savings accounts if we had rented instead of buying our home) a copy!"*

Preface

I originally wrote this book in late 2009 – in the wake of the Housing Crisis, at a time when it was rather easy to take a potshot at housing. As hindsight would show us and if buying low is the right thing to do, buying a home between 2010 and 2012 might have been ideal. However, hindsight is somewhat irrelevant for people who plan their home purchase with a life event such as getting married, moving jobs, or changing schools.

Here in late 2017 as I write this, news outlets such as *USA Today* are ripe with headlines such as: "Renting homes is overtaking the housing market."[1] Alternatively, others say: "The biggest mistake Millennials are making is not buying a home."[2]

Yet, the pendulum is swinging back toward renting. Homeownership hit a high near 68% during George W. Bush's administration. It's now at 63% and on its way lower[3].

What is happening and why might this book be of interest to you?

Housing is one of the most significant contributors to quality of life and the largest investment/expenditure most people ever make. Thinking deeply about the rent vs. purchase options can help one more fully consider the housing expense as a component of lifestyle preferences and a long-term wealth plan.

Popular news articles tell us that rentals, even of single-family homes, have increased by 30% in the last three years.[4] They don't, however, typically have the space to dig through the subtleties of why renting may not only be more appealing, but why it might even be (contrary to popular opinion) a wise financial move.

Yes, it's true! Renting could be a BETTER financial and personal decision than buying!

What is going on here?

For decades, we've been led to believe that buying is the best investment we can make. Many financial gurus advise that working to be able to live in a paid-off house is a primary goal of attaining financial peace in life.

True? Is the rent vs. buy decision purely a financial matter or is it a lifestyle choice? Could it be a mix of both? Can freedom be found in renting?

We associate renting with sacrifice (which it may be), but not all sacrifices are necessarily negative.

Sacrifice might indeed be a very positive thing when viewed in the light of giving up something of a lower nature in order to get something of a higher nature. The famous Marshmallow Experiment, a Stanford University study demonstrating the value of deferred gratification, comes to mind. It showed that those who defer early gratification (delaying the reward of one free marshmallow in favor of waiting for second) prove to have better life outcomes.[5]

Since my original draft, I have updated this book with my additional data, insights, and experiences. However, where I generally completed my original analysis based on long-term data (like 30-year data plus), I have kept some of the analysis from the Census Bureau dating back to 1940. That data stands the test of time, even amid tectonic shifts in the economy.

We'll take a deep dive to consider the fully purchased house as more of a luxury to be retained *after* achieving financial freedom, rather than the conventional view of the house being a means to wealth.

We'll look at the renting of a house as a means to access nicer homes and reduce expenses (yes, you read that right: nicer and less costly) while meanwhile freeing up cash for other investments.

Thanks to different accounting rules and the investment horizon, we'll see how you can win as a renter at the same time the landlord is also making money.

We'll also learn how reduced expenses (lower housing costs) leave room for financial options that appreciate faster than a house would and also for compound wealth – winning financial freedom.

I'm no financial adviser, but I've researched and crunched some numbers. I'm very aware that plenty of people have made hundreds of thousands, if not millions, on their house. I know, and it is clear, that you *can* make money on your house. Heck, I've even owned a home – on which I made money. But, over time, I have grown more attuned to the value of renting.

I've come to find renting is NOT as bad as it is often maligned. In fact, it is even cheaper than owning in many cases.

I've also found that owning and renting are both, in a sense, "throwing money away" [in housing expenses].

I've come to find that houses do not appreciate (net after expenses) as much as one might hope and that other investments can more effectively increase wealth over the long term.

While I've seen plenty of people make some money buying, owning, and selling their house, I've also seen others desperately "underwater."

I've noticed that making money on a house has as much to do with the purchase price as it does with the selling price. As they say, "well bought is half sold."

How we use our money, either by over-spending on houses and the "stuff" to go in 'em, or by controlling expenses and building investments, has a tremendous difference on an individual's wealth account.

No doubt, a house can be a great place to "make money," but it's not true for everyone.

It seems many people feel inferior as "renters." It's as if they are wearing a "Scarlet Letter" and are somehow second-class compared to the owners' "Red Letter Day."

In my experience, there's more to the story.

Renters might actually have a great deal more freedom than owners and are quite likely able to get themselves on a path to building wealth, through true investments, more easily than can a homeowner, who may be strapped to and bled dry by a mortgage payment.

My experience with renting has grown since 2009 and many things have changed to make renting far easier now than it was historically. This book is as much about an alternate path to financial freedom as it is a lifestyle choice.

Three Themes

There are three basic recurring themes to this book:

1) Don't buy a house until you can afford it – it's a luxury;
2) A house is not the asset you think it is – it's housing;
3) There are other, better ways to invest.

This is not an anti-ownership brigade as much as it is a pro-rental endorsement. That is NOT because I have a vested interest in real estate as an investment, of any kind. In fact, in full disclosure, I currently own zero percent interest in real estate of any kind – except perhaps through some shares deep inside some mutual fund or deep within a 401(k).

However, that does not mean I believe people should not own or owning is bad. Indeed, everyone should aspire to own something, but people should do it at the right time.

To that end, renting should *not* be maligned. Government (tax) policy could be changed to establish renting as a solid and financially responsible alternative to contribute toward good, stable, and safe housing – as a home!!!

I currently rent a chateau in Belgium. The owner wants to sell it to me, but I'm holding off. I prefer renting! Why? Many reasons, but just consider one rhetorical question: if he's making money off of me, as well as appreciation, why would he want to sell it to me as his standing offer to me would suggest he does? One day, maybe I will buy it. For now, it's…

All good things in time!

Introduction

Over time, I have grown out of love with owning houses and in love with renting them. Not only out of personal preference for the freedom renting provides, but also because I have witnessed so much financial and personal loss over homeownership.

As a wedding present, a dear friend gave me David Bach's book *Smart Couples Finish Rich*[6]. I didn't get through the Introduction before learning that "financial infidelity," or even straight-up stress over money matters, is the leading cause of divorce. That is a powerful life lesson that has stuck with me.

Another great financial life lesson comes from George Samuel Clason, author of the classic *The Richest Man in Babylon*[7]. He teaches the value of compound interest as a secret to wealth accumulation: start early and only spend from the interest on the interest.

It wasn't one year into my marriage and I understood exactly why my friend had given me Bach's book – he was getting a divorce! It seems the book was his way of giving a fair warning about money management. Now in our eighteenth year of marriage, I more profoundly understand the value of building wealth. Life is more expensive than we can imagine.

There have been tight times in our marriage and financial stress is indeed tough. But my wife and I have always had a shared vision on life, money, and how we spend/invest. On the other hand, my friend and his ex-wife were divided.

Knowing them, I guess he actually read Bach's book and had a difficult time getting his wife to crack the cover. She is like many of us who want to believe they know everything just from the soundbites.

As their practical counsellor over the years, I know they disagreed on both saving and spending. Innocent enough in small matters, the failed alignment showed up when the going got tough.

Their marriage had started in the mid-90's with reasonable enough housing and it ended in the early 21st Century divided over a $1M mansion. Ironically, they accessed both houses in the way most would dream. As some sort of a modern day upper-class dowry, her father provided them rent-free housing.

I tell their story as an opener specifically because it is an extreme case. Clearly, not everyone is like this; but their story is instructive because extremes point a spotlight.

The mansion, their second house, was in perfect condition when they moved in. Bought from a reputable doctor, there was practically zero deferred maintenance. It was a massive upgrade from their first home and her father provided it rent-free as a helping hand to their growing family. Her dad paid the mortgage. All they had to do was live in it and pay the maintenance, taxes, and utilities.

Their scenario was what most people spend their life working toward: the hope of getting a house "paid-off" and living in it "rent-free." Though they'd arrived to the panacea, the "keep up with the Joneses" pressure overwhelmed them.

He wanted to squirrel away investments into the corporate-sponsored stock plan. She wanted more stuff to complete the package: cars, clothes, and private schools for children, along with the house.

Expenses were high all the way around. They lived to the edge of their means and were unable to save money or build wealth. The house they occupied was a point of personal pride, even if acquired as a gift. *Note: rent-free housing as a gift may seem strange, but providing use of stuff (or even free baby-sitting of the grandkids) is one way parents pass wealth and give a helping hand.*

Their situation typifies the two extremes of the housing paradigm. He saw it as something to be accessed within their means, after paying themselves first in an investment account. She, like many of us, had her identity and self-worth inextricably linked to the house, at all costs.

He grew up in a middle-class environment, paid his way through college, and saved/invested in his corporate-sponsored stocks and 401(k).

She grew up in a rich environment. She didn't finish college, and she never worried about money (until she got married).

They lived in the starter house rent-free for a few years. It was not perfect by any means and was nothing to build a self-image around, but it was nice enough and in a great neighborhood. With one full bath and three kids, it was growing tight.

Generously enough, as their family grew, they were upgraded to the mansion – the one that eventually broke them.

Her father bought the place in 1997 for $850,000. The idea was that they would live in a bigger, nicer house in which to raise their family, rent-free, while they built savings. She loved the idea. He could see the writing on the wall and was reluctant. They lived in the mansion – rent-free – for only about three years before divorcing.

During that period, ancillary expenses high and no savings accumulated, somewhat out of the blue, her father dropped the whole weight of the place on them – they were soon to be sunk.

He had them on the hook living in it and turned it over to them for $925,000 in 2001. It was for a higher price than what he had paid, but he required no down payment of them. In essence, they got the place, including a 20% gift of about $180,000.

Her dad felt he'd done them a massive favor with a few years of rent-free living along the way and a nice gift, but it was a poisoned chalice.

There was no change in behavior or shift in perspective, although something massive had changed in their situation. The outcome was a forgone conclusion, as they would soon be up to their eyeballs in housing expenses/debt, which is all too common these days. He wanted to sell, downsize, and take the cash. She wasn't going anywhere… it was going to take dragging her out of there, kicking and screaming.

They got in a house that was too big for their financial britches, too early. They could have cashed out and liquidated as he wanted to access the "gift" and get to a lower cost base, but that was not meant to be. Like the frog bathing in some warm water (the fire underneath bringing the pot to a boil), it eventually boiled their situation. Just as frogs don't jump out, we too don't tend to take drastic measures either – after all, it's our house!

Stress mounted. What started out as a nice gesture ended badly. Like most of us, they could afford life. They had enough money at the end of the month, but there was not enough left over for the retirement savings he wanted and all the stuff and lifestyle she wanted. The divide was deep. Credit card bills slowly mounted and the divorce ensued.

She got the house and he moved out – compromising some of his deep "till death do us part" beliefs. The income remained the same. With a second housing expense to cover between them, that meant even less to go around.

It's not just them. Our identities are tied to bricks and mortar. Houses easily become a pattern of attachment.

Another guy down the street, after selling his house, was literally forced out by the police – he'd inherited the place that looked something like Tara from *Gone With the Wind*, but he could not afford it.

Then, there's Stone Cliff. This place was built by a bootlegger during prohibition era, something out of *The Great Gatsby*. It was amazing – at one time. But, the house overtook the owner. When it went up for sale the house tour (for which they literally organize busses) was shocking. You had rooms full of lamps, literally, and others full of old vinyl records. The owner wouldn't detach. The house, massive as it was, was so stuffed with crap that overflowed into the yard. Parked out front was a *Brady Bunch*-era station wagon packed full of more stuff and papers. I never knew a car could be used as a storage unit.

These owners, again extreme cases to shine the spotlight, refused to detach. They possessed the houses – or should I say the houses possessed them.

The woman in the first case stayed in her home scraping along for another ten years or so before being forced to sell as drops in income and alimony took their toll during The Great Recession. Her life was a constant complaint about money problems. Yet the solution was right in front of her and all around her.

Not willing to solve the problem by downsizing, she, as many do, justified staying in the place (which she'd landed in too early) under the pretense of providing a "family home" for her kids. I can tell you, the kids would have been fine (perhaps even better off) with less financial stress – even if it meant a smaller house.

Between them they had not only two separate houses to maintain, but also the kids' school and college fees over which to disagree. If they'd found alignment on housing and spending, life might have been different. But alas, mindsets were inflexibly set... like bricks and mortar. He didn't like the idea of divorcing but just could not go on. So he drastically detached from the situation.

His next house was a purchase supported by the second income from his new wife. He got on reciting his daily positive affirmations expressing the joy of being freed from his "million dollar jail."

When she eventually sold the house she got a little over a million, walking away with approximately $150K – after paying off the 1st and 2nd mortgages. But she was still attached. The new owners had to forcibly remove her, literally, crying and screaming.

Consider that! After nearly ten years of ownership and contribution to a mortgage all the while, she only got back what effectively amounts to the original down payment. There was no return. Effectively, she threw away money on "rent," in the form of a mortgage, for ten years.

Her next step was a rental.

Finally, she had some cash that *could* have been invested. If invested in the market, that $150,000 of hers would have grown 41% between June 2014 and 2018 to $211,500. But, rather than investing it or setting it aside for the kids' education, she earmarked it as a down payment for a new house.

As will happen with many of us, the equity was burning a hole in her pocket. Free to leave her rental on 30 days' notice, she eventually plunked down the money for a house. Though far more reasonable than the previous mansion, she once again found herself "house poor" and stressed with no capital or cushion invested. To top it off, soon after, she found herself battling with contractors over kitchen improvements.

For her, it was out of one expensive mess and into another. She remains stressed to this day, trying to subsidize the kids' college and lamenting the absence of the mansion she once had.

He, on the other hand, remains downsized in a modest house and is apparently happy while he builds his investment account.

He has not "Rented [His] Way to Freedom," but he does sit comfortably in a reasonable ranch home, supported by the dual income with his new wife.

Rented or bought, he has applied an important key: he kept housing expenses low and built investments on the side.

She was, for a moment, well positioned with a pool of funds for investments to "Rent [Her] Way to Freedom" on a single income. She could have been building her future investment portfolio. However, she could not resist the siren's call of her homeownership paradigm. So, she shopped and shopped until she bought.

Now she is strapped again with no plan in place for building a retirement. She has all her eggs in her new house basket.

Who knows…? Ownership might not be a bad thing for her. Though not accumulating much, all the expenses keep her on a short purse string unable to afford much else.

He, on the other hand, might find himself well-off enough owning, as long as he continues to pay himself first in the form of investments.

If she'd been able to keep the mansion, she might have made more money in the strong housing market from 2014-2018. But she couldn't service the mortgage debt. She was forced to sell and take up a rental. She could have stayed in the rental and used the 'down payment' to build a cushion for herself. She didn't.

Growing earnings is a key part of putting some space between earnings and expenses. Life is not about simply reducing expenses. She needed more. Similarly pressed, people are taking up "side hustles" as part of the new normal in today's economy. To get ahead, people make sacrifices and do more. Millionaires tend to have multiple sources of income. They also have assets. Sangeet Badal reports from Gallup that 10% of the people own 84% of the stocks[8]. Getting something else growing on the side is the key to having more.

Consider housing from another angle. A decision to control housing expenses, in order to leave space to invest, could create a virtual "side hustle," generating a passive income in the background.

Everyone wants another $100 to $500 per month of passive income. Right? Thing is, an investment account of $10,000 or $50,000 could generate that and more! So, just get a $50,000 investment account started and you have what most strive for from a side hustle.

Nonetheless, the $24,000 question remains: where do we get $10,000 or $50,000?

In her case, we have an example. That $150,000 she had could have been generating nearly $1,200 per month of income. Viewed as a "side hustle," this could have subsidized a fair bit of rent. Instead, her money sat there waiting to get tied up in the down payment. She decided to buy, yes, because she wanted her own house with a vision of security down the road, but she justified the purchase because a mortgage payment was $500 less per month than the rent. In essence, she exchanged the down payment and got the house. She gave up $1,500 per month of side hustle income in favor of $500 "savings" on rent.

She got the house, yes! She got a lower monthly payment and fewer bathrooms too. She also got a ton of other (what I call "New House Tax") expenses to go along with it. She went from being in a bigger nice-enough rental, with money in the bank, to having buyer's remorse and stress from being "house poor."

However, she wanted a house. She had to have it. And maybe the house, with all the projects that give her something to sink her energy into, will appreciate…?

Now, before some kettle calls my pot black, I've got to admit: I too struggle with the same thing. I look at MLS listings all the time. I get tempted to buy, even if I'm not living in the same city, state, or country as the listing. Daily at the store and online, I make consumption decisions that put a preference toward spending now, as opposed to deferred reward later.

I don't do all the exact calculations on every dollar, but I know that spending now means less savings, now, which means less retirement in the future. Fine! I know that. However, I justify because I rent. I have my cash invested. My "down payment" is invested in the market and it's growing there for retirement. It could be invested in other places besides the market. There are even better investments than a 401(k) or low-cost fund, but those are simple enough for now to grow, and my asset pool is growing, every month. I pay myself first, adding more to my income-generating "side hustle" (otherwise known as my automatic deposit to my investment account). I live more freely renting, unattached to housing.

In the end, just because one side is right doesn't necessary mean the other is wrong. Life is a series of choices. You may land on one side of the argument or the other. Homeownership and the market may not work out for him, but the house alone might for her. Maybe rental plus investments would have been better for her. Who knows what the future holds? That's why we have Bears and Bulls. Two people look at the same thing and see something different.

You may side with him, or her. You may side with ownership or rental. But either way, the point is: renting leaves your down payment available for you. You can access comparable housing as a rental more cheaply than purchased. With more liquid investments working in your favor on the side providing calm and security, renting can be a great solution to give people the means to finally start investing for compound growth.

Not six months into ownership, she was already back at the bank looking for second mortgage. I guess the kitchen renovation was calling. And that's the dangerous part. Houses are expensive. Uncontrolled consumption plus chasing a certain kind of lifestyle equals mounting debt!

Save now, build investments first, and buy stuff later.

In the book we'll explore all these issues more deeply, including the idea that you're throwing away money as either rent or mortgage. Consider: she didn't make anything on the house though she paid the mortgage, principal, and interest every single month.

There are multiple approaches to life's preferences, housing decisions, and finances. These are very personal choices. Do what you want! My friends did that. She did it her way and he did it his. I do it mine.

However, what we consistently see is that starting investments early grows wealth over time, and buying a house too early tends to strap people to a lifetime of house poor servitude. Keeping our biggest expense, housing costs, low can leave more cash freely available for application to investment accounts that grow – free from anchors of homeownership, including the mortgage, property tax, and maintenance.

Sure, you can flip houses and make money on them as you move. That is doable. People can and do make money on houses.

But, you can also **Rent Your Way To Freedom** and enjoy these benefits:

- keep your wealth building in an investment account
- have better cash flow and fewer monthly obligations
- access nicer housing (*by definition, people who can't afford to buy at any price are at least able to rent*)
- build a bigger investment account in the long term
- have more freedom from and fewer obligations to bricks and mortar

You can do those things with ownership too, as long as you keep your costs low.

But what I find, as do 60% of the new households being created these days, is that renting provides more freedom and greater liberty.

Maybe you will find that too!

Lifestyle Freedom

Take my Polish-born, London resident friend who at one point also spent time in Connecticut. She, now in her mid-life, just bought her first home.

Actually, she bought a year earlier and spent twelve months of renovation effort. Finally moved in, she's ecstatic about the place she crafted as the fruit of her dreams. She believed in a vacation vibe as home and created that in the middle of London. The house has clapboard window shutters reminiscent of Bombay and a view of the water harbor.

When I first heard she bought, a cool settled over me. I cringed inside. I was thinking: "If only she knew" the house is NOT a great investment.

What I've come to find out is that she did know and her story exemplifies two major points: 1) renting buys freedom; and 2) buy when you're ready.

Interestingly, she didn't jump right into homeownership. At the outset of life, she didn't know where she wanted to be. The idea of tying down roots with a house and mortgage was not something she wanted to do. Live in London or move back to Poland, the path wasn't clear? Every time she was in one place, she missed the other.

Even if all her childhood friends bought houses and her family-centric Polish background encourages ownership, she didn't go down that path. She valued freedom – freedom to live where and how she wanted, according to the pace of her life. Her friends in her home country have constricted options, tied to the ball-and-chain of a mortgage. In Renting [Her] Freedom, she has experienced the world. Maybe she's missed out on other things in the homeland, but it seems renting has been both a good lifestyle and financial choice for her.

As mentioned in other places, mid-life (age 40 +/-) seems an ideal time to buy. It has worked for her. Before buying, she rented – exclusively. Though she'd considered buying a couple different times along the way, what she'd found was that, at those stages, all she could afford to buy was some kind of dingy one-bedroom house in a less than ideal location. So she didn't. As she says, "I realized I could rent a nicer place than what I could afford to buy."

She applied herself to her profession, shaped her thinking, and worked on building capital until she found and could afford a house of her dreams.

Numbers Previewed

For starters and though we'll dig through much more later, it might be worthwhile to put a few numbers on the table to explore how renting can be cheaper/better financially than owning, even when the average mortgage ($1,190/month) on the median home is *less* than the median average rent ($1,468/month)[9].

First, in renting, you don't pay property taxes and maintenance which are roughly 1% per year or $312/month – each – on a $375,000 house. Those "hidden costs" quickly make ownership more costly than we think. Add both of those to the average $1,190 monthly mortgage and you get to $1,814 per month for the house. That's about $346 *more* per month to hold a house than the average $1,468/month rent. That's one way houses can be more expensive than renting.

Next. Appreciation, it doesn't grow as fast as we believe.

As reported by Lisa Smith on Investopeida.com, *The Truth About Real Estate Prices*[10], we all want to see the average 6.4% annual housing appreciation over the 36-year period from 1968 to 2004, for example, with no decline in any year. However, the full picture is not so rosy. The reality is: housing saw significant declines before and after that period. The long-term average is NOT 6.4%, but rather something less. Below we use 4.5%.

As a preview to what we'll explore in the following chapters, here are some numbers to consider.

For argument's sake and to keep it simple, let's assume the mortgage and/or rent on a $375,000 home (the average selling price was $375,500 in the 3rd quarter of 2017[11]) was the same. That is to say, let's say we could get a place, purchased or rented, for the same monthly payment. That's not the actual case, because ownership is more expensive overall, but let's assume parity on cost.

Then, let's compare appreciation on a $375,000 home versus what the corresponding 20% (or $75,000) down payment would do if invested.

A compound interest calculator shows $75,000 invested in the market, at the average long-term rate of 9.5%, earns less in year one than does the appreciation on a house – generously calculated at 4.5%. In year one, the investment account grows $7,125 in interest versus the house gaining $16,875 of appreciation[12]. So, the house wins – right?

Well, maybe…

If a house is just "housing" and the investment profile doesn't matter; we can just get housing any way we want, within the cost profile that suits us.

And, if the fact housing appreciation is illiquid and investment income by comparison is more liquid doesn't matter either, once again, we just throw caution to the wind and blindly retain housing based on preference.

Unfortunately, in this life, we know that is absurd. We do have to concern ourselves with the finances, as well as the personal preferences to housing.

Do we invest in a house for the short or long term? Is wealth planning something we do over the next year or over our lifetime?

Over time, by year 29, the $375,000 house adds $969,013 of total appreciation. By comparison, the one-time $75,000 investment grows too. It adds nearly $900,000 and arrives at $967,487[13] in total.

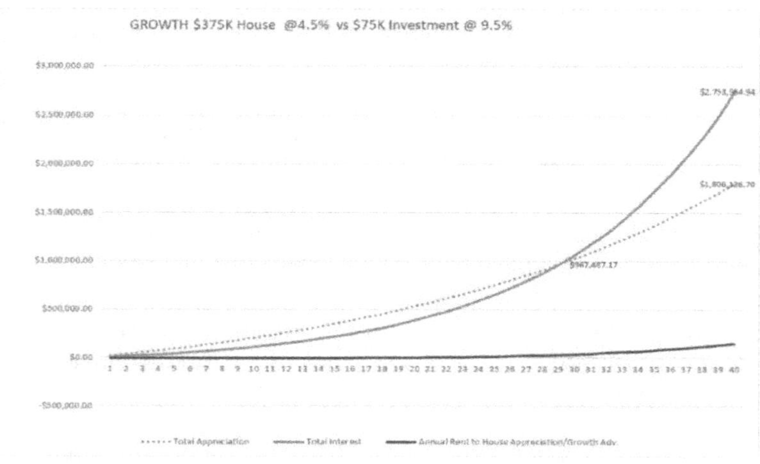

Figure 1 Housing appreciation versus growth of an investment account based on data in Appendix: Housing Versus Investment Account

Thereafter it gets interesting. The interest on the $75,000 investment takes off. Through to year 40 the investment income grows to become almost $950,000 GREATER than the amount of appreciation on the house.

In total, over 40 years, the house adds $1,806,136 of appreciation, but the investment account accumulates $2,753,954 in interest[14]. I don't know about you, but I'll take the more liquid, extra $1M in the investment account.

The challenge is, during the first 18 years, the house appreciates faster. The house outstrips the annual growth of the investment account, year after year, up to year 19. Therefore, if you're in it for the shorter term and want to speculate, then a house might be a better place to take a risk.

However, as can be seen on the charts, the difference during those 18 years is rather small – about $7,620 per year, on average[15].

That means you commit to all the maintenance, property taxes, and mortgage owning a house to gain about $635 per month, on average, during the first 18 years. Fine!

However, in year 19, a little less than halfway through, the investment account pulls ahead - putting more and more on the table annually. From year 19, the investment account is growing by more than $52,028 per year, on average, to over $245,434 annually in year 40[16].

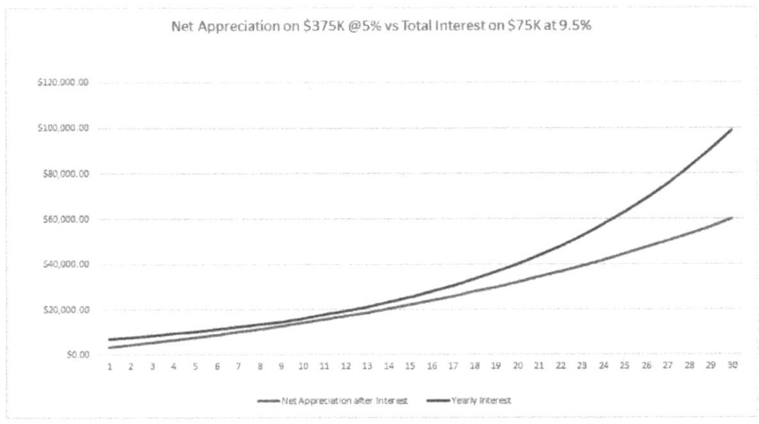

Figure 2 Rate of annual increase in housing appreciation versus investment account based on data in Appendix: Housing Versus Investment Account

I know skeptics are saying all kinds of things right about now, including:

- "But I've thrown away rent!"
- "But it is a long time to wait!"
- "I want my own place in which to live!"
- "What about taxes and market fluctuations?"

To all that, I respond: Fine! Because I know: you can *Rent Your Way to Freedom* and *Live Well Now While you Build Your Future.*

Here's the kicker.

As we saw, property taxes and maintenance on a house are estimated to each be about 1% per year, or about $312 per month each, on a $375,000 house. For nearer parity, let's assume we took just $300 per month and added that to the investment for 30 years.

If done, the investment account takes off.

The house remains at $1.4M after 30 years and gets to $2.1M after 40 years; but the investment account grows to $1.7M after 30 and $4.2M after 40 years[17].

That is over $2.1M more money in the investment account – and you're more liquid and free all the while since you're not tied-up in the house.

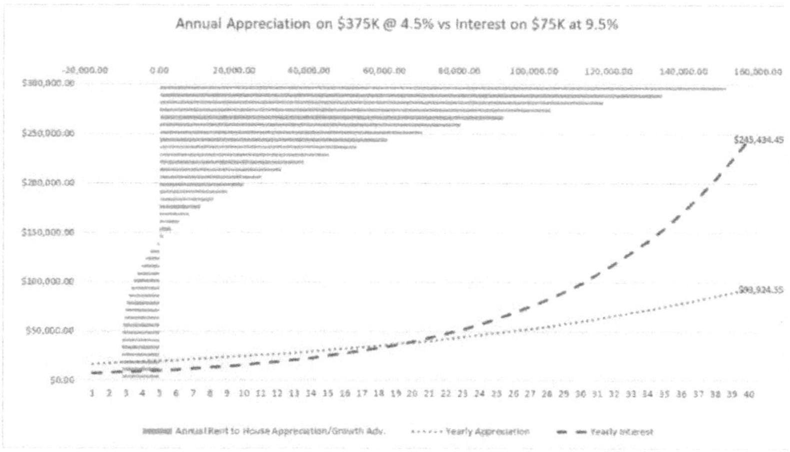

Figure 3 Appreciation of a house versus investment account growth with $300 added monthly, based on data in Appendix: Housing Versus Investment Account

And yet, the common refrain of: "Yeah, but in renting I'm throwing away money and in owning I'm paying myself" still resounds.

Why we buy!

We've seen, over 30 years, the $375K house appreciating at 4.5% grows to over $1.4M in value.

Meanwhile, excluding the extra $300, an investment account starting at $75,000 growing at 9.5% trails…never topping $1.14M in 30 years.

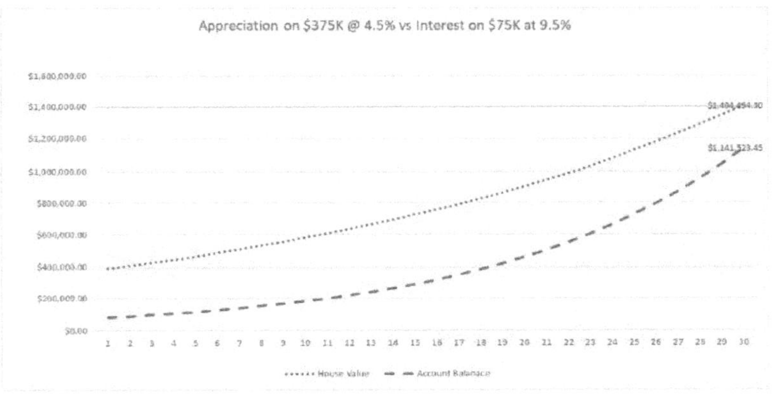

Figure 4 Analysis based on data in Appendix: Housing Versus Investment Account from The Calculator Site: Compound Interest Calculator

So owners are vindicated because, in terms of absolute value, the house grows <u>*larger*</u> than the balance on an investment account.

We put $75K down on a house (pay the mortgage, property taxes, and maintenance along the way) and 30 years later have a house worth $1.4M.

Nice deal! The house wins. That's what we generally see and so we buy!

However, that is with no consideration of the annual maintenance and annual property taxes. The $1.4M is total gross value of appreciation, and it's over 30 years - with no consideration of the mortgage principal contributed and interest paid. That's the problem. We think we pay $75,000 + $300,000 for the house; but, in reality, we pay a lot more

Why we invest!

With each mortgage payment we are reducing interest expense at the same time sink more and more money into the house.

Take the interest, property taxes, and maintenance into consideration too and we get the Net Total Appreciation- the solid line which is actually BELOW the investment Account Balance line.

Considering the house on that basis, the investment account wins.

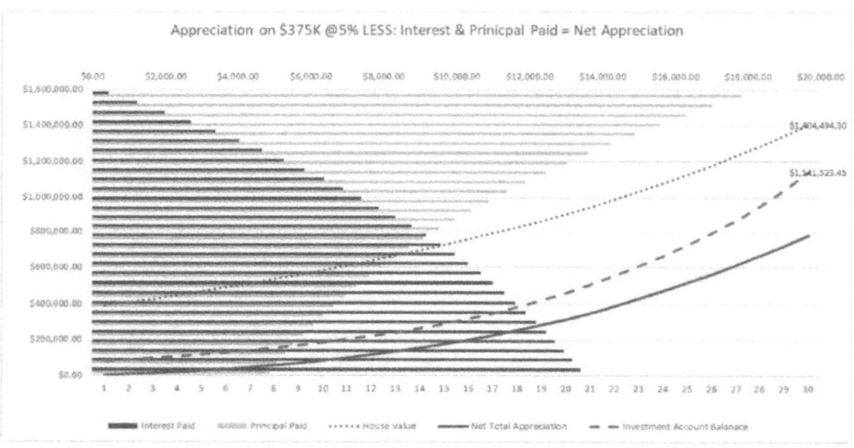

Figure 5 Housing appreciation net after of holding costs compared to investment account based on data in Appendix: Housing Versus Investment Account

Rent versus buy

Financially, the choice might be as simple as a one-time investment of $75,000 in the market, growing to $1.14M or a $75,000 down payment, PLUS contributions through a monthly mortgage payment for 30 years growing to $1.4M.

On the one side, we put in $75,000 in an investment account and choose to rent. Doing that you'd pay about $838,088 in rent over 30 years[18] and, in essence, pay for the house more than twice. That is the so-called "throwing-away money" which repulses people.

On the other side, in buying, you put in $75,000 and pay: the full house $375,000, plus interest of $247,220, plus $356,244 of property taxes and maintenance over 30 years[19].

Once again, we pay for the house twice. In fact, almost three times as we pay $978,464 – about $150,000 *more* than comparative $838,088 rent.

We might grow a million dollars of appreciation in the house, but what we pay along the way is very expensive. Also, we tie-up much more than the $75,000 one-time investment sunk in an investment account.

Of course our inner skeptic says: "Well, at least with a house I get a place to live." Okay, but you pay a pretty price to own the place. Alternatively, we can pay rent, less out of pocket in total, and have an account balance growing on the side.

Apples-to-apples comparison

For a more true apples-to-apples comparison, we need to net out rent from the investment account and net out property taxes, mortgage, and interest from the house.

Rent of $1,468/month is $17,616 per year. Taking this out naturally reduces the Net Return on the investment account. The return drops to $228,434 when rent (increasing at 3% per year) is taken out[20].

Similarly, when we take property taxes, maintenance, and interest out of the appreciation on the house and we net far less than the $1.4M imagined - just $426,029 in net appreciation over 30 years[21].

Nonetheless, on a net basis, investment in the house is $200,000 better over 30 years. To boot, at that point, at the end of 30 years, you're living "rent-free" in a house that is appreciating – meanwhile the guy renting is still paying rent.

In fact, worse still, early returns from the investment account are frighteningly small. The investment account does not even return as much as what rent costs – in the first years. The annual interest earned in the investment account, net of rent paid, is in fact negative for a long while.

The investment account returns just $7,125 in year one, yet rent costs $17,616. That leaves you $10,128[22] behind when trying to use interest income to pay for rent.

The same, however, is true of housing. Appreciation on the house in the first years does not pay for all the costs of ownership.

The house appreciates, but he appreciation fails to cover $4,014[23] worth of property taxes, maintenance, and interest. That is why we must work! We're not living for free and we must cover the shortfall.

This chart paints the scary portrait of this grim scenario. If a picture paints a thousand words, what should we do?

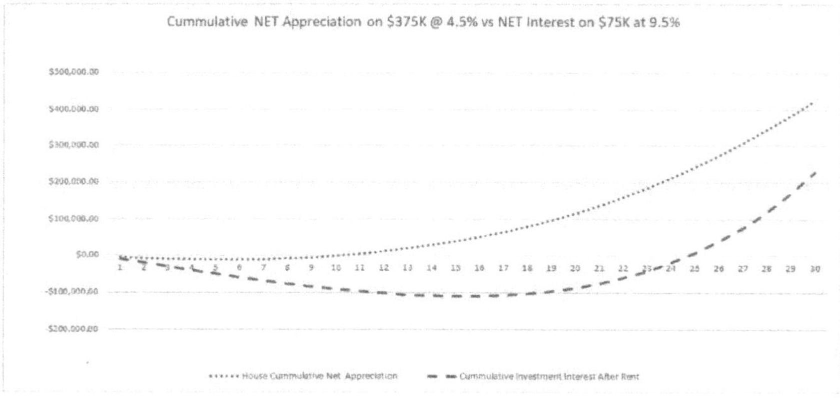

Figure 6 Housing appreciation net of holding costs versus Investment Account net of rent based on data in Appendix: Housing Versus Investment Account

Turtle versus the hare

Before we call the race in favor of the house, let's remember, both the house and investment accounts continue to appreciate. Just when all seems so well in favor of the house is right when things start to get interesting.

In year 31 the house appreciates $63,202 ($45,026 net of tax and maintenance – there's no more interest since the mortgage is paid off), but the investment account adds $108,444 (or $65,686 after the $42,758 of annually adjusted cost of rent) [24].

Continue that scenario of an investment account gaining steam for another few years and in year 40 we have a house that adds $70,209 of appreciation (net of tax and maintenance) as compared to an investment account adding $189,644 (net of rent paid) [25].

Put it all together and after the 40 years the house has had a Net Cumulative Appreciation of a little less than $1M ($994,331 to be exact) and the Investment Account Net Cumulative Growth has $1.425M – even after having paid rent all the while[26].

It takes the investment account some time to start winning and through the process, especially in the early years, it seems paying yourself by owning a house works better. Over time however, the investment account beats the house by 43%.

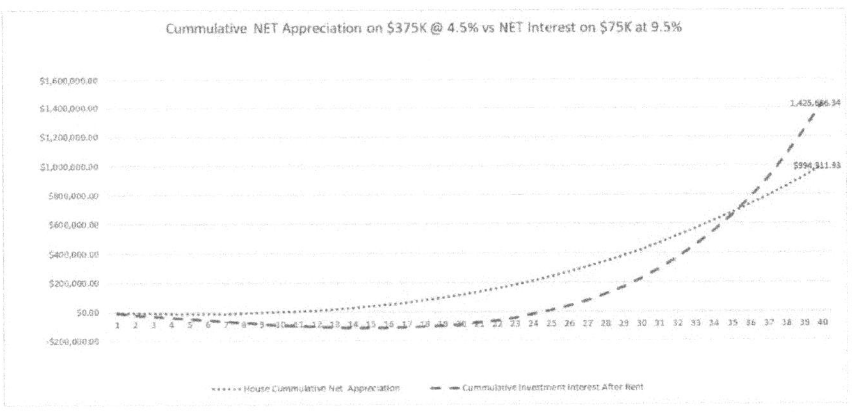

Figure 7 Net housing appreciation versus net investment account appreciation, based on data in Appendix: Housing Versus Investment Account

That is a night and day difference. The irony is that, historically, people embrace the house as a long-term investment. What the data seems to suggest however is that, over the long term, the market wins and in the short term owning is perhaps better.

If well bought and well sold, the house might, in the near term and when leveraged, be a good investment that can be flipped. There are plenty of courses teaching about flipping real estate and how to make money relatively quickly.

With an investment in housing, one could very well beat the returns in the market - in the near term. Where compound interest and reinvestment of capital comes in however, returns in the market beat the return of the house in the long term.

There is more to it all than just finances, oversimplified calculations, or one couple's story. There's more to it than just running it through a rent vs. buy calculator.

That is why we go into far more detail in the book.

Chapter 1

Freedom

Back in 2009, friends of mine would discount the perspective I offered in favor of rental (and many still do) because I was renting a rather large house from my father.

My parents, stuck with a house they did not want to sell at depressed prices during the housing crisis, offered the family home (in which I had grown up decades earlier) to me as a rental. It was great for them and for me. Onlookers, conditioned to owning, believed rental worked for me because of "cheap rent."

Fact is: it worked for me because I prefer freedom (from a mortgage) and I like renting accommodations that best suit me at the time. It was a big house, with a big yard, and that worked for my wife, eight kids, and me.

While that arrangement was great and the idea of raising my kids in the house in which I grew up was nice (while it lasted), it was inaccurate to believe my rental was a freebie.

Even if I did have a more flexible landlord in the form of my father, after four years I was pressed with the decision everyone fears in renting: "buy it or move out." A normal landlord can't do that as easily, but your dad can.

Attachment to the house of my childhood almost caused me to buy it, but fortunately … I came to my senses. At the last minute, I decided to move out, within 30 days – with eight kids and no sight of future accommodation.

Two times since I've managed to find rental situations that enabled me to treat my housing like a home! The last move was a transatlantic hop.

All told, I'm a renter by choice! This book explains why I enjoy renting my freedom.

Travel Freedom

In the fateful summer of 2013, my wife went on a European vacation for a few weeks – I stayed home at work. She and the kids visited and decided they liked Belgium. Of all places, she convinced me too and we moved here.

The backstory was a little more complicated, but my wife literally went on vacation with the kids and stayed. That's what I call freedom.

The fact that we transitioned to homeschooling and had a flexible work situation added to the feasibility, but if we'd owned a home we couldn't have taken such rapid action.

Arranging the work permits and work transfer was the more complicated part, but disconnecting from the house was as easy as calling the moving men and sending a letter to the landlord. We were moved out within 30 days and all our stuff (and I mean *ALL*) was on a boat to Europe.

Some people don't value that kind of freedom. Clearly, we do. As one friend asked, "Eric, do have a little Bedouin in your blood?"

As renters (by choice), we feel we hold far more cards in our favor – landlords can't really kick us out, but we can leave whenever we want.

Before renting from my dad, I'd been renting from third parties for almost a decade beforehand. In total, I'm 5-for-5 with my rental luck. Though a house I owned for a brief period was my single largest payday in life (though I am not sure how much I made in net profit including all the remodeling costs over the years), all told, I am a renter by choice – not of circumstance.

Thus, I share my perspective of renting, based on both "soft" (personal values and preferences) and "hard" (financial) factors.

Liquidity Freedom

In reviewing this material with a colleague who was approaching retirement, he conceded that all he has from his homeownership and many years of "investment" was some bricks and mortar – which can't be spent as easily as an investment portfolio.

Many don't see it this way, but after years of working to pay off a house, what do you have … equity? Yes! You have equity value: stored in some bricks and mortar, along with the right to live there – as long as you pay the taxes and maintenance.

After his wife passed away, my father-in-law recently found this out. He needed liquidity and a few less rooms. He had a house, all paid off, but it was a lot of work and was consuming cash (taxes, maintenance, and utilities).

Facing the next step in life for a widow at 82, my father-in-law tried to get a reverse mortgage or equity loan on the house (which he'd owned in full), but the rates were so poor that it didn't work.

He needed more freedom in the final stages of life and preferred to liquidate/sell the house to free himself from the things that were tying him down and wearing away at his time and money, and adding stress.

The selling process was a stressful six months. De-junking. Tons of last-minute improvements. Weathering a hurricane and praying for no damage. Thanks to a very helpful sister-in-law and oldest daughter, he did it. He has now moved into a condo that can, eventually, if need be, transition him to intermediate or long-term care.

He's all set! He has rented his way to freedom! A 13th floor view of the Tampa Bay and social life to boot! I didn't convince him – he decided on his own – but I commend him.

Spend a lifetime working to pay off a house to only eventually need the money; sorry, but I just don't get it. I prefer to consider a house as what it is: a housing expense. Or as an investment – when it provides rental income. Or maybe as a "luxury" to be bought from investment income.

Many people talk about "living abroad." We did (and do) it. That would have been far less possible attached to a mortgage.

Possession Freedom

This book serves to expose another side of the finances and soft factors in the rent vs. buy decision.

My current landlord has offered to have me buy the house I'm living in but, as I told my wife when we moved in, I'll rent it but I'm not buying it!

Possessions can own you more than you own them. The Bible warns against being attached. This book exposes some ways to live with a little more detachment from the house, but to still have a "home."

It's not to condemn anyone who buys or to say it is always wrong or never good to buy. No! There are many good reasons, personal and financial, to buy a home. And many people make money on their house.

On the other hand, many people are locked out of the housing market. They feel badly they can't buy – and perhaps they shouldn't!

Renting might not be a villain and buying might not be the panacea.

While some people may need to buy in certain housing situations, I find renting can provide greater liberty, detachment, and freedom.

Location Freedom

It is a little unnerving living here in Europe as an American because of the need for residence permits and all. It's not like everyone is fleeing the USA or like living abroad isn't without its hassles.

Truth be told, governments (at least some of those outside of America) aren't so open. The "open borders" of the EU are more closed than one would be led to believe.

If residence permits aren't renewed here, we're kicked out – fast. And come to think of it, we live in Belgium – The Heart of the EU.

Getting to the right place can be some serious work. After we finally moved in, my wife laid in bed sick for three weeks – suffering from exhaustion! And, staying here remains a challenge.

In Belgium, they want to see your college degree before granting you a right to start a sole proprietorship (which is like a 15-minute process in America) and they want proof of contribution to their economy as a prerequisite to gaining a residence permit.

Some people couldn't live with that uncertainty. For us, we favor renting so much that we live with the uncertainties and do what it takes to stay.

But, there's another side of the location issue. About one-third of people have "neighborhood regret." As detailed by RISMedia, that means: "they would have moved to another neighborhood than the one they reside in." And, "the issue is heightened in metros, where 46 percent are dissatisfied with their pick."[27]

That's incredible! Pick a house you think you *love,* move in and then come to realize the neighborhood is not your liking. One major benefit of renting is that it is much easier to change if you made a mistake.

In fact, it happened to us…

In the "idyllic" American neighbor in which we lived, some neighbor kid kept coming over uninvited, expecting to be entertained or play. With eight kids of our own, we couldn't take another. That imposing kid, who's parents we never even met, was part of the reason we moved away.

Home Freedom

Personally, I like the idea of being able to live anywhere and respect people's interests to seek a better life.

Here in Europe, we rent a chateau built in 1778 – probably the most prominent house in the town. As I said, the owner wants to sell it to me, but why would I buy it? Are you kidding? That's like asking a philanderer to get married. Married forever to the woman of my dreams, no problem (done and doing that) – but strapped to some bricks and mortar … no thanks!

Now it's true that many people don't wash their rental car and don't treat their rental house like a home. But I do!

I make improvements, of my choice, in ways that benefit both the owner and my family – from both a cash perspective and quality of life. If the owner hasn't trimmed the hedge in a while, I do it – even if it means buying a hedge trimmer. A true win-win! I've got a "home," the way I like it, and he has a good tenant – and all the while I'm paying less than owning.

I might be missing some appreciation or something else in not buying. There's always more certainty of about what's given up, rather uncertainty of the potential of what might be gained. But, that's the way it is in life. You take one road and you can't take another.

Like the famous Robert Frost poem, *The Road Not Traveled* (which I had to rewrite by hand many times over in high school detention – thank you, Mrs. Fultz) – "you keep the [other] for another day, Yet knowing how way leads on to way, I doubted if I should ever come back." Though I may "somewhere ages and ages hence" be "telling this with a sigh" I've taken "the [road] less traveled by, and that has made all the difference."

I may be missing out on something in not owning, but I don't have to come up with a down payment and I don't have to worry if the pipes need replacing. I have my principal free for other investments. I can change houses whenever I want. And, if a major appliance breaks down, I'm not the one scrambling for cash to replace it.

Original Freedom

Houses are a cornerstone of the American Dream. Perhaps that's where we get the potentially misguided idea that the house is the best investment we can make.

The path which many followed in the 20th Century was to buy a house with a small down payment then build equity over time by paying down the mortgage and watching it appreciate. That was the plan.

Thanks to the house, with a mortgage being a leveraged investment, you could soon double your money on your down payment. Then you could sell that house and ratchet-up the investment with a house of a higher value, thus making more money. Rinse, wash, and repeat– retirement assured!

We'll see how this worked and worked well during the Keynesian stimulated economy launched after WWII. As US Census data shows: "Median home value increased in each decade of this 60-year period"[28] from 1940. It worked really well, especially if you had a fixed rate mortgage when inflation took off in the 70's.

Home values were "rising fastest (43 percent) in the 1970s." Still, even if it worked, that's just 4.3% per year on average and things have changed since. Home values were the "slowest (8.2 percent) in the 1980s."[29] That's just 0.82% per year.

Housing may still be excellent in certain markets. Nonetheless, the economic model has been changing significantly over time. Today people seem to be more strapped with housing and credit card debt (a relatively new invention). Something seems to have changed in this original freedom plan.

Change Freedom

In the 80's, people transitioned from the historic notion and default practice of buying a car to leasing – which is basically renting transportation.

Famed financial guru Dave Ramsey hates the idea of leasing. He calls it "fleecing." But in 2016, auto leasing hit an all-time high of 32%.

Leasing is appealing because it enables you to buy more car (i.e., lifestyle) than you can afford. The logic would be: why settle for less when you can have more?!

I'm not sure Dave Ramsey would be too keen on that idea; after all, he hates debt – period – and embraces the idea of getting your house fully paid off.

Ramsey gives great advice. He has said leasing and credit cards are two of the three things (with whole life insurance being the third) that keep the middle-class in the middle.[30]

I don't doubt Dave Ramsey. He's smart and correct. What's interesting is why he hates whole life insurance[31].

Investment Freedom

Insurance analysis shows that "for 30 years, from 1940 to 1970, whole life insurance was very common."[32] - the same period buying a house was a great investment. But "in 1981, the Tax Equity and Fiscal Responsibility Act (TEFRA) became law, and… Individuals questioned putting money in whole life insurance instead of investing in the market where return rates were upwards of 10 to 12%." Times change and things changed – people moved their money out of whole life and into the market.

Why?

Whole life insurance has two major components. The insurance companies carve out a portion of money you pay in for the death benefit and another portion accumulates as cash value. In the end, the interest earned within is so insignificant that it acts more like a savings vehicle.

Whole life is nice because you can borrow against the "cash value" of what you've paid in, but what it is really is a "commitment device" that stores your money. It does a little savings (paramount to building equity in a house) and a little investment accumulation (paramount to appreciation on a house). It worked, and people lapped up whole life insurance!

Where incomes were continually climbing and other investment options were more limited, in the past, whole life might have been great – back then. However, as other alternate investment options came on the scene, "the majority of individuals, at that time, began investing in the stock market and term life insurance"[33] and whole life fell out of popularity.

Locking money away into a low-yield product is one reason why Dave Ramsey is contrary to whole life insurance[34]. I agree! That is also why I'm contrary to locking my money away in a house – a low-yield investment.

Asset Freedom

In essence, like whole life insurance, there are better investment alternatives for building cash value than paying down the mortgage.

I've found renting a house is a bit like buying term life insurance and buying a house somewhat like buying whole life.

Renting a house enables one to forgo sinking funds into bricks and mortar – which, like the cash component of whole life, appreciate at a very low rate. By renting the bricks, so to speak, one can save cash to build equity in other investments that grow at higher rates and compound earnings.

Nonetheless, some people want to "own." Some people want whole life. They feel they need a place to live, so they may as well own it. They feel they need security and they still buy whole life insurance, –but they fail to consider the low rate of return on the allocation of their cash.

Or they just love stuff. They *need* a good house for the family and a reliable car to get them from A-to-B, in style. So they buy the house and, in Dave Ramsey's words, "fleece the car"!

We believe it is an "asset" because it is tangible, but the house (and whole life) are principally a store of value.

We'll see how housing, rented, can make sense for the tenant even if the landlord is making money. We'll see what money, freed up by renting, can do if applied to other investments.

We'll also see how renting might be a good financial decision.

Choice Freedom

In the end, how we retain housing is a personal choice.

Today, people are opting to forgo a car and are choosing to share/rent their transportation. That is becoming feasible with companies like Uber.

The tech elite are now moving out of Silicon Valley – to the Midwest, of all places – because prices and lifestyle are becoming irrational in California. You can get more bang for your buck elsewhere. They move out of California to save on housing and reduce taxes – with all they save in taxes they nearly "live for free" elsewhere.

Times change and big companies are making our lives easier in so many ways. People now seriously consider the idea of renting their car and never owning one – like they do when they ditch their landline in favor of a cell phone-only policy. It might be more expensive, but some things are liberating. Or, for safety's sake, maybe we should stick with our bricks and mortar and landline …

A friend in Atlanta recently got rid of his Porsche in favor of perpetual Uber! For him, this means better cash flow, freedom, and quality. In a certain sense, he's opted for being chauffeured.

Yet people cling to the idea that their house is the best investment they can make.

As Robert Kiyosaki says in his book *Rich Dad, Poor Dad,* "I find so many people struggling today, often working harder, simply because they cling to old ideas." [35]

Financial Freedom

Where the public sentiment has us so strongly conditioned to buying a house, one may be justifiably skeptical towards the idea of renting.

For both the credibility and summary aspect of the ideas to be explored in this book, we can look to Dr. Harold Pollack, a Helen Ross Professor at The University of Chicago School of Social Service Administration.

Dr. Pollack put together 9 simple rules on a 4 x 6 index card that went viral and eventually wound up in his book *The Index Card: Why Personal Finance Doesn't Have to be Complicated.*[36]

As reported on Freakonomics Radio[37], Rule #7 is: "buy a home when you are financially ready."

He clarifies: "That means when you have a nice 20 percent down payment … buying a home that you can afford and still have a strategic reserve if you move in and your hot water heater breaks, or a raccoon eats its way through your roof, or all the things that can happen to a home."[38]

As encouraged here, the view is not to permanently swear off ownership, but just to consider the rent vs. buy alternative in light of the fact that we're buying housing (rented or owned), not an investment.

Some of the ideas herein, such as the suggestion that an interest-only loan is paramount to renting from the bank, *could* be a solution for people who feel they MUST buy/invest in a house. Having an interest-only loan (essentially renting from the bank) would surely NOT agree with Dave Ramsey, who suggests paying off an owned house as fast as possible; nor would it agree with Dr. Pollack, who says to get "a vanilla-ice-cream fixed-rate 15-year or 30-year loan." They may both be right, as heavy leverage on a house is indeed very risky.

Either way, loan or no loan, "you don't want to rush into buying a home and you want to buy a home in a very sensible way."[39] To that end, if now is not the time to buy, you should *not* feel bad (and even good) about renting in the meantime. It's like the Marshmallow Experiment proved: good things come to those who wait.

Emotional Freedom

Dr. Pollack sums it up well when he says: "We should think of our home as something that we use and consume and something that helps us with our life, not as the major pillar of our wealth."[40]

If that's the point of this whole book, then why all the hubbub? Well, because, as Dr. Pollack says: "We've been conditioned from birth to believe that you're not a full adult until you own a home. You have to be careful about that."[41]

It's not just Dr. Pollack who warns of the housing trap. Dave Ramey's whole recommendation seems to be one of encouraging people to forget "The Joneses" and save consumption for a time when you can afford it.

Though from a different school of thought, best-selling author Robert Kiyosaki frames another perspective where he cheers "Repeat After Me: Your House Is Not An Asset."[42] Like Pollack says, it is something we consume.

In fact, it is exactly because these ideas are so disruptive to our pattern of entrenched belief that we should explore them in detail. The book goes through the topic because:

a) the concept of buying a house is so ingrained in us that it takes some reflection on alternate perspectives to challenge (or change) entrenched ideas;
b) many other authors cover personal finance, more broadly, while this explores the rent vs. buy question of housing, specifically;
c) houses are people's single largest expense item and a large percent of people are financially stressed – renting may be a way out.

Though the more bombastic side of the argument, namely "that your house is not an asset,"[43] is endorsed herein, a more stayed and academic view of the ball-and-chain aspect of a house is what economists call a 'commitment device.'

Commitment Freedom

A Commitment Device is a way to lock yourself into a behavior you need some help getting locked into. "In this case, your mortgage payment is a forced savings plan."[44]

As Pollack further expressed on Freakonomics radio: "A home is a good commitment device although it's a less effective commitment device than it once was" because people "dip into their home equity."[45] It's one thing to pull money out for investments, but it's something else to pay for more consumption. As reported on the Freakonomics episode Everything You Always Wanted to Know about Money, "that could really blow up on you"[46] when values dip.

If you don't want to hear it from me, at least listen to Pollack when he says: "buy a home when you're financially ready"[47] because, as Robert Kiyosaki might be fast to tell us, "Very simply, an asset is something that puts money in your pocket"[48] and a liability is something that takes money out of your pocket. Think about it: homes consume cash – in at least taxes and maintenance if nothing else.

Question: outside of it being a store of value commitment device, why sink money into bricks and mortar when there are other investments available that provide much better returns?

"Because I need a place to live" is NOT a valid answer! You don't ***need*** to buy housing, you ***want*** to buy it. You ***can*** rent a (very nice) place to live.

Or "because it appreciates" is also not foolproof. The true appreciation on houses just barely beats inflation.

The house might have been a great investment in the past, at a time when savings accounts actually paid interest, but today and with the exception of certain markets, the house might be the new low-yield savings account – a store of value.

Unfortunately, people stick with houses remaining terrified of the stock market, based on some outdated belief of the need to pick and choose stocks and guessing when to buy and sell them. Unfamiliar the safer forms of generating longer term returns from well-diversified, simple investments in low cost index funds which can be bought with literally, pennies.

In Favor of Owning!

It's a little odd to come out in a book firmly in favor of renting and concede that *there are times it is better to buy.*

Given the predisposition people have toward purchasing a house, it's worthwhile to overtly acknowledge the fact that there are many excellent reasons to buy a home. *Note: I'm not against homeownership, per se; I just believe in the concept of all good things in time and have seen that there are many underappreciated merits of renting.*

I get it. I too am tempted to buy, every day with small stuff at the store and every time I see a nice house. So a word of caution: Restraint!

There are many lines of logic to convince the emotions to buy. People have the buy button ingrained in their psyche from a very early age and the MLS listings on the internet are tempting. Very! The inclination is to enter blindly in the joyful bliss of homeownership.

However, moving forward to buy a house without a good look at the rental option could be like buying the first car you see – or marrying the first person you kiss. While the same caution should be made with regard to signing too quickly on a rental, at least, mistakes with the rentals can be more easily rectified.

It has been proven over and again that what the mind focuses on it seeks to fulfill. Thus, one needs to be careful when looking at houses (even on the web), as the natural instinct is to *want* to buy.

After you read this book and go to consider rentals but don't immediately find a great rental at first glance, persist. Don't throw in the towel on the rental option. As with many things in life, patience is a virtue. Just like searching for the perfect house to buy, it pays to search for the perfect house to rent!

If nothing else, the data and views presented might have you consider housing with a little more emotional distance!

In Favor of Buying: My List

Though it is very hard (for me) to endorse the idea of actually "buying" a home, I can see a few reasons where buying might be good.

Location! Location! Location! – The old adage is true. Location makes a big difference. Virtually any house can be rebuilt, but there is a limited amount of land. So for me, it comes down to the piece of property – more than the actual house.

Sure, some houses are beautiful. However, as a good real estate broker will tell you: "Don't get emotionally attached – there's always another house."

What a View! – If a house had that "million dollar view," in my mind, that might be reason to buy it. The next person might have different reasons (proximity to the office/school or living next to friends), but any way you start to justify it, be careful, because it is easy to rationalize the purchase.

Sale! Sale! Sale! – Other times I might buy a house is if it is a very, very, *very* good deal; something I could be 1,000% sure on which to make money … even if it had to be sold tomorrow, so to speak.

But, I'm not talking about "flipping" – that is the business of professionals and they, having their finger on the pulse, will access the best deals first. One needs to know what they're doing in that field. It takes just one house going bad, especially for a small-time landlord, for that whole plan to crumble.

When Money's No Object! – When money doesn't matter, then housing is different. Then it becomes purely consumption, like coffee at Starbucks; we know it's expensive but we like it (and can afford it), so … we buy it anyway. Where there's money to burn, then I might go ahead and buy! Until then, I'm holding on to my down payment.

The Best Life Stage to Buy?

Is it better to buy a house when you're younger or older? As we'll see, the decision to rent vs. own is very much influenced by the question of: How many times will one move in life?

Moving every 5-10 years, one never gets to really accrue the cash flow benefit (lower costs which often happen in later years) of owning. And moving a lot, one keeps paying the "New House Tax" – that's my term for the realtor fees, closing costs, and repairs, etc. incurred upon contracting a house.

On average, Americans move 11.7 times in their life – that is 9 times after they turn 18 and just 2.7 after they turn 45.[49]

In the 27 years between 18 and 45, people are moving on average about once every three years. Clearly, with this type of nomadic lifestyle, the best way to avoid the New House Tax [50] votes in favor of renting.

The average life expectancy is now about 74 years. After age 45 people will move 2.7 times on average, or about once every 10.7 years[51]. So, even in later life people barely get started into the cash flow positive years of owning before they move. And by that time, they're less nimble.

It might seem, based on timing, that it ***could*** make sense to buy a house right before or at mid-life – maybe about the time the kids are in primary school and you're settled down. Then, satisfy the mid-life crisis with a house, not a sports car. Before and after, give renting a closer look!

THE ADVICE I'LL GIVE TO MY KIDS:

KEEP YOUR HOUSING COSTS AS LOW AS YOU CAN, AS LONG AS YOU CAN. LIVE WITH MOM AND DAD. SAVE YOUR MONEY AND COMPOUND IT. DO WHAT YOU CAN TO BUILD YOUR FINANCIAL INVESTMENTS FIRST. THEREAFTER, WHEN YOU HAVE SOME CASH AND CAN AFFORD THE MORE EXPENSIVE FIRST YEARS OF HOMEOWNERSHIP AND ARE SURE WHERE YOU WANT TO STAY, CONSIDER TAKING THE LEAP AT THAT TIME … NOT BEFORE.

OR, IF GOD MAY BLESS YOU, BUY WHEN MONEY IS NO OBJECT.

Personally, I have moved about every 5 years. So, not just for the freedom (from bankers and brick-and-mortar), but renting make sense for my life's pace. Think about your life: how often have you moved or will you move in the future?

On the Back of Rentals

Though most everyone is, by definition, either a renter or "living at home" with their parents just before buying a house, some people choose to take an ownership sabbatical.

Here we have two examples of people who, having previously owned, went back to rental as they built strength and waited for the house of their dreams.

The first was, of all things, a builder and former banker, so he presumably knows rather well how the housing and finance industries work. When I first met him and his wife, they were temporarily living in a beautiful house he'd built on speculation. He wasn't a big-time builder, just one-sies and two-sies. He lived in this one until it sold. He had small kids at home, and he could have just kept it. But he stayed in it knowing he could be gone any day. Once it sold, he then rented a rather nice condo in trendy Buckhead, Atlanta.

As his success mounted and children grew, he upgraded and started renting a proper (and I mean "proper") house from a private owner. It was a wonderful place with a back covered terrace and, after a few years, he eventually took the owner up on the offer and bought the place. It is very nice house – a place for generations, which I guess he envisioned because within 5 years of buying his kids were off to college and starting families of their own. He and his wife will soon be empty nesters. What's next? Who knows…? But the rental period while he mounted success enabled him to confidently buy a place of his dreams.

Another friend owned a beautiful house on Davis Island in Tampa, Florida. He sold it and then rented a massive 5-bedroom condo, on the beach, for a few years while his business success grew and he took time to search for the house of his dreams. Not strapped to a mortgage, he was able to patiently wait as alternatives showed up. Eventually he was able to buy a practical chateau in Florida. He got it for pennies on the dollar from its original $8M construction price.

Believe me, even if it meant uprooting to Orlando, they're happy they rented for a while. They are now settled in a beautiful house, on the lake, at the end of a private drive. And we love visiting, as they are wonderful hosts, it is a stone's throw from Disney, and they have room to accommodate our whole family.

Chapter 2

It's a Rental

You've heard it! The colloquial expression "It's a rental" has often been used as some sort of justification to mistreat an object or overlook its imperfections.

Often a car or apartment is the subject of our disregard and mistreatment, because, after all: "Who cares?! It's a rental." The logic suggests that it's not mine and I'm not responsible for it, so what do I care if it gets a little mistreated?

If you'd look in that back seat of some family minivans, you might think nothing other than: It's a rental! Yet, it's owned (or maybe "fleeced"). Moldy Cheerios and spots from dried gum or doughnut icing are enough to disgust even the most hardened vacuum worker at the carwash.

Personally, I get a sense of freedom from obligation by renting. However, I don't treat something badly just because I'm renting it. I take care of my stuff, owned or rented. I wash my rental cars if I'm going to have them for a while because I have to live in it. I pull the sheets up on the bed in a hotel room even if I'm checking out that morning. I take care of and improve houses I rent because, even if it is not my house, it is my home! I want it nice.

The idea of being a "renter by choice" is relatively new for me and very much "out-of-the-box" thinking in my social circles. It is something I've warmed up to over time. From my youth, all I ever knew was the concept of homeownership.

My parents didn't talk about money or their mortgage, but it was clear that my family and all the friends in our neighborhood owned the houses in which they lived – aspiring to ownership was ingrained in my paradigm. I'd later find out a couple friends of prominent families were living in houses their parents got (presumably with a family discount) from their grandparents. Helping their kids with the (expensive) house was a means of transferring wealth.

While, the super wealthy conservatives (think top one-percenters with a closet full of Gucci loafers) were transferring their house to their kids, to keep housing expenses low, my upbringing (though exaggerated beyond the average) was like that of most Americans: an indoctrination in how to spend and consume.

My dad liked books, clothes, cars, and…houses. He grew up in poverty and rocketed to massive business success in the 70's. With his newfound wealth, he would go out on a Saturday or Sunday and come back with a new car, a sunburn from golf, or a new house – literally. Fortunately, his success afforded him that luxury.

Though an extreme case, our family's penchant for English Tudor houses and nearly collectable cars (which we used as everyday drivers) mirrored, or should I say *magnified*, the American situation more broadly – make money and spend up to (if not beyond) your limit.

If they can agree on anything, financial gurus agree that needless consumptions is, well, needless (and wasteful). But, it seems people tend to get some money and immediately go out and buy "stuff": cars, clothes, and HOUSES too. Problem is, we don't tend to see a house as "consumption." We tend to file them away in our mind as an "investment." Thing is, of all the consumption we do, houses tend to consume the most money the most quickly.

The super-rich know the house is an expensive luxury, but at the median we don't tend to see how expensive houses are, really. We see the mortgage payment, but we don't tend to keep close track of the real outflow. We overestimate the appreciation and underappreciate holding costs.

Where cars with big tailfins were the iconic representation of American lavish in the 50's, in recent times our excesses have shown up in our houses. Fortunately, houses are good for more than just housing; they also provided access to second mortgages – to fund more consumption. No wonder there's such a movement to get us attached to a house/mortgage.

The alternate plan here suggests there is merit to sustaining an interim period of low-cost housing (i.e., rental) in order to route funds to investments that will grow wealth more substantially over time than does an investment in a house. Grow wealthy first, then fund housing luxuries.

Real Concerns

In coming around to the idea of renting, there is this whole question of: What am I to do? After all, I have to live somewhere!

The Rent vs. Buy consideration raises some immediate questions:

- How can renting be good if landlords make money?
- Why do financial gurus differ in their recommendations?
- Why have ownership rate trends reversed in recent decades?
- What will "The Joneses" think?
- Is renting really cheaper (and owning more expensive)?
- Don't I *need* to own my home?

Those are all very real concerns.

As a quick rhetorical response to many conceptions of the house, as an asset, I ask: if the house is such a great investment, why is it the first thing to be sold when Grandma dies? Why is it that massive estates of the super wealthy have to be liquidated, broken up, and subdivided?

Answer: houses are expensive to maintain. They are a better store of value than they are income-producing asset.

Another rhetorical question would ask: why is that Romania, Slovakia, and Cuba each post homeownership rates at 90% or above,[52] yet none of those countries can boast a rank in the 1-to-49 of "Top countries with the highest average wealth per adult in 2017."[53] And Switzerland ranks second in highest average wealth per capita, yet ranks 50th in homeownership by country with rates below 45%. Clearly, ownership is not the means to wealth.

Unless money was no object, I would have to LOVE, love, love that particular house before buying it. For me, that means a place with woodwork and materials from that Old World that would cost more to rebuild than for what it can be bought.

But, even still, I'd have to have a surplus of cash and generational wealth reassured to do it.

Freedom Revisited

It may not have been previously considered as such, but money tied up in a down payment (which is hard to access) can be confining, illiquid dead weight.

While one can move from one rental to another rather easily, many people can't move until they sell their house.

Some people live in fear of renting – concerned their rental price will go up or the landlord will push them out. Thus, they *want* to own. I don't see it like that – even if I've been pushed out and had my rent increased.

Maybe you'll like freedom!

- Freedom to live where you want;
- Freedom to move when you want;
- Freedom to scale up and down as you need;
- Freedom from obligations
- Freedom from a mortgage debt;
- Freedom to access more house than you can afford to buy.

Those bits of freedom have value, for me. And they outweigh the so-called benefits of owning and offset any negatives of renting.

These softer sides don't fit too nicely in a financial equation. They are not addressed by the conventional wisdom – especially not in an economy which is largely dependent on the housing and mortgage industries. Don't think debt is important to America? Consider that the $1.5T of student loan debt is one of the government's largest assets.[54] The government lives off debt and **Uncle Sam Wants You** too!

Even if I were paying more to rent a house than own it (which I don't), I would still rent – you may be different.

I was sold on housing for the first 30 years of my life. I was "bought in" to homeownership and at times am still tempted to buy. Breaks while writing this book are consumed looking at MLS listings of beautiful homes. There ARE beautiful houses to buy. But there are also beautiful ones to rent. As I remind myself (in those moments of weakness), there's always another house AND I prefer liquidity to bricks and mortar.

Benefits of Renting

Presuming everyone will build their own rationale for why they *want* to own, here's a summary of my rationale in favor of renting.

- More house for your money – Just like "fleecing" a car, which enables you to afford more car, so too can renting enable you to afford more house. Many houses rent for LESS than the mortgage itself. Clearly, you can rent more house than you can afford to buy.
- A house – without the loan – Many Millennials are opting to rent because they're strapped with college debt and can't get a loan. Renting cuts the emotional stress of mortgage debt.
- Liability is on the owner – If something breaks, the landlord fixes it. However, I don't call the landlord for every little thing. Clogged sink – go get some Liquid Plumber!
- Even billing – Renting eliminates the risk of unforeseen major expenses; you just need to monitor the annual rental increase.
- Better quality – If you look, you will find very nice houses for rent … often better than what you can afford to buy.
- More options – Considering you can always move, your rental choice does not have to be the "house of lifetime." When you go looking for a rental, you'll have more flexibility because it won't be so permanent in your mind.
- No "upside-down" risk – Clearly, if the market goes backward, it's the owner's risk … not yours.
- No strings attached – sure, you can always sell a house you own and you do have lease obligations if you rent, but many times it's more difficult to sell a house than one thinks and less complicated to get out of a lease than one imagines.
- More upgrade/downgrade options flexibility – If something ever changes (more/less kids at home, more/less money), it's easier to move. When a family is small, you need less house. As they grow up, you need more house (and more yard). As they go off to college, less house again. All that in two decades.

- Fewer Joneses to keep up with – Like Facebook envy, there's always some weird competition between homeowners – which eats at the ego. Renting clears that up. You can take pride in good decisions ("Yeah, didn't I rent a great house?") and offload the bad things about the house on the landlord ("Who cares… it's a rental"). Shifting the blame protects the ego!

- You CAN improve it – Many people say they want to own a house because they can then make changes and improve the place. I have made MANY improvements to houses I rent – and the owners usually love them. Of course, you have to be prudent. Don't spend on improvements beyond the value you get out of it during the time you live there.

- You can paint it — Don't like the color of the living room in a rental? Paint it (and paint it back when you leave). I've put in new bathrooms, kitchens, and do extra maintenance all around. The owner naturally loves me (and the rent doesn't go up)!

- A governor on spending — On a rental, spending is naturally more metered – that's a good thing, considering "improvements" to a house you own are usually very difficult to recover. They help sell the house, but check online and see just how long it takes to earn a return for improvements made on a house.

- The spiritual reason – Our time on Earth is borrowed from God and everything here is a gift we are using. Renting helps detach from the material side of owning something. As renters, we just use what God makes available to us and take care of it in the meantime.

- The bottom line — In renting, expenses are offloaded to the landlord and money is freed up for other investments – hopefully in things that make a significant return.

"A House is a Home"...

The housing decision is an emotional one. There are many very powerful motivators to sign on the dotted line.

However, the deeper consideration lying under the surface is that buying can strap one to the "house poor" path and renting can take one down the path of freedom.

People nonetheless tend to justify the desire to buy, citing reasons like:

- "everyone is doing it"
- "a house is an asset"
- "it's the house of our dreams"
- "we can make it our own"
- "it is the place where our family will grow up"
- "but I'm different"
- "renting is throwing away money"

The challenge is, rented or owned; life's expenses may be such that people still don't have enough to start allocating to investments. Often a matter of limited earnings, looming student loans, or lifestyle choice in the first place, an interim period of lower cost rental might free some cash more quickly.

People tend to consume as much house as they can possibly afford, not having the willpower to hold off and save. Overconsumption is probably the first evil. And housing is the pound foolish siren's call.

A trick to starting saving/investing is to reduce housing cost. Shop 'til you drop on your housing (not at the mall). Get a good deal on the house to free up more cash more quickly.

Those who've studied him know that Dave Ramsey has laser focus on auto expense. He zeroes in on the cost (and overspending) of the car. He often recommends reducing it. That is good, even great! Here we're raising our scope of focus to the housing expense line.

Saving 20% on a house will go much further than saving 50% on some clothes or useless stuff at the mall.

OPM (Other People's Money)!

There are, of course, scenarios in favor of buying. A certain location or buying cheaply, perhaps with low interest (only) loans. Maybe buying a suitable house for $150,000 is better than renting a $350,000 McMansion.

If you can get credit from the bank, then you're using their money. It feels really nice when they give you a bunch of money. Renting is another form of using other people's capital. In renting, you leverage the landlord's capital. It feels good when people give you the keys to the castle.

One (major and alluring) advantage to borrowing from the bank is the simple fact that the mortgage provides money not previously available.

You borrow money and the bank is a partner in the deal – as is the government a "partner" in not only the taxes you pay but also with the mortgage tax deduction they provide.

In fact, the mortgage deduction, which acts like a "20% money-back" refund coupon on income taxes, has the government subsidizing your lifestyle. Perhaps ill-advised, but people will keep a mortgage just for that purpose – they want to get something from the government. But, as Dave Ramsey says, that's an expensive way to get a discount.[55] Like getting 2-for-1 or 30% off, the deduction helps afford larger payments to the bank for their mortgage. See that? The deduction helps the bank sell more debt!

Nonetheless, getting OPM (Other People's Money) to fund your housing might be a way to your capital (principally the down payment) for investments until you can really afford the house. Taken to an extreme, one could get an interest-only loan.

By definition, an interest-only loan pays back only the interest. No principal is paid, so it never builds equity – you just pay interest and the monthly payment is lower. But, at the end of 5, 10, or 15 years, you still owe the full balance of the principal. That's not too bad if the house appreciates, but it is *terrible* if you experience depreciation. *Note: there are certain varieties of interest-only loans that charge "interest only" for a certain period (providing a lower payment for 5, 10, or 15 years) and then automatically convert to traditional loan terms at a higher payment including principal.* An interest-only loan, excessive borrowing in general, is a good way to find yourself in a bad place "underwater" – still on the hook for the mortgage note.

Real Cost of Ownership

Owning is cheaper and houses appreciate, right? Well, that's all relative to the true cost of ownership.

No one knows the future, but here in mid-2018 The Federal Reserve is pointing to rate hikes to offset inflation. News outlets like *The Washington Post* talk about how "Mortgage rates have been rising at a pace not seen in almost 50 years."[56]

What that means is that the cost of ownership, presumably with a mortgage, goes up … as in percentage points up. People with an Adjustable Rate Mortgage (ARM) can find themselves short on cash, and those previously considering a purchase scale back demand when monthly payments increase by a few hundred dollars.

Sad but true, this is a real problem. People get locked out of housing or find themselves behind on mortgage payments. Where the difference between doable and not is a few hundred dollars a month, one might seriously reconsider their preparedness for the full responsibility of ownership.

But it's not only mortgage rates, as CNBC relayed in a report from Reuters that an acute shortage in affordable homes has prices projected to increase *faster* than wages or inflation in 2018.[57]

That is not just a "West Coast" problem. In the report produced for the Urban Home Institute, the John Burns Real Estate Consulting firm also "[assumed] home prices and rents will increase slightly *<u>faster</u>* than incomes each year" (emphasis added). As if that is not bad enough, they suggest that "mortgage payments will grow faster as interest rates rise." And on top of that, "Increased regulation and supply constraints around the country will continue to limit supply, and housing affordability will get even worse."[58]

So, while one might correctly take a tightening of supply and rise of projected prices as reason to buy. Another view might suggest that, where costs are going up, it will be even more critical to get investment dollars routed to assets producing higher returns – faster than wages and enough to offset increasing housing prices.

Renting is Freedom

There are certain people who will never see renting as freedom. Kind of like sticking money under the mattress, owners get peace from their bricks and mortar – even if they're attached to a mortgage. Some renters will never envision ownership. Renting provides them peace of mind that owning doesn't.

There's peace of mind that tends to accompany life with money, in the bank – and no looming mortgage obligation.

Renters have freedom to build an investment portfolio or relocate, rather than attaching to bricks. Renters can find peace of mind in watching investments grow, not in repairing bricks and mortar.

Ironically, sooner or later and in the end, most people come around to renting their last space in this life – in the form of a retirement home or hospital bed. When funds run thin, the house eventually gets liquidated to cover expenses – Medicare will kick in, but only after all personal funds are exhausted (and the service they pay for isn't necessarily ideal). Oh, if only the investment account were larger!

If nothing else, by avoiding the house purchase, one can avoid money going to: closing costs, ongoing repairs, and maintenance – possibly freeing up enough for side investments.

Investment growth can enable one to:

- vacation more often
- develop financial independence
- send the kids to college
- live with more (not less) every day
- peace of mind, no mortgage (debt)

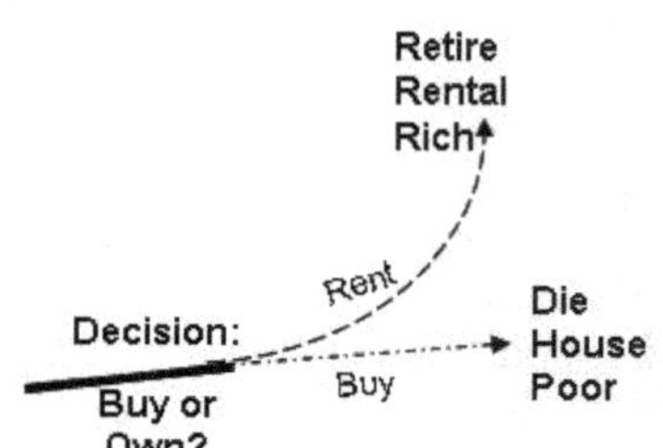

In essence, houses are expensive. They tie up money – money that could be routed to investments.

Heck, if it's the long term we're worried about, compounding wealth is an answer that works well with money invested in the market, but not so much with houses. Renting can buy freedom.

Bricks and Mortar vs. Investment Account

To take an extreme example, consider the idea of buying a house outright – in cash.

Though unrealistic practically, the theory of living in a fully paid-off house is not too far off the end game of what most people have in mind when they buy. The plan is to work a lifetime to pay off a mortgage and own a house they can live in "free and clear." That's fine, but there are other ways to live rent-free.

Imagine a $119,900 windfall used to buy a $119,900 house, in cash. Thanks to appreciation, 40 years later the house would be worth about $385,698[59]. Nice! Not bad. That's nearly 4x in value. You'd have "lived for free" for 40 years and *only* paid taxes and maintenance along the way.

Alternatively, imagine you took that $119,900 and put it in the market where it could average 9% for 40 years. Instead of $385K in bricks and mortar, you'd have a liquid asset account worth $3.765M.

The difference is extreme: a $385,698 house versus an investment account that is worth $3.76M – which would be earning nearly the full value of a house ($338,939 in interest) in year 41?[60] By comparison, what would the house be earning in year 41? Some appreciation of maybe 5% (or $19,285), which is probably barely enough to cover the taxes and maintenance cost of holding the house.

In one scenario you'd pay taxes and maintenance to keep the roof over your head, and in the other you'd pay rent. So to be fair in comparison, with all our money in the market, we'd need to pay rent along the way – perhaps $800/month for a total of $811,683 in rent over 40 years.[61] That rent would need to be netted out of the $3.76M. In the end, we'd have something less than $3M.

Nonetheless and though a good rent vs. buy calculator handles all the math, with basic math we see that, already in year one, the $800/month is covered by the interest earned. At 9% the $119,900 generates $10,791 in interest income, where monthly $800 rent costs only $9,600 per year.

If even just by a little ($1,191), thanks to interest income you're "living for free" in year one.

Investments Beat Bricks and Mortar

Though it seems comparably fair as what a rent vs. buy calculator defaulted to for a $119,900 house, one could say $800 in rent might be too low.

What if we said rent started at $1,800 month – costing $1.8M in rent over 40 years?

Even if everyone says rent is "throwing away your money," after all the rent is paid, thanks to compounding interest growing the investment account larger, renting would still work out better than owning outright – starting in year 31 and every year thereafter[62].

By year 40, a $901,622 advantage would have accumulated in favor of renting – including investment income of $232,900 in year 40[63]. Who knows what the value of a dollar will be worth in 40 years, but it seems to me $232,900 is more than enough to cover the inflation-adjusted annual $82,628 in rent that would be due in year 40.[64]

Is it clear what's happening here?

On the one side, a fully paid-off house in which one is "living free" (as long as they cover maintenance and taxes) is growing in value on a near straight-line basis – 3.5% in this example – to about $385K.

On the other side, a fully funded investment account is growing in value, faster, at higher rates of interest. Further, in an investment account, interest is reinvested such that the account starts compounding wealth (the interest earning interest) in ways the house doesn't.

The investment account generates tangible, real, spendable cash at massive rates over time. The house generates appreciation, which is somewhat illiquid and harder to spend. The investment account is the better long-term play.

This example shows, even when someone is "living for free" in a paid-off house, they still pay maintenance costs and generate only illiquid appreciation. Alternatively, income from investments can be used to really "live for free" by having the interest income pay the rent over time.

Long-Term Benefit of Compounding

Gains from investments can be leaps and bounds ahead of gains for housing over time thanks to compounding. Charts can show that. But the conditioning against rental and past history with our house and investment decisions is so strong we don't want to see it.

We talk about the house as an investment, for the long term, but if it is the long term we're interested in, investments growing at higher rates, with compounding, are the way to go.

Don't want to hear it from me? Ask the world's third richest man Warren Buffet[65] about the value of compounding and then ask yourself: did Buffet make all his tens of billions from the investment in his house? Maybe he borrowed against it in the early days, but Buffet clearly didn't make his wealth off his house, as he is reputed to live in the same house he owned when he started Berkshire Hathaway.

The potential alternate use of the down payment for investments is a big thing – many people just don't consider it. They think they *have to* buy a house and the down payment is a necessary part of that game.

Perhaps we're conditioned this way because (in the past) people didn't have good investment alternatives. Even if Buffet found a way to start an investment fund, there weren't mutual funds and low-cost index funds that could be bought back in the 50's as they can today, inexpensively and easily, with a couple of clicks and the swipe of credit card.

Today, that is NOT the case. There are SOOOO MANY great places to invest, literally dollars at a time. Today, one would do well to more carefully consider the use of money applied to a down payment vs. applied to investments.

The "buy it outright" scenario is a little unfair; however, it shows that buying outright (paramount to what most people are working toward in paying off a mortgage) *might* not be as financially prudent as we think, and spending money on rent (especially if we're building investments on the side) might not be as wasteful as we're led to believe.

Rental Rich Plan

By controlling housing expenses (renting more inexpensively), money can be routed to grow bigger and larger over the long term in an investment account.

Given that idea, one might be better off to put money (otherwise used for a down payment) toward investment assets. And then, when assets starting generating a return that grows wealth, at that point buy a house and other luxuries. Until then, keep expenses low and pay yourself first in the form of investments. That plan can work.

Yet in considering rent vs. buy, people will overlook the $3.76M distant end result of an investment account and focus on the rent "thrown away." Starting at $1,800/month, it mounts to $1,826,6286 total over 40 years. That IS serious money. But focusing on that is like getting caught robbing the gas station while you're on your way to a heist at the bank. Don't get distracted – eye on the prize!

Some will still choose bricks and mortar – they're just so tempting. Others will chose rental to maintain greater access to their capital and grow their investment base. This book exposes both sides, with a preference for the later Rental Rich Plan.

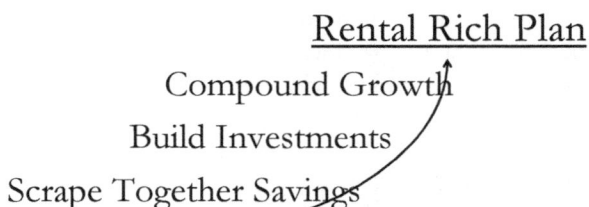

Rental Rich Plan

Compound Growth

Build Investments

Scrape Together Savings

The research the famous Marshmallow Experiment shows is that those with the discipline to sacrifice today (rather than consume today) end up more successful in the long run.

So knowing what we know about life with hindsight, wouldn't you love to have put more money away sooner?

If so, the good news is: it's never too late to start.

Chapter 3

Rent? You Can't Be Serious!

A very dear longtime friend and I got to talking at a party. While catching up, I floated the idea of renting, not buying, his next house. Where guys can tend to be especially sarcastic and dismissive of each other, this time was no exception.

So firmly rejected were my rental ideas, I started to second-guess my own ideas. Perplexed, I took to research.

While the initial experience (and many others since) raised my awareness of just how personal the housing decision is and how attached people are to buying a house; further research has only reinforced my belief in the merit of renting, as opposed to buying – at least for my family and our preferences.

Though people do warm up to the concept of renting over time, the initial reaction is typically filled with skepticism. Our entrenched belief system, indeed our whole life, seems to serve the goal of buying a house. Challenging fundamental beliefs throws people off – to say the least.

I'd floated the idea of renting to my longtime friend casually, while chatting at a wedding party – shortly after I'd read and grown favorable to ideas promulgated in the book *Rich Dad, Poor Dad* by Robert Kiyosaki. Needless to say, not everyone shares the same ideas about personal finances and housing, or freedom.

I shared Kiyosaki's views but repeatedly found people didn't understand housing the same way or had a litany of objections to the idea of renting. I've got to admit, doubt can creep in.

I'd already been a renter by choice for a long time by this point but started to wonder … was I wrong? Was I missing something in homeownership? Am I still? Ownership opportunities forgone might never be regained, so I had to look further.

I needed to address my doubts and wanted to make sure the facts behind my beliefs were correct. I wanted to make sure the statement "your house is not an asset" was correct and justifiable, as I saw it and lived it.

Now, when I talk about a house or housing, I'm talking about the primary residence. The house we live in is completely different as an "investment" from investment in non-primary residence real estate.

When considering the idea of renting their housing, almost verbatim, people repeat what my dear friend retorted over cocktails: "It's a home, not a house." Then you hear: "I want to fix it up." After that, my next favorite is: "It's an investment." The most common objections, however, are: "Renting is throwing away money" and "I need a place to live."

We'd known each other for 35 years, but my friend didn't know I was a renter by choice. After all, most everyone in our social circle was/is of means to buy a house. My friend would have naturally assumed I was, like everyone else, going along one of life's inevitable paths: to buy a home and settle down.

It seems we, in some passive aggressive or clandestine way, start showing off our success in life by the size of our house. The settle down part I get, but the homeownership component … not so much!

Back in 2008, I'd already lived in Europe for 15 years and had grown accustomed to renting. My friend and I had not seen each other too much over the years and we were catching up at that wedding party. As they will with old friends, things picked up right where they left off. So there was no problem in being candid. I shared my views and he did too.

At the time, he was looking to sell his house. He mentioned interest in buying in the neighborhood where we were for the wedding. Seeing his starry eyes, I leapt at the opportunity to give him some unsolicited advice – hopefully, in my view, saving him from being strapped down by another house.

As far as I could see it, needing to move provided him the opportunity to make a clean break. He could take a different course in life: rent (reduce expenses), increase freedom, save money, make investments, and get money working for him – not the other way around (working just to pay the mortgage).

Needless to say, with all the conditioning through the years (and having already sized up a house he was emotionally committed to buy), he wasn't too keen to jump on the *Rent Your Way To Freedom* bandwagon. Asset or not, the house was going to be his "home" and the rental concept got in the way of that specific house. His emotions were leading him – or maybe I'm not a good salesman.

Either way, there was no convincing him. No light bulb went off that night and, frankly, I grew concerned about my own position on the matter.

As he tossed out all the typical rationale ("it's a home", "it's *mine*", "it appreciates", "I'm not throwing money away to a landlord", etc.), he, like most of us, had deep-seated beliefs in the <u>need</u> (actually "desire") to *own* a house as his home.

While I left it at that with my friend, I've come to recognize (and don't criticize) that people tend to buy. We all have free will. Nonetheless, I wanted to know, at least for myself, if the rental ideas had merit. So I set about researching the matter, which resulted in this book.

Originally, the research was just for him/me, but then I got a little absorbed. I wanted to make sure what I believed was indeed correct, from my perspective, and that it was founded in data.

As a dear, dear friend, I didn't want to adversely impact his finances with some offhand advice or flippant comment. And I didn't want to screw up my own life with some blind, foolish attachment to renting – perhaps missing out on windfalls in the housing sector.

While I did own a house for a period, right at the height of the market run-up (1999-2005), I only lived in it myself for about three years. I rented it out to corporate execs while I lived in Europe. So in a sense, my house served as more of an "investment" than a home.

I made good money on that house – but that was mostly thanks to the luck of having bought in at a time when it was hard to go wrong. And to top it off, I sold to a guy who was, seemingly, counting on more upside (or living on a housing allowance as part of a job transfer). As hindsight would show, he paid too much.

Outside of that ownership experience, on which I admittedly made good money, I've been a renter by choice.

I recently talked with my lifelong friend. He has been going through a brutal bout with cancer but is still in good spirits. Though his health prevents him from keeping up with the yard work, in reminiscing about our previous conversation he told me: "Just five more years and I'll have a $2,000 pay raise. I'll have this house paid off with the mortgage behind me." So, he's well rationalized in his housing decision. Not only that, but thanks to the insurance plans our mutual friend advised, he has a couple of accounts of five figures saved up.

As my friend said, "Thankfully, I don't have stress of the top one percenters. I'm happy where I am and won't be living in a shack down by the river either."

In his situation, it's worked out. But I wonder. How is he going to get the money out of his house if he has to pay medical bills?

In his book, Robert Kiyosaki explores many facets of building wealth and getting out of the Rat Race. Of the many things he touches on, one of them is how we consider our choice toward housing expenses. While he quickly and accurately challenges the idea of the house as an asset (and exposes it as a liability), he didn't dig too deeply on the housing rent vs. buy issue.

Same with Dave Ramsey. In his work, Dave also touches on the house, suggesting an alternate path – get in one you can pay off. But he doesn't explore the facets and alternatives of housing more generally. Dave is bent on eradicating debt and living in a paid-off house.

It seems the purpose of their books, each excellent in their own right, are to get people to think more broadly about financial freedom, in general. Consideration of housing was just one of many examples and topics they touch on. Perhaps you're already forming your own ideas, objections, or agreement. If so, this book explores the details as I see them.

We'll see why your house may not be the asset you think it is and how renting might be a better alternative than previously considered.

Eye-Opening Experience

In all this I have my wife and mom to thank (or blame – for the sarcastic bunch in the crowd).

My wife bought me the *Rich Dad, Poor Dad* book by Robert Kiyosaki and my mom introduced me to Dave Ramsey. After that, I thank my friend (who divorced over money issues related to housing expenses), who gave me David Bach's book *Smart Couples Finish Rich*.

By the way, for those who know them, can you imagine the shock of Dave Ramsey and Robert Kiyosaki being mentioned, positively, in the same sentence? Some years ago in an interview I arranged with Kiyosaki, in which he was promoting his book *Business of the 21st Century*, he highlighted use of debt and optimization taxes as tools which propel the rich. Dave Ramsey views debt as the evil cousin to kryptonite.

My wife eventually convinced me that a mortgage is actually debt after all, but it took me getting away from the belief that "a mortgage is not debt, it's normal – everyone has one!" Apparently a better saleswoman, my wife also convinced a girlfriend at church.

The girls would go out once a month and do what girls do: talk! At one of these dinners, in 2008, just as we were moving, her friend asked, "So where are you going to buy [a house]?"

My wife proceeded to explain, "We just sold our [previous] house and we're ***never*** buying. We'll rent." Upon hearing the idea of renting, my wife's friend was taken aback.

"RENT! That's unheard of … how insane!" There was a hush over the whole table.

In most everyone's mind, "renting" was something for *poor* people – with no other options. So how is it that we would do such a thing?

My wife proceeded to explain the theory behind the decision, as prompted by Kiyosaki and supported by the rationale that would later be compiled in this book.

Regardless of finances, views on housing are deep-seated and my wife made little headway in convincing her friend that night – at least that's what she thought.

A little while later, just before the housing crisis (notice their fortunate timing), that friend sold her house and took up a rental contract on a builder's "model home" in the community next door.

I saw the friend's husband a couple months later and he told me, "I want to kiss your wife!"

Leaving the awkwardness of that aside (my wife is a former Miss Illinois and these were church friends), he said, "We would have never considered the idea of renting and yesterday we just closed on the sale of our house. I couldn't be happier."

He told me, "We have a stack of cash in the savings account and are taking the family to the beach tomorrow!"

By renting, my wife's friend was able to lower expenses, free up money, pay off credit cards, boost investments, and substantially upgrade houses and quality of life – all in one fell swoop.

It turns out another reason they wanted to sell was because their house was starting to need repairs. It was starting to show age and they were making a list of things they wanted. Renting their freedom got them a showroom new, builder's model home – granite countertops and all.

True story! And I couldn't be happier for them. They have since gone on and, from what I know, bought a house. But that was after a few good years of renting, paying down debt, and building an investment portfolio.

Just like this family, you might look at your finances differently with this information. You might consider how your "down payment" could be otherwise used if not pinned under a house, tied to a mortgage.

Or you might be like my childhood friend. You might look at this information and decide to "press the buy button" on a house you love.

Either way, the choice is yours! From this book, you'll have another perspective – perhaps another side of the conventional wisdom.

To Each His Own

As some may take pleasure in pointing out, I'm NOT a Financial Adviser. I am NOT a Certified Financial Planner, in any way, shape, or form. I just believe in Robert Kiyosaki's view (your house is NOT an asset!). And I like Dave Ramsey's prompting to get fighting fit, reducing costs everywhere possible.

At the same time, I value freedom – personal and financial. That's why I like what renting provides. While the house may be an "investment," it seems rife with problems – especially in comparison to all the investment alternatives available today.

However, more importantly, I am the personality type that tends to, deep in my being, want things orderly. I like to have facts and weigh my alternatives before making a decision.

For example, when my wife shops, she finds the item that suits her needs and moves on. I, on the other hand, find the item, check my alternatives, compare, and then choose the one that best suits my needs. We go about things differently. I can't stand to live in regret.

Thus, I've compiled the facts, in detail, as I see them, colored with my commentary and opinion. Available here for consideration.

My childhood friend didn't take my advice when I shared an early version of this with him. He went and bought a house – actually, the bank bought the house and he is living in it as long as he pays the monthly "rent" in the form of a mortgage.

That is his choice, of course. And, considering he weighed the alternatives, it's presumably the right one for him. I've got to admit he got a nice place, in the middle of the woods, swimming pool and all. It suits him.

Renting is not for everyone. Ownership makes some people more comfortable. To each his own!

Favorable to Flexiblity

I get it – some small towns or other locations may not be ripe with rental options. Comparatively, others (like San Francisco or New York) might be rental-only. Renting has greater merit in some markets more than in others.

Millennials, strapped with college debt, have less choice in the matter. For me, I started in a rental-only environment, Monte Carlo, and had few other options. I warmed up to the idea over time.

Finances aside, it can be a simple choice between connection to a bank (that owns most houses) or preference for cash and location freedom.

On the cash side, $10,000 barely secures a down payment on house. As an investment, $10,000 can build in the market. Build investments growing in the market, first – even if it means renting a house in the meantime.

I prefer to rent a house that suits where and how I want to live, during the particular phase of my life. Perhaps you too prefer liquid investments, growing, as opposed to a mortgage connected to brick and mortar.

Housing needs often change over time. A small apartment to start; a bigger house with a yard while the kids grow up; and a condo with a first-floor bedroom as an empty nester. Above all, I count on the fact that St. Joseph, patron saint of families, will look after us.

Friends of mine are now "empty nesters" at 70 years old. They'd move to a condo, but they can't seem to sell the house they've owned (now "free and clear") for 30 years. They rationalize their attachment to their house as a preference but, in reality, they're stuck!

When you rent, all you have to do is send a termination notice to the landlord – that's what I call freedom. Try selling a house in 30 days. Forget the hassle of showing it and the six months and thousands spent to stage it – it will minimally spend 30-60 days in escrow.

Your House is not an Asset

It's hard to accept, but I guess we can understand why a realtor might not want you to be of the idea that housing, as an asset, is a misnomer.

Author Robert Kiyosaki provoked the idea (rephrased here as: "Your House is not an Asset") 20 years ago in his 1997 best-selling book *Rich Dad, Poor Dad.* [66]

Summarized in two simple sentences in an article on the RichDad.com site (*Rich Dad Scam #6: Your House is an Asset*) he says:

"The simple definition of an asset is something that puts money in your pocket. This is accomplished through four different categories, one of which is real estate. When I say real estate, I don't mean your personal residence, which is a liability" (Kiyosaki, 2013)[67] .

I have nothing against realtors, title companies, or the building and banking industries. I have friends in all those sectors and wish no harm on any of them. They provide great services. We need all of them. Suggesting a preference for rental does not mean we don't need houses.

Swayed by popular opinion, many de-facto believe: "The house is the best investment you can ever make." Investment, maybe (on a good day), but not the *best* one you can ever make!

The house, as paid down via a mortgage, can be an excellent way to "save" – but that is a bit like sticking your money under the mattress. Saving is different from investing, and analysis shows houses do not grow as nicely in value, as compared to other financial alternatives. Moreover, they are expensive.

According to Robert, the house fails his basic litmus test. The home is not an "asset" because it takes money *out* of your pocket – minimally in just the repairs and taxes.

According to Robert, it is more likely that the house you live in is more of a liability than an asset.

The House Owns You

A great misconception in America, as I see it, is the idea that: "A house *is* an asset." Or, as is often said, a house is the best investment you can make.

The second greatest misconception is the idea that "renting a house is throwing money away."

We're led to believe that buying a house is "paying yourself" or "investing in an asset." Unfortunately, it's not so straightforward.

> 1) You're "throwing money away" (on housing) whether you rent or buy, with a mortgage.
>
> In one case your money goes to the landlord; in the other case it goes to the banker.
>
> In a certain sense, money "thrown away" on a rental might not be much more than what's "thrown away" in maintenance and property tax on the house you "own."
>
> 2) The house owns you. Expenses associated with "owning" a house are much higher than one is led to believe.
>
> Granted, you may own the house, over time, when you buy it. But, then again, in buying it, "you own [the responsibilities of] it."

Thus, when you buy the house, you're throwing money away every month too … and the house "owns you."

Remember, paying rent is not throwing money away – it is buying housing. You do get a place to live in return.

Every Rose Has its Thorns!

People make money, great money, on houses all the time. That is true.

The problem with recognizing the profit potential on a house is that people will perhaps mistakenly believe: "I know what I'm doing." And then, in a bold, brash move, they will make an emotion-filled decision and put an offer in on a house one Saturday afternoon. They fulfill their emotional need, saying, "Watch me! I'm going to do this and make a bunch of money on my house" without really considering the finances.

Emotion, as with all rash purchases, is a big risk …

It's easier than one believes to get wrapped up in buying a house. It's also easier than one thinks to find oneself "house poor." Getting out of a house can be harder than you think – especially when you see money bleeding out from your wallet.

Very experienced developers and builders go broke on housing investments, daily. The myriad of home improvement shows (heck, there are channels dedicated to it) psych people up to believe flipping houses is easy.

Keep in mind, people who run housing businesses as investments are professionals. The little guys get killed. Even the big boys, who supposedly know what they're doing, go broke all the time.

Developers are like the average homeowner: highly leveraged – one misstep and they take a mortal wound financially. Ask Dave Ramsey; if I'm not mistaken, real estate troubles caused him to go broke early on.

Warren Buffet is known to quote his partner Charlie Munger, who jokingly says that the only way an intelligent man can go broke is ladies, liquor, and leverage.

The 2008/2009 housing market weeded out many investors and left many people underwater on their mortgage. Housing is a bed a roses, very appealing – but it has its thorns.

A Man's House is His Nest Egg

The house represents people's principal "asset." True! For many people, the house is their retirement nest egg. As such, it is sacred to them. Understood!

Thankfully, buying and holding, as with any investment (ask Warren Buffet), is often the best approach.

But what if people, rather than pouring money into their house (to cover the mortgage for 30 years), were pouring money into investments?

What if people took to looking at the house as a true expense (like they do their car) and left their "nest egg" to grow in other assets?

In paying off the mortgage, people reduce their interest burden and, after 30 years, they "live rent-free." True! However, taxes and maintenance remain.

The house, what people sink their money into, is appreciating at only about 4.3% [68] – and it then locks up their cash.

The appreciation on which people count is a great misnomer, as it doesn't often take into account the effect after property taxes (which can be 2%) and inflation (which is also about 2%). You've got to net those out and account for maintenance and repair along the way. People don't do that.

What if money, even just that spent on a new fridge, dishwasher, and water heater (not to mention the new roof, painting, etc.) was invested in in the market?

In virtually every 30-year period (the length of a typical mortgage loan), the stock market has returned about 9% on average.[69] So we need to consider the alternative of 9% (in the market) vs. 4.3%, for example, on a house. The 4.7% difference might be enough to fund a nice retirement, and that doesn't even consider reinvestment potential.

4.7% interest on just $200 per month comes to $155,306 in 30 years. **That is roughly equivalent to what the average American has in total wealth today – including their house!**

The Sacred Cow

The house, like the car, is sacred in the American psyche (Europeans too, for that matter).

People just can't seem to accept that a house (especially not *their* house) is *not* an asset. It is embedded in our paradigm. It's not a house, it's a home. With all the money sinking into it, it must be an "asset." Right?

Yes, maybe.

The house can be a store of value and, in that sense, an "asset." But it is not an "asset" according to Robert Kiyosaki's definition – his assets don't consume (but rather provide) cash flow. A house can be a "home," but you can have a home without owning (the obligations of) it.

A change in perspective might come when people see their house as an expense or, more dramatically, as a liability – limiting mobility and freedom.

For example, consider phrases like "house poor" or "chained to my house." Those are real expressions that put the house in a different perspective. People use those phrases loosely, but there's more truth to them than we know.

Facts are, even free and clear of a mortgage, there are liabilities associated with owning a house. The roof, leaky basement, insurance, taxes, etc.

There's a lot of s**t to shovel around that sacred cow.

A Car is Definitely an Expense

Okay, how about the car? This should be easier.

A car can be a store of value, it is true. In that sense, it's an "asset," according to accountants. But it is NOT an *appreciating* asset.

Ask Dave Ramsey and I think he'll agree: cars are expensive to buy and though getting less so, expensive to maintain. On top of it all, they depreciate in value every year.

However, many people will still say "my car is paid off" – as a means to somehow suggest their (expensive) car is an "asset." An essential component of life, probably. But, even if the car is a store of value and may appear in the "Asset" column of an accountant's balance sheet, it is NOT (except for Uber drivers) putting money in your pocket.

Sure, you have equity in it, which can be converted to cash. It is a store of value. On that everyone agrees. But it is not Robert Kiyosaki's "asset" – it is NOT something which makes money for you, and it costs money to hold/operate. That's why Dave Ramsey often recommends that you sell the car and get a beater as the first step in rebuilding financial might.

Robert Kiyosaki taught and teaches:

- **Assets** add to your cash flow.
- **Liabilities** drain your cash flow.

In fact, the car (and house too) consume money, every month, in maintenance and taxes. Yes, they're needed … We need a place to sleep. They're expenses, however. Basic rules of personal finance suggest expenses should be minimized.

Sure, there are certain cars which do appreciate … there are exceptions. The '57 T-Birds or '59 Corvettes, etc. They *may* appreciate! So too may certain houses, in certain markets.

But they are expensive (very expensive) to maintain and (outside of certain markets) they are not appreciating much beyond the costs. They're also not nearly as easy to sell as a couple of shares of a stock portfolio.

A Short Mental Leap

Seeing a car as a store of value (but NOT a cash flow-generating asset), it should be easier to recognize the house as a store of value, a liability.

Fact is, we often invest more in a house than it gives back in appreciation, and the mortgage is just the tip of the iceberg.

Sure, money can be made off a house. It's appealing and rather seductive. Robert Kiyosaki loves real estate as an investment. He has great courses on real estate, as an investment.

However, the house, the one we live in (unless you live in a two-family home or rent out space via Airbnb and other units) consumes cash like a bottomless pit.

To the contrary, we see stories like: "My parents bought their house in 1950 for $5,000 and it is worth $225,000 now." Or "I bought my house in 1998 and made $50,000 on it – even during the housing crisis. So, houses are great investments!"

Yes, that's true! Houses do appreciate!

There will be certain periods where one can't go wrong on a house. There are certain markets that seem to do nothing but go up, up, and up. California Dreamin'.

There are, indeed, diamonds in the rough. One can make money on a house, granted!

But that is where the danger lies. People want to believe they can make a profit on a house and so … they buy it!

You *CAN* Make Money on Real Estate

The house I made money on was purchased from my dad. I got the "family discount." It needed fixing up, so there was plenty of upside. That helped, but dumb luck – actually, my wife's prompting – helped even more. I bought in 1999 and was fortunate enough to have sold in 2005.

Stories of friends or family members who just killed it in the housing market are not only incredible, but true.

For example, some friends in California paid an exorbitant $950,000 for a two-bedroom in the mid-2000's, only to sell it two years later for $1,500,000. They cleared $550,000 and made about 150% on the down payment they had in the house. Nice deal and hard to beat – especially if you look only at purchase price and exit value.

Another friend, in an even higher-end housing market, Monte Carlo, made $4 million dollars (or was it $5?) in six months on an apartment. One apartment! He was living in Monte Carlo and had been paying rent of $10,000 a month for a two-bedroom (yes, you read that right: $10K per month, in rent). The landlord told him to "buy it or move out."

So, though his monthly payment went up to choking levels (note: he was paying *less* renting and *MORE* after buying), he bought it because he liked the place. Well, six months later, Russians started pouring into Monaco and prices skyrocketed. He sold for $9M and pocketed millions.

Nice move! Especially considering that apartment has lost its Mediterranean view thanks to construction. It now looks at the back of a 40-story building and has lost millions in value.

Donald Trump and Steve Wynn are great examples of people who make money on real estate. You probably have other personal examples all around you. Money can be made – in bundles – but you have to know what you're doing.

Problem is: most of us don't.

Most People are NOT Good with Money

With both financial investments and real estate, most of us are novices. Yours truly being no exception.

Sean Hanlon, reporting for *Forbes* in his article "Why the Average Investor's Investment Return Is So Low," says the average investor has made less than 0.7% over 30 years.[70] Should we imagine the housing market is any different?

Is it not that most people only buy a couple pieces of real estate in their life? If so, then how are we, if by nothing other than luck, likely to make a killing on our house?

In his book ***Unshakeable: Your Financial Freedom Playbook,***[71] Tony Robbins pointed out that most people are better off buying low-cost, low-load market index funds than trying to trade. I agree!

We don't do all the research we need to on houses. We might think of the house as an "investment" or "business decision," but we often spend more time deliberating the color of the paint or price of the dishwasher than the purchase decision on the house itself – not to mention the type of mortgage we get.

Many times we get swept up in the emotion of the purchase: "I love it" or "Someone else is going to buy it" and end up in a house that may not have been the greatest for us – nor the greatest deal. In trading, we tend to buy a stock because "we like it," only to eventually get killed. Tony Robbins advises: "buy and hold" with market index funds – and the same advice may be true with homes. Buy and hold, or rent and buy index funds as investments.

Most people never compare the mortgage for better offers and most don't really consider the type of mortgage: traditional, ARM, or interest-only. They tend to go with a friend or recommended broker.

As a savings vehicle, the house might make good sense. It is a solid, tangible thing that won't lose value dramatically. It is a store of value … and as long as you don't trade houses too often (and get killed on fees with each transaction), it might just turn out to be worth something in the end.

The Rising Tide

The rising economic tide of the mid-20th century, which went out changed in the 70's, regained some strength in the 80's and the 90's. But in 2008/2009 the housing component burst – many washed up on the shore or found themselves underwater.

In the run-up to the housing crisis, it was practically impossible to go wrong on a housing "investment." People felt like champs – including yours truly! One didn't need to be all too swift with the investments: buy high and sell higher. In that boom-time, making money on your house was easy.

Consider the impact of the 2008/2009 crisis.

In 2016, *Fortune* magazine reported "3 Charts That Show the Housing Market Has Finally Recovered" from the 2008 crisis.[72] Eight years is a long time for a market to recover.

What's also interesting is how they measure the recovery:

1) New Construction

2) Mortgage Debt Growth

3) Service Payments of Percent of Income

Take note, all three items (construction/debt/payment) stand to benefit from the blind belief in housing.

Hmmm …

It causes me to wonder: is there a vested interest in pumping up our interest to buy a house? One with more square footage than we ever use and one we buy a little too prematurely?

A Mortgage is Free Money

Most everyone is aware the Federal Reserve is NOT a government organization but rather a private institution that *creates* money and loans it to the government and other large institutions. People are also aware that fiat currencies, like the US dollar, aren't based on anything. It's money that is "created" out of thin air.

There's not even much actual "printing." Some 1's and 0's are added to an accounting ledger, somewhere, and the process begins. One side creates the money, as creditor, and loans it to another side, who becomes the borrower of record, in debt, promising to repay.

Interestingly, in taking a mortgage one often participates in the process of "creating" money. The mortgage "note" is nothing more than a promissory ***note*** to repay. They check credit worthiness and all that, but when they find the debtor makes enough money (from other places) to service the debt, the bank gives a loan. That's why banks have their "charter." They're the ones with the right to write a "loan" out of thin air.

According to Household Debt and Credit Report by the Federal Reserve bank of New York, in Q1 of 2018 there was $9.38 trillion of outstanding mortgage debt[73]. Approximately 1/3 of it is owned by government agencies, like the Federal National Mortgage Association, and another 1/3 is owned by major financial institutions.

To put $9.4 trillion into perspective, consider the total US GDP is only $18.57 trillion, China's is about $11 trillion, and the total debt of the US government (which everyone says is excessively high) was, in January 2016, about $18 trillion. We have mortgage debt equal to about half of what we produce (and the government owes) – as a nation.

Mortgage Servitude

If addiction to debt is what keeps a fiat currency system afloat, is it any wonder people are encouraged to buy a home?

Is it any wonder banks are so willing to lend? It's a virtuous cycle. Like Vegas, the house always wins.

As a borrower, we make a promise and take on an obligation to re-pay – or they take your house. We sign up for that deal.

But it is a rather nice thing when you think about it. One day you don't have money and the next, the bank gives you hundreds and hundreds of thousands of dollars – often created out of thin air.

The weight of the note we write with the mortgage obligation is, in many senses, what gets people to wake up early and submit themselves to the treadmill of generating new income in the Rat Race.

In communist countries, the deal was a little more obvious. The government gave you a job and told you where to live – the housing came with the job.

A somewhat sadistic view, but in our capitalist society we voluntarily sign up for the servitude by taking on a bank note.

The Real Estate Game Changed

People who realize that housing is an expense and treat it as such are a step ahead of the game – in my opinion.

People who look at their house as "their single best (and only) asset" are potentially missing much better alternatives.

At the most basic level, you make money on a house in, essentially, one of two ways:

1) Value Appreciation

2) Rental Income

In either case and especially now, where the free markets have cleared out the easy money, you need to know what you are doing to make money on your house.

Simply trying to pay down the mortgage, over 30 years, is essentially a bet on the value appreciation of the house. That idea presupposes, for most people, that there are no other (better) alternatives. I protest against this because there are better investments.

The thing is … we're house poor and don't have any money for them. All our money is being poured into our biggest monthly expense, housing – which can be even more expensive when "owned." Not to mention there's a subtly here. Paying down the mortgage reduces leverage and decreases the percentage return on invested capital (ROIC). More of our capital goes in it, yet the appreciation remains the same, so the ROIC declines.

Do we get that?

As homeowners, we have more obligations, which leaves less cash at the end of the month for other investments. And every dollar paid toward principal is a doubling down on the house – which grows at low relative rates.

So the idea of paying down the debt, as our parents or grandparents used to do, can reduce the return.

What Can $500 Get?

What would happen to just $500 per month if routed to the market?

Even if you start late, investing $500 from the time you're 45 until retirement at 65, at just the difference (4.7%) between the stock market's average return (roughly 9%) and the average return on a house (roughly 4.3%), and you'd have $199,324.73. That's ***more*** than the $150,305 of equity the average person is reported to have in their house.

Think about that.

Reduce the housing expense/investment by $500 per month, put it in the market, and … *voila* … nearly $200,000 in the (cash) account twenty years later.

Also consider, the $200,000 would then be earning nearly $1,500/month in interest income. $1,500/month buys a fair amount of housing.

If that holds true and excluding inflation, where the average home equity is about $150,000, building one's nest egg in the form of home equity provides about $49,000 ***less*** wealth ($199K-$150K) than investing in the market.

Ah … but we still need a place to live and thus it makes sense to "buy" a house, right? Well, not so quick …

Where renting can be cheaper, especially in the first few years because of the New House Tax (realtor fees, closing costs, and repairs, etc.) and where an average person moves 11.7 times in their adult life, this "New House Tax" is hard to recover from. That alone (especially if you move once every half decade) can be reason enough to rent.

Not only are there great rental options these days, but you can often get more house by renting than you can afford to buy. What do we mean? As an extreme example, consider the impoverished. They can't afford to buy a house, at any price, but they ***can*** afford to rent! You can rent more house than you can afford to buy.

It's the same with you; you may not be able to afford a $500,000 or $1M house, but you might be able to rent it.

Chapter 4

Why Housing?

One might ask: "What's the beef with housing and why such concern over renting or buying it?"

Housing represents people's single largest expense on average AND housing may be the single largest determiner of quality of life. Thus, it makes some sense, if we're trying to improve our lifestyle, to focus on the housing component. Certainly, one's underlying earning potential is an even greater determiner of financial capacity, but how we choose to spend what we earn is fundamental – housing is one very large consumer.

As a teenager, my dad taught me a simple lesson about personal finances. It went something like this: "Make 20 and spend 21 … life is nothing but sorrow and misery; make 20 and spend 19 … life is bliss."

It is often recommended that housing expense should never exceed 30% of one's earnings. Yet many people find themselves living on the edge, bouncing up against or over that number. It may be because earnings are too low, but, in an effort to keep up with The Joneses, many people prematurely try to fulfill dreams.

For whatever reason, people often end up buying too much (house), too soon, and find themselves "house poor" – in servitude to a mortgage. If not spending 21, we're often spending every bit of 20.

Housing is an enormous determiner of quality of life. Everyone should aspire to quality and secure housing – no doubt. However, the notion that quality and security are somehow uniquely retained through ownership or that renters are somehow second-class citizens is fast changing in the "sharing economy."

Upon closer examination, we find housing alternatives. We find previously under-considered options that reduce monthly expenses and meanwhile they improve quality and flexibility as they free up cash for investments that can grow wealth more fully over the long term.

A Near Inalienable Right

Everyone is well-served with good, solid, stable housing. Rented or owned, stable housing is fundamental. A college student, for example, might more happily sustain less comfortable accommodations, but there are certain periods of life, like while raising kids or in older age, that good, solid, stable housing is important.

Owning a house or building a home has been the near exclusive means of attaining that good, solid, stable housing – in the right neighborhood, with the right level of security and comfort. Historical stereotypes shape a vision of renters, taken advantage of, sifting through scraps.

Indeed, governmental public policy has, since the mid-20th Century, been slanted in favor of homeownership. Tax credits and tax deductions have stacked the deck in favor of homeowners. It's a little dirty secret that ownership benefits accrue more fully to the wealthy, with larger houses, bigger mortgages, and larger deductions. The middle class thinks it's getting the deal, but the National Housing Institute reported that over half of $59B mortgage tax deductions in 1995 went to those making over $100,000.[74]

The thing is, approximately 60% of people, irrespective of political affiliation, believe that public policy should, in fairness, incentivize rental and ownership equally. However, the policy enacted in the 1940's remains largely unchanged.[75]

Why does the government give first-time homebuyer tax credits and mortgage deductions, but yet doesn't give individuals a deduction for rental expenses – as it does for business? A deduction for rental could definitely help those of lower incomes.[76]

For those who can afford it, ownership is a great program. Buying into housing is like getting into a special club. Keep the chicken and egg problem in mind. It is not the club that makes people upper class; it's the upper class who are welcomed in the club. But, being in the club can have its advantages.

Thus, it is no wonder and perhaps with good reason that people aspire to own a home. Too often, however, people chase the dream (too soon) and find themselves "house poor" – a member of the club, but unable to afford Sunday Brunch.

The American Dream

Though everyone should aspire to stable and secure housing, owning a house may not be the one-size-fits-all answer to attainment of the American Dream.

Note: while we may casually think of the "American Dream" as consumption and everything Americana, more strictly speaking, the American Dream is a reference to the idea of later generations being able to improve their situation (attain great social affluence) as compared to their parents.

Attitudes toward housing and the paths to attainment of the American Dream are changing. Social habits are changing along with economic times. The housing crisis made people more brutally aware that housing is a leveraged investment. Great when it works, but rather painful when it doesn't. People are also starting to realize and envision renting as a rational means of attaining good housing.

What was once a cornerstone of the American Dream is not so necessary anymore. Nearly 61% percent of people now feel that attainment of the American Dream can be equally had by renters and/or owners.[77] Further, people believe that the home is no longer the ticket to wealth (through equity development) that it once was.[78]

Times have changed and it is not only the young Millennials that are more prone to rent. People with advanced degrees and those making over $75,000 are also more likely to consider the rental option – 51% see renting as a viable option, versus 44% of those earning less.[79] Apparently, the more sophisticated are now more likely to lean in consideration of renting. Think about this: only 43% of Swiss own their home.[80]

Ironically, it is the poor and undereducated that swear off renting, and those over 65 who are anyhow likely to find themselves "renting" a condo or room in a retirement home. While others are changing to a more favorable perception of renting, these groups (who perhaps benefit from and need to rent most) hold more strongly to the idea of ownership.

Strange, isn't it? Those who would be most well served by renting are the very groups that don't want it. And those who have ownership are more comfortable considering life without it. It seems we humans really do tend to want what we don't have.

Times they are a Changing

People these days believe less in the merit of ownership and are less antagonistic toward renting. Approximately 60% of all new households created will choose the rental option.[81]

Times are changing. People place a higher value on freedom as compared to previous generations. People are more likely to move to another city and less likely to remain in the same town as their parents.[82] Renting is well suited to a transient population.

Just as you would rent, rather than buy, a car for vacation, so too can it make better financial sense to rent a house (and I'm not talking about Airbnb) if one will be moving more frequently.

While the cost of moving may be more dramatic when changing cities or countries, the moving men are not the expensive part. The real costs and negative impact of ownership show up in the "New House Tax" (principally real estate commissions) one experiences whether they're moving across the street or across the country. The value of renting shows up in avoiding this "tax," which is especially heavy if we're moving every few years – even within in the same city.

Some people are locked out of the housing market because of the growing perception, if not reality, of being unable to afford the 20% down payment. They are renters of circumstance. However, there's a growing population of renters by choice. Perhaps not so coincidentally, there's also a growing population of those opting out of buying.

Nonetheless, renting does have its stigma. We associate renting with "throwing away our money" and as something "only for the poor,"

When we consider it more fully, we find we're not throwing away money; in fact, we can be saving/investing it in the market and for other amounts we pay in rent – we get housing in return.

Living on the Edge

The rental stereotype is often trying to classify people who, for whatever reason, find themselves "living in the edge."

My wife was an activist for the homeless during her reign as Miss Illinois. She explained to me that the stereotypical "homeless guy," as the older aged drunken bum, is overplayed.

Yes, a majority of homeless are single males (51%) and about half of the homeless have a co-occurrence of substance abuse, but the fastest growing segment of homeless (23%) are families with children.[83]

Indeed these are single women who find themselves in a difficult situation, trying to raise kids on a low income.

Statistically, those most commonly "on the edge" are women, over 40, raising kids, on less than $40,000 income. They end up facing housing expense as something over 30% of their income and life gets tough.

Where housing is expensive, perhaps the growing segment of those on the edge is best served with a hand up. George W. Bush made a plea to help the economically disenfranchised access ownership – and we know where that ended.

Governmental policy might do well to help people get good, stable housing more inexpensively – and I'm not talking about 0% down loans that strap the unsuspecting to what ultimately becomes a very expensive house. Rather, how about assistance with good rentals?

Good, stable housing leads to: a) better relationship with parents b) mental health and well-being of family c) better performance in school and d) physical health of family.[84] Ownership with elevated expenses (taxes and maintenance and mortgage service) might only compound problems.

A nice rental solution (or tax deduction assistance) might be a real hand up as cheaper housing reduces expenses AND gives the aforementioned emotional, lifestyle benefits – which can lead to more confidence, peace, and in turn improve income.

Not Your Father's Housing

The housing situation is not the way it once was. As time has marched on, what we feel we *need* has grown to inflated proportions.

We've gone from a time in the 50's when just 980 square feet of housing was enough to raise a family (even with more kids and one bathroom) to our current average house of a 2,500 square feet, for just 3.2 people.

Still, all the *wants* we have and things we *need* don't fit in our house, literally – storage units are bursting across America, along with belt buckles.

We now have more and better stuff, with TVs in every room, yet we live in houses we can barely afford. How did we get here?

While our parents struggled, no doubt, it seems something was different. They were able to retire with equity, yet the current generation keeps pulling everything out via second mortgages.

In the past, thanks to public housing policy (enacted before 1950) and the expansionary Keynesian economics previously at play, people were able to buy their house with 20% down and build equity over time – by serving the mortgage and benefitting from appreciation as the economy inflated.

That worked and it worked well for generations. They had a leveraged investment they would ratchet up. They didn't pull money out, as we do now, but rather they graduated to larger and larger houses, expanding their equity base over time as housing appreciated.

Not to say that can't still be done. The house, as an investment, still works in some markets. A commenter on one of my channels recently reported how he, over 30 years, ratcheted up twice and finished the race in a fully paid-off house with $1M profit to show. So it can still be done.

Perhaps that's why we still envision the house as the "best investment."

However, getting rich off the appreciation in the house, as an investment, is not the same as it as in the thirty glorious years which kicked off from 1945 and lasted until about 1975.

Close to Home

Take my parents, for example. They started in an apartment in the 60's. To save money, my mom cleaned the common areas and my dad took out the garbage of the 4-unit building.

With success in his business career, they were able to buy their first house for about $15,000 in the mid-60's – that's $66,916 in 2016 USD. They even made double payments along the way to build equity more quickly. Soon, with some cash in their pockets, they were able to graduate to a larger house that they bought amid an economic crisis in 1975 for $115,000 – that was $513,026 in 2016 USD. They got a loan and "moved on up" a la *The Jeffersons*.

Today, according to Zillow, the house they bought in 1975 is worth over $1,486,417 and the first house is worth $503,034. So, as it has for many others, housing has been good to them.

The plan, as underwritten by favorable governmental policy, was simple and safe: buy with 20% down, service the mortgage, wait for values to go up, sell when equity builds up. Then, use the profits from the first house to buy a second, more highly valued house (that will appreciate even more in absolute terms). Rinse wash repeat – secure your retirement. It was the ratcheting up of the American Dream, underwritten by a Keynesian stimulated economy.

In current dollars, my parents' first house appreciated 7.5 times (from $66K to $503K). Yet the (bigger) one, which they bought 10 years later, went up less than 2.9x (from $513K to $1.5M). Both were nice and the plan worked. They made more money on both houses. But, on a percentage basis, the juice was running out as time moved on and as they moved up the value chain. More recently, the second house, at $1.4M on Zillow in December 2017, is down from a high of $1.8M in December of 2009. Thanks to the housing crisis, that house is worth *less* today than it was 10 years ago. But, on the bright side, it's up about 4% per year from the $1.2M bottom in April of 2013.

Houses are just not the great investment they once were. There's risk with all investments and houses may be relatively safe, but it's harder to make money as markets top out. Investment alternatives available now are easier and more plentiful than what they were in 1950. Heck, my stupid 401(k) (a relatively new convention) returned 30% in 2017.

The Almighty Dollar

The winds of economic policy have been at the backs of America since WWII.

The economy was humming with continual GDP growth and full employment into the 1970's, stimulated by expansionary Keynesian Economic policy – which is the government printing and spending of money to stimulate demand.

As detailed in my second book, *Bypassed: GenX's Vanishing American Dream*, massive economic changes set in starting in the mid-70's. Until then there was tireless printing of the USD.

The US dollar was the literal "gold standard" pegged to gold at $35 per ounce. While that lasted, they printed US dollars, which were consumed/used worldwide as the practical base standard. It was a great boon for the American economic expansion. It was a virtual license to print more money than America needed, because there was worldwide demand for the almighty dollar. Like selling carnival tickets at the fair, anyone who needed to transact business internationally needed dollars to do it.

But the excessive printing and Vietnam War caught up with America. Other countries didn't appreciate the devaluation of the dollar (their base counter-currency) and started to demand the underlying gold. The game was up (as there was not enough gold in the vaults, literally) and President Nixon was obliged to pull us off the Gold Standard. Things changed.

At that point, as power shifted to the Middle East as the Petro-dollar was introduced and replaced by gold, tides swelled as Asia strengthened. The Middle East got rich supplying oil (priced in US dollars) to the rest of the world and Asia became the beneficiary supplier of goods to feed America's insatiable appetite for consumption, underwritten by easy money.

But, starting with the decoupling of the dollar from gold, things changed in the finances of the word economy and in housing too. Tides shift. Growth of GDP slowed and secular stagnation (sustained periods of minimal economic growth) set in. Some suggest cryptocurrencies could usher in another mega shift.

Baby (and Housing) Boom

The period we know as the "Baby Boom" was in Europe more commonly called the "Glorious Thirty" years.

The economic period from 1945-1975 saw unprecedented growth in GDP – some say it was the greatest economic period *ever*. The 80's and 90's might have seen a boom of shopping malls, where we could blow our money, but the "Glorious Thirty" saw the building up of industry and houses in suburban America!

We say "Baby Boom" and understand it to mean that people came home from the war, reunited, and had more babies. And we understand that the population boom drove expansion in the economy.

But it is actually the other way around. The economics drove the booming baby population.

The comfort of economic growth, thanks to a stimulated economy and rebuilding of Europe under The Marshall Plan, provided a more stable future. That more stable economic future gave people the confidence to have babies.

It is NOT that babies drove the economic "Boom." Rather, it is that economics stimulated expansion and that led to babies, which led to building of houses and industry across America.

It was a different and wonderful era. A swelling of the middle class.

Generational Change

The term Secular Stagnation ties its origins back to the 1930's when people feared a general economic malaise coming out of the Great Depression. But, not to worry, war spending followed by rebuilding under The Marshall Plan solved the problem. Take my grandparents, for example. They were born in the early 20th Century.

Thanks to inflation and economic expansion, my grandfather went from making $12 *a week* at the start of his manual labor working career to earning over $12 an *hour* at the end of his career. They had a house, paid off, and retired with an RV and a piece of property in Florida. The booming economy worked for them, but it is not the same anymore.

Sure, some people are getting fabulously wealthy off the internet and real estate, not to mention the stock market. But, for the most part, the period since the 70's has been one of slowing economic growth and wages – a great stagnation.

Economist and former President of Harvard, Larry Summers, suggests we've been under the curse of Secular Stagnation. As laymen, we might think of it as the Great Unwinding – a hangover after the Baby Boom period. This can be some explanation as to why it is so hard to make ends meet these days and why the American Dream is a vanishing mirage.

We might blame economic cycles or increase in conspicuous consumption, but the observable sensation of Secular Stagnation shows up at checkout counters in the levelling off of the average American's purchasing power. Simply put: where the basket of stuff we buy gets larger (and more expensive) faster pace than the economy or wages grow, purchasing power declines.

The economy is still growing, yes, but not as it was in the Glorious Thirty Years (1945-1975). We're growing, just at slower rates today.

Suffice it to say here that the Keynesian economics worked to promote growth since the mid-40's. Americans, with the dollar at the helm, were able to buy a house with a fixed rate mortgage and do very well. But things have changed since the 70's. The economy and housing markets have seen some bright periods; however, there have been some major busts too.

Investments Changed

The easy money has been made. You can still make money on a house, but you need to know what you're doing. It is not the same "great investment" it once was – especially not for the house you actually live in.

Changes have been subtle, but one day we woke up and realized we were not able, on average, to build equity in our houses as our parents and grandparents once did. They too had difficulty making ends meet and building savings, but it was a lot easier with the rising economic tides lifting all boats. The older generation after WWII experienced practical "full employment" (meaning low unemployment rates) and had personal discipline in guarding their checkbook.

Quality of life is better now. No doubt. We have more stuff, but an easier path to the servitude of debt. We have higher incomes, but a harder time affording all the stuff we're supposed to have and feel we "need" – which incidentally might be part of the problem! Everything gets paraded in front of us in advertising and subliminally through social media posts. We're supposed to have everything our friends have (all of them) and the celebrities too. Everything in our face, all the time. It's incessant!

Perhaps one solution is to stave off the appetite for stuff, bricks and mortar included, and get ourselves into more affordable housing. This means housing better suited to our finances and particular state of life.

We may do well to view "owning" a house as the luxury it is – like all luxuries, it's expensive. A rental payment can consume more cash than a mortgage payment, maybe, but even still … you don't own the risks.

Rent doesn't have to be more expensive. In some rental-only markets, renting may be far cheaper month-in and month-out than owning. Remember my friend in Monaco? It was MORE expensive for him to own (than rent) the apartment. Avoiding many associated (higher) costs of homeownership can provide better cash flow in the interim, freeing up money for higher earning investments.

If it can be had at more affordable rates, renting might be something to consider. And if ownership is deemed better for stability and growing wealth, it too should be considered. Depending on the circumstances, they are both valid options. Keep in mind, circumstances are malleable.

A Holistic Perspective

Comparing the average mortgage on the median home ($1,190/mo.) to the median average rent ($1,468/mo.)[ii] suggests that, on a monthly cash flow basis, that we're clearly better off owning. In fact, $278 better. So, why even consider rental?

First, beyond the down payment, owning has more expenses and cash flow requirements. A holistic consideration would take into account other factors. We need to consider the real estate commissions, other potential uses for the down payment, preference for freedom, and tolerance for risk. We must also consider that houses don't always go up in value – they are subject to the market and need TLC (Tender Loving Care).

We might also consider people will tend to overspend on a house in which they have a vested interest.

A holistic consideration of alternatives might include not just the houses available for sale, but also similar situations available for rent. Not just by style, type, price point, and school district, but also taxes and preferences toward soft factors like quality, ease of moving, and tolerance for maintenance.

Taxes are a real issue – and not just property tax. People are fleeing California because of income taxes and retreating to Texas, Florida, and Nevada, which have no state income tax. They can get to a market where income tax savings might pay for housing. Thinking more holistically, one might consider the New House Tax, including 6% of real estate commissions (3% coming and 3% going) and be less absorbed with the *need* to buy.

People seem so squarely focused on buying they don't tend to think <u>*IF*</u> they should buy or just how great an investment buying is. They get some money and seem blinded and bent on buying a house, without seriously considering alternatives. I get it. I may be biased the other way.

I've had such good experiences renting I ask myself: With the money I have, how much housing can I afford? Where do I want to live? And I blindly think: With all the alternatives out there, why would I sink my money into bricks and mortar? Where I'm biased in my perspective, a dose of holistic thinking might prove beneficial all the way around.

Rules of Thumb

From a financial perspective, the rent vs. buy calculation can be rather straightforward. Simple Price-to-Rent ratios can give an easy answer too.

For example, Zillow shows that payback (buying vs. renting) often pays off in under three years. But does that take into account the New House Tax and how often we move?

Alternatively, Michael Bluejay offers a simple metric on his site. I call it his Rule of 240. He says that if you can buy the house for less than 240 times the monthly rent, then buy it.[85]

For example, $1,000 per month or $240,000 purchase would, in theory, be a toss-up. That is to say, pay rent for 20 years or buy it with a mortgage. According to the Rule of 240 they are, in theory, the same.

How often will you move? What other alternatives do you have for your down payment? What type of loan will you get? Are you sure it is the right neighborhood? Will you have more or fewer kids at home over time? Could you save income taxes living elsewhere? The answers to all these questions have important bearing on the rent vs. buy decision, and calculators can compute many of those factors.

Investopedia explains the Price-to-Rent ratio differently. As they calculate it, when it goes over 21, it is usually better rent. They take the annual rent and divide that into the price. They use division where Michael uses a multiplication-based ratio.

For example, a $240,000 house at $1,000 per month ($12,000 per year) would have a ratio of 20. So, under 21, it makes better sense to buy. Different calculation method, but same basic result as Michael Bluejay.

Looking at it from another perspective, consider a consistent fixed rent of $1,500 across various housing pricing points: $200K, $300K, $400K, $500K, etc. A $500K house available for $1,500 – no brainer, rent it! A $200K house for $1,500 however, that takes a little more noodling. This is why there is no single perfect Price-to-Rent ratio or Rent vs. Buy calculator.

Affordability

A problem with the simple calculation is that it "does not provide information about the overall affordability of a market or individual property"[86] or even *if* we should afford it. They typically don't consider things like how often one moves or preference for freedom or what else you could be doing with your down payment. Further, they don't consider availability.

One gets locked out of the housing market in cities like New York, Long Beach, and Anaheim. They are all basically rental-only markets. The price of real estate is so high in those places that it almost always makes better financial sense to rent versus buy – even paying a rental premium.

Good online calculators take into account "mortgage principal and interest, property taxes, insurance, closing costs, HOA dues … tax advantages for owning."[87] They consider the advantage of appreciation in ownership. But many, indeed most, don't take into account things like: moving, real estate commissions, and the opportunity cost of your down payment (that is invested in the bricks and mortar and not in the market).

In the end, most people make their housing decision not so much based on a rationalized Price-to-Rent consideration (how much housing can I get for my money?); but rather on a purchase affordability index (how much house can I buy with the money I have). They're geared to buy. It's like the American Dream has us conditioned to buy the maximum amount of house we can, rather than what we need or what we want to spend.

As with the nice Affordability Calculator on Zillow, we tend to put income of $78,500, for example, and with their base assumptions, *voila* … we are told we can afford a $375,142[88] house – the average selling price was $375,500 in the 3rd quarter of 2017. [89]

People tend to consider and rationalize that they can afford a $2,081 payment (including insurance, taxes, and PMI) because it's not much more than rent. But they provision less for the maintenance, real estate commissions, and they virtually never consider the opportunity cost of money – locked into the down payment.

A Great Calculator

The rent vs. buy decision has some soft factors that come into play. Kristin Wong says, "Individual Factors Make It Impossible to Simplify".[90] That why rent vs. buy calculators on their own aren't enough.

"You have to consider affordability" of a house purchase, including all the ancillary costs. It may be more prudent for a period of time to avoid ending up "house poor." Though good deals are to be had (making renting cheaper than owning), it may even be acceptable to pay more (than a mortgage) in rent.

Why? Because owning a house has other expenses.

It might be helpful to understand the cost/benefit of freedom. As my friend realized, she's paying a premium to own. You may also want to know: Are you paying a price (or saving) per month to rent?

Hands down, the best calculator I've seen is on *The New York Times* interactive site.[91] It is one of the best rent vs. buy calculators, in my mind. Among all the other thigs, it takes into account what your money could be doing for you if invested elsewhere.

Further, I like that calculator because it paints renting vs. buying in a realistic perspective. It addresses many of the issues raised in this book, like how long you plan to stay. We'll see later that owning has its 10-year sweet spot, between about years 5 and 15.

Backdoor to Investing in Houses

People rebel against the idea of a landlord "making money off them" but tend to overlook that he is: a) providing a service/house, b) is subject to different, more favorable, accounting/tax rules c) invests over a longer period.

We surely might do well to get on the landlord side of the fence, but the house we live in does not qualify for the items just mentioned – tax laws are more favorable to business owners (landlords) than to home owners.

If a key to solid investing is diversification, sinking all of ones' money into a particular house might be the antithesis of diversification. However, most people's single largest (and practically only) place they put money is in their house. Most people are poorly diversified!

If we want to invest in real estate, that is not exclusive done purchasing a house. There is a backdoor. We don't even have to clean toilets or manage property either.

Instead of sinking all of your money into a particular address or mortgage, you can simply buy into REIT (Real Estate Investment Trust). In the stock market you can buy a Housing Index Fund or ETF (Exchange Traded Fund) REIT and you own a broad basket of housing.

By rules of regulation, a qualified REIT must[92]:

- Invest at least 75% of its total assets in real estate, cash, or U.S. Treasuries
- Receive at minimum 75% of its gross income from rents from real property, interest on mortgages financing real property, or from sales of real estate
- Pay a minimum of 90% percent of its taxable income in the form of shareholder dividends each year

So these are not only well regulated, they are also professionally managed and generate cash flow.

With no maintenance or mortgage burden or tenants to manage, you can invest in housing. And you can sell whenever you want.

For example, rather than investing in a down payment on the average house, $75,000 used to buy the HGX index at $100 per share in 2012 would have grown 3.5x to $262,500. That's excluding the possibility of trading with leverage or on margin.

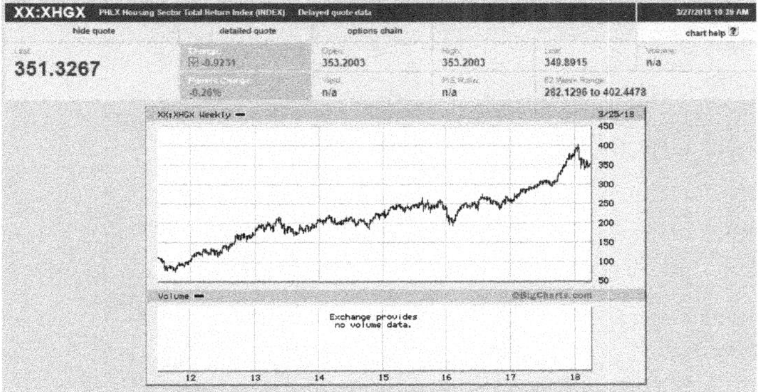

8 Image Source: bigcharts.marketwatch.com

The $75,000 could grow to $262,500 in about 5 years.

But as we saw earlier, the $375,000 house does not grow by the same $262,500 (to $637,500) in 5 years. From the section Numbers Previewed, we saw the house grows from $375,000 to only $467,318. Those housing index funds are managed differently than a simple buy and hold, as we do with the houses we buy.

The house is, in many senses, the "put all your eggs in one basket" approach. Take and watch that basket. The market has the endurance of the turtle.

Consistent investing in the house pays back equity and appreciation on *that* house. Consistent investing in the market builds a wealth portfolio.

But don't forget, if one wants to "invest," in housing there are other ways to do it than buying rental units or flipping your home.

Housing index funds are always an option. If you're bullish on housing, they can be bought/sold with a couple of mouse clicks.

Rent vs. Buy Real Life

Curious, I ran data for a $375,000 house with my criteria.

The New York Times interactive calculator[93] said I would be better off renting for under $1,949. So what can I get for under $1,949?

Having some affinity for Florida, I compared a few houses in Lutz – a suburban city north of Tampa.

The Rent Zestimate on Zillow.com suggested the following real-life examples, in early 2018.

House Value	Mortgage w/ 20%	Rental		Freedom Factor
		Zestimate	Breakeven	
$ 379,900	$ 1,517	$ 2,295		$ 346.00
$ 388,236	$ 1,556	$ 2,365	$ 1,949	$ 416.00
$ 376,172	$ 1,654	$ 2,406		$ 457.00

In essence, there a monthly premium of $346 to $457 to rent.

The calculator said $1,949 was the suggested break-even target in favor of renting. However, what the market will actually accept is between $2,295 and $2,406 for those houses. So if I were to rent, I'd be paying a freedom premium. This is a 15-20% premium per month to be worry-free and to have my down payment liquid. Is that worth it?

Interestingly, if one shops around, the premium does not necessarily need to be paid.

Besides the fair rent on those particular houses, Zillow also shows the market average of rentals being available, in the same zip code, for $2,086 or in the same city for $1,684. So one could rent for less than $1,949.

It just goes to show, for very comparable houses, you can have significantly different prices. And other, cheaper rentals are available for LESS than the price of a mortgage.

People will go through much to buy the perfect house, but not invest the same energy to find good rental housing. There are surprising opportunities in renting when you look.

Chapter 5

Conventional Wisdom

The preponderance of opinion is clearly NOT geared to the idea of rental. Rather, we're geared to homeownership.

So much so that it would seem life's joys, happiness, and financial fortunes will all be found in the attainment of a house – attaching use, via a promissory mortgage note, to those bricks and mortar.

Renowned author and financial adviser David Bach, whose book *Smart Couples Finish Rich* [94] had a tremendously positive impact in my own life, suggested in a 2018 *CNBC* article that: "The biggest mistake Millennials are making is not buying a home." [95] Clearly, that got my attention.

I greatly appreciate David and his 2001 book, which came into my life just as I was getting married – at a time I was feeling particularly broke (thanks to, coincidentally enough, overspending on a home).

With much thanks to David for having opened my eyes to the value of building wealth and the amount of stress lack of money can put on a marriage, I eventually sold the house in 2005 and made good money on it.

The 2018 *CNBC* article reported: "Homeowners are worth forty times more than renters."[96] I appreciate the value of the shocking headline to raise attention, but it got me thinking … homeowners, 40x richer? Really?

Forty times wealthier – that is a *very* BIG number. So big I took to carefully reviewing the source material: the September 2017 *Federal Reserve Bulletin* Vol. 103, No. 3 "Changes in U.S. Family Finances from 2013 to 2016" issued by the Board of Governors of the Federal Reserve System.

That report provides some great insight.

True! Homeowners *ARE* 40X Richer

No doubt, homeowners are in fact wealthier than renters.

91% of the top 10% of income earners own their home.[97] Thus it would seem: homeownership is a necessary step on the path to riches. Right?

Right! But, there is more to the story than meets the eye …

Just as David Bach has more room to explain in longer books, here too we look at another view of housing – different from what conventional wisdom might have us believe.

Specifically, the *Federal Reserve Bulletin* states: "Those in the top 10 percent, by income, have a homeownership rate of 91.4 percent." [98] However, ownership rates overall never topped 70% in America.

So rich people own their homes. Great!

Is it, however, perhaps that homeownership is more a consequence of elevated income, rather than a means to it?

In looking at wealth, which eventually buys luxuries like houses, it needs to be considered that people in the top 10% of income brackets are more likely to be business owners too.

In fact, on average, business equity contributes up to $1,190,700 to their wealth. [99]

The cause and effect is not so clear. It definitely seems there's more to the 40X number than meets the eye.

It may in fact be that these homeowners are also wealthy owners of business and other real estate assets. Perhaps it is these other assets that give them a few X's of boost.

The Median vs. Mean

It is nonetheless true, as noted on page 13 of the *Federal Reserve Bulletin* cited in the *CNBC* article that, in 2016, the *median* wealth of families not owning their house was just $5,200, compared to $231,400 (or about 40x greater) for families owning their homes.[100]

This statistic seems to be the one that proves the point that people who own their home ARE 40x wealthier, at the *median*.

Now, we must revisit some math and realize there can be a big difference between the *median* and the *mean*.

As we'll remember:

- The *median* is the middle number in a string. For example, 2 would be the "median" number in the string: 0, 2, 10.
- The *mean*, however, is what we would know to be the "average." In the preceding string of numbers, the *mean* is 6.

There can be a big difference between the median and mean – a 3x difference in that simple example. Thus, it might be a bit quick to sway opinion citing the fact that homeowners are 40x richer, as measured by wealth, at the *median*.

The "average" homeowner is NOT 40x wealthier, at the *mean*. And, even if they were, I am not sure the home made them so much richer.

Is it the increase in home equity that gives them the boost or growth of other investments? Is it earnings from business which makes them wealth and affords them the house, with equity? Is it the man that made the money, or the money that made the man?

At the *mean*, homeowners are only about 11x wealthier.[101] That is still important, but about 75% less significant.

As the report cited shows, people who own their home have a mean (i.e., "average") net worth of about $1,034,200 versus renters, who come in at $91,100.[102] So that is an 11x difference. Still profound, but not as dramatic as the 40x statement based on the median.

Chicken or the Egg

It may be true (and I cannot deny the facts) that homeowners are 40x wealthier than renters, at the *median*. After all, the Federal Reserve reports that to be true. However, as we see, it is not a foregone conclusion that the home made them 40x wealthier.

Conventional wisdom continues to suggest it is the house that makes people rich. After all, it is said [people] who don't buy are "making a big mistake."[103] Frankly, I'm not so sure.

Imagine if I said: People who own a Mercedes are X times richer than those who, for example, rent a car. Does that mean you should believe the Mercedes made them rich?

Of course not! The Mercedes is an expensive, luxurious form of transportation. Owning a home is an expensive, luxurious way of retaining housing.

The homeowner is about 11x richer than the renter, on average. Yes! But rather than looking at the current state of wealth, a more telling indicator may be the pace of wealth production.

That is: are homeowners getting richer more quickly than the renters? If so, then it might just be that the house is a faster path to riches.

What we see is that from 2013 to 2016 both renters and homeowners increased their wealth, on average. The owner at 28% and renter at 26%. So, owners *are* getting richer, faster – a whole two percentage points faster (sarcasm intended).

But seriously, two points is a big difference, especially considering the absolute numbers. Two percentage points equates to a 7% better pace ((28-26)/26 = 7%).

Growing 7% faster means doubling your lead every 10 years. Said differently, at that pace, it will take a homeowner 10 years to get 2x ahead. But, the numbers show homeowners are 11x ahead – which would require a couple more decades of sustained lead.

Does the lead come exclusively from the house?[104]

Fly in the Ointment

When we look at data regarding income, wealth, and asset ownership, we see the largest gains in median net worth, between 2013 and 2016, were of families ***without*** a college degree. And, those without a high school degree experienced the largest percentage increase in median net worth.[105] Given that, are thus conclude the way to improve net worth is to forgo an advacned degree?

What is going on here? Homeowners are wealthier and richer, but the less educated (who presumably have a lower rate of homeownership) are improving more quickly. How is that possible?

Missing out on home equity, stability, and value appreciation may indeed be a BIG mistake in foregoing homeownership, but it is not sure that homeownership is the ideal finanical decision or best lifestyle choice.

Yes, rich people tend to own their home. In fact, rich people tend to own many luxuries. As income increases, it becomes easier to be a little looser with the purse strings – spending on luxuries more freely.

A house, like many other luxury items, is expensive to own. Similarly, advanced degrees are expensive to get. Is it perhaps the weight of college debt that is holding back wealth and mortgage approval ratings?

Consider that, while 63.7% of people own a home,[106] it is also reported "nearly half of Americans have trouble finding $400 to pay for an emergency." [107]

College and house debts strap people. That is not to, however, say we should skip college or the home.

The competitive standard of expecations are increaseing. A college degree is fast becoming the new minimum standard. The advantage a Bachlor's Degree used to provide seems to now require a Master's degree. So we need education and skill (just as we need housing) … we just need to control the costs of getting those things.

High Homeownership Rates

The financial plan driving America, the one we've been fed (go to school, get a job, and buy a home) which is largely rooted in debt, does not seem to be working for a large chunk of Americans – or folks from other countries for that matter.

For example, when you think of Romania, Slovakia, and Cuba … what comes to mind? A rich population, thriving? Or, poor people struggling?

Well, only one of those countries ranks in the top 50 (Slovakia is 50th and Romania 73rd, Cuba doesn't make the top 100) of the "Top countries with the highest average wealth per adult in 2017."[108]

And yet, those counties (former communist countries, by the way) are all in the world's top 5 when it comes to rate of homeownership – each posting homeownership rates at 90% or above.[109] Perhaps a coincidence, but it would lead one to wonder: is homeownership a ticket to wealth?

Now, what comes to mind when you think of Austria, Germany, Hong Kong, and Switzerland? Poor or Rich? Well, they rank as the bottom four in the Top 50 when it comes to homeownership rates.

With some exceptions (the three blips being Singapore, Norway and Iceland), the below chart suggests an almost inverse relation between wealth per capita and homeownership rates. The further right we go, the lower the rate of homeownership and higher the rate of average wealth.

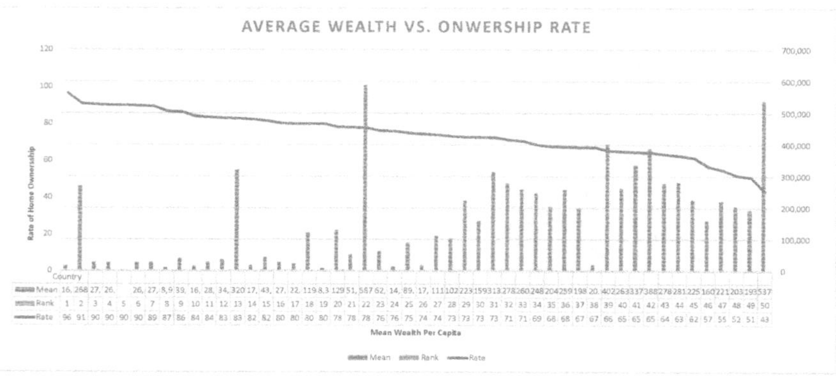

Figure 9 Data Source See Appendix: Homeownership By County

Housing Crisis

In our own country we saw the "[George W. Bush's] drive for homeownership fueled [the] housing bubble"[110] and led us to the brink of Armageddon.

"Eight years after arriving in Washington [Bush], vowing to spread the dream of homeownership ... with roots in the housing sector he so ardently championed. There are plenty of culprits," but even President Bush, when briefed on Lehman Brothers and Merrill Lynch 'faced with the prospect of a global meltdown' and the bail-out he'd sign, "wondered aloud, '[how] did we get here?'"[111]

Is it any wonder that ownership rates are said to have gone from about 62% to nearly 69% in his presidency, when he was pushing "a plan to increase the number of minority owners by 5.5 million"?

In fact, "Bush persuaded Congress to spend as much as $200 million a year to help first-time buyers with down payments and closing costs."[112] Noble, I'll give him that, but rather than helping them get strapped to debt, perhaps he should have been helping them with a rental tax deduction.

It seems the "mortgage bankers and brokers" had their way in 2004 when they "more than tripled their contributions [from] 2000."[113] Maybe the earlier mentioned thought of a "conspiracy" is not too far off?

It can be said that people make a big mistake in ***not*** buying a home, I agree. Everyone should aspire to something. However, a house is not the ticket to riches and wealth – nor is it the right choice for everyone.

Affordability and Debt Service

The only home I ever owned (and then sold) was one of my most lucrative "investments." I've got to admit, it felt good spending all the money the bank loaned me through the process of renovation – sinking money into bricks, mortar, plumbing, electricity, etc.

Truth is, however, I was constantly at the edge of my means. I got lucky. It worked out in the end, but it was tight – even with a second mortgage.

The housing crisis proved people can get behind on payments and find themselves "underwater" – which makes it really difficult to "service debt" (or downsize when need be). You can spend the money you borrow, but you've got to feed the mortgage. As one of my private equity investment friends was quick to say: don't forget to service the debt.

In fact, the BIG mistake people make might not be renting, but rather overspending (on a house).

Affordability is perhaps the key component of the housing decision. Not just whether one *can* afford to buy it, but whether one *should* buy it. Houses are expensive to hold and maintain. Some people work out a budget for that, but many underestimate how quickly a house consumes money.

The problem with not keeping a budget is that, without a budget, people are less likely to save and more likely to spend, now – leaving less to build investment capital for the future. A 10% miscalculation on the housing can mean the difference between solvency, or not, at the end of the month.

A 2013 Gallup Poll shows: "only 32 percent of U.S. households prepare a monthly budget."[114] On average, the US household spends about $54,000 per year, in 2013, including about $1,415/month on housing. That's 33% of total expenditure and the largest of all expenses.[115]

Too many people have too much month left at the end of the money – and use credit cards to fill in the gap.

Owning is Cheaper

Conventional wisdom implies and would have us believe that owning is cheaper than renting. After all, "renting is just throwing away your money."

Where other sections of the book expose why owning may *not* be cheaper, neither in the short or long run, one quick rhetorical question might be: well, if owning *is* cheaper, why aren't all the poor people buying?

The economically underprivileged are locked out of homeownership because it is expensive (and they lack credit). So, in many senses, the house is an expensive luxury item. And one questions the sanity of strapping people down with them.

My veterinarian comes from Spain. She made the point rather well. In order to get work, she had to move from her own country because pets were a *luxury* and the Spanish (after their own housing speculation crisis, coincidentally enough) couldn't afford pets.

There are two points here: 1) housing (ownership) speculation broke Spain and 2) certain items, pets in that example, are luxuries that avail themselves to higher incomes.

The Fed's data shows it is the rich who tend to buy homes as income goes up. That's perhaps the way it should be, as they are expensive. As a friend says: "It's one thing to buy a Ferrari, it's another to be able to afford the oil change."

We see how well government sponsorship of homeownership's path to wealth and riches has worked out, so why do more of it?

Well, maybe because we're wising up to the facts: a) houses are expensive and people need to be aware of what they're getting into b) it doesn't always provide a positive return and c) oh yeah … the government already tried that massive experiment which ended in the Housing Crisis.

So, though conventional wisdom would have us believe owning a house is cheaper, it is kind of like a pet … the "free puppy" is not so "free" once you get it home. Maybe we'd all be better off with the government providing some tax deductions for renters.

Probably the Worst Financial Advice

Back in the 2009 era, before Google bought YouTube, I posted at least one video about this topic. You might still find it, under the brand 401kNo, entitled: "Get out from under your house." The video summarized many sentiments from earlier editions of this book. I posted it back then and never looked at it until recently – when I was shocked to find it has over 24,000 views.

Along the way, that video got a sarcastic comment from a user named "Telegram." He took pride in saying: "[my video] was probably the worst financial advice."

Telegram's comment: "It's funny, but in 2009 after the housing collapse it appeared every video on YouTube was about houses not being an asset. Actually, that WAS the best time to buy. I bought my house in 2010 and have made a killing while this guy [a.k.a. me] is still renting." Telegram added a "lol" at the end to show how smart he is and how stupid I am apparently. Fine!

As admitted in so many places in this book, there are plenty of ways to make money on a house. Indeed Telegram, if he'd read this book, would find that 2010 was just about the absolute bottom. As he says, he did well, very well, to buy then. Indeed, a secret to making money is buying well.

Many people have and do make money on their house – all the time! After all, the house is the single greatest (and perhaps only) investment for most Americans. On the other hand, people get hurt badly on houses too. Consider, it was only in 2016 that the market recovered from the 2008/2009 Housing Crisis. Telegram is smart to have held his house. But, is it not the time to sell? Who knows?

For example, I sold my house in 2005 for $527,500. Per the info from Zillow, my house was sold twice since. My buyer, who bought with zero percent down, eventually sold for 33% less – he lost about $150,000. And imagine, he was professor of accounting at a large University.

It just goes to show how costly housing can be. This is one clear case where renting would have been the MUCH better option.

How Growth Compares

Insight to the economic profile of homeowners versus non-homeowners might be better measured by the *rate* at which wealth increases. How fast wealth is increasing for homeowners versus non-homeowners is indicative of the role housing choices play in wealth creation.

Again from the Federal Reserve: from 2013-2106 "The *median* net worth of homeowners increased 15%..., whereas that of renters and other non-homeowners fell 5%…explained by growth in housing prices…." So, we're back to the point where the house seems to be ticket to wealth.

But wait ... because the "*mean* net worth of both homeowners and non-homeowners rose substantially over this period…partially attributed to other asset prices rising."[116] Other assets! Ah…! Other asssets.

Increasing *median* net worth for homeowners and *declining* for non-homeowners – if anything, it indicates that people at the bottom end are perpetually locked out of the housing market. Non-homeowners are missing the opportunity to climb up a rung on the *median* ladder through increases in housing value. That alone would suggest it is worthwhile, at the median, to own a home – if one wants to grow wealth. And it would substantiate the belief that wealth is attained through housing.

At the median, in not buying, one misses out on wealth creation. However, it is not so cut and dry.

As previously noted, looking at the *average,* we see wealth of non-renters is increasing at about the same pace (just 7% less) as for homeowners. So, non-homeowners are growing wealth too, almost as much as homeowners, as the report says: "partially attributed to other asset prices rising."[117]

Where renters may be locked out of buying a house (or, in the case of Millennials, chosing to not buy), those groups are nonetheless growing wealth. Homeowners get growth from increases in their less liquid brick and mortar; renters get growth from reduction of credit card debt and increases in other investments.

Homeownership Follows Higher Income

Deeper inspection of the Federal Reserve report to which David Bach was referring provides other insights.

People who buy a home are, as judged by *mean* income, far richer ($134,000 mean income verses $47,800) than renters.[118] In and of itself, that piece of data is not necessarily a conclusive indicator to suggest homeownership makes you rich. It does, however, suggest the likelihood of buying a home increases as you earn more.

As the report says: "Families with higher levels of … income reported greater levels of net worth" which has "a relationship reflecting a higher level of savings among higher-income families"[119]. That means people with more income have greater liberty to save, and they might spend more readily buying a house.

One rather conclusive fact is that people who live in metropolitan areas tend to earn more than double those living in non-metropolitan statistical areas.[120] *Conclusion*: if you want to make more money, move to the city! However, remember: housing is more expensive in (big) cities.

In making more money you can afford more stuff, that's for sure. Beware: too much consumption and a higher cost of living might leave you no better off at the end of the month. Again, it's a lifestyle choice.

In theory, if you make more (and control your expenses), you can afford more. More savings. More stuff. More housing. More investments in assets. The data confirms the rate of homeownership correlates directly to income. And it seems the first place people tend to spend is on housing – perhaps prematurely.

Interestingly, as regards income growth, from 2013-2016 incomes for renters went up by 10%, while incomes for homeowners went up only 9%. So, renters are starting to make more money. This suggests incomes are, on a percentage basis, increasing at the bottom end faster than at the top. However, in general and for the moment, homeowners still have about 2.8x the income of renters.[121]

Brown Bag It!

David Bach is a very smart and rather successful financial adviser. He gives some advice in the video attached to the *CNBC* article: "Use this simple trick to save $44,000 on your mortgage."

In essence, the article suggests making a 13th mortgage payment every year – funding the bet on the house more quickly and reducing the interest paid on the house over the lifetime. My parents employed this sound advice in the 1960's for their bet on housing. Pay off the mortgage faster and you reduce interest expense. Bach estimates this can, on average, save $44,000 over the lifetime of a mortgage.

For those who like the home as an investment, that is indeed GREAT advice – no sarcasm intended.

In a linked video on the CNBC site, Bach even suggests brown bagging lunch, to be able to save up the money to afford the additional the 13th payment per year. He was apparently joking, which is good because needing to brown bag it might mean one in a house that is beyond their means.

Indeed, saving money and paying down debt is GREAT advice. However and while scrimping to pay down the mortgage does increase equity, it also reduces leverage – it is the leverage that provides the higher returns on capital. Paid off completely, the house loses the multiplier effect of leverage. Save and brown bag, maybe, but in order to fund an investment account – not a mortgage.

Dave Ramsey wouldn't agree, but some say there is good debt and bad debt. Good, low-interest, debt to bridge cash flow shortfalls (like paying off credit cards every month) and for investments that pay you (perhaps using debt wisely to buy income-producing assets). Bad debt is used for wasteful consumption or investments that "consume" money.

There's another perspective that suggests: save and don't get into debt in the first place. Feed savings into investments, before getting tied to the obligation of mortgage interest debt. Get to the bottom right of Kiyosaki's Cash Flow Quadrant, fast. And then, with cash flowing from investments, consider plunking it down on a house.

Burning a Hole

I have eight kids. Some save, some spend. One can't seem to spend money he gets fast enough. He's generous, but he just blows through it.

Similarly, it would seem when people get a little bit of money saved up, they run as fast as they can to sink it into a house.

With that housing choice, one signs up to the mortgage, potentially excluding themselves from the freedom to access other (potentially better) investments and wealth-building options.

The data seems to confirm that, strapped to expenses related to homeownership, people have very little left over to save.

The Federal Reserve Bulletin of September 2017 says that of "families in the middle of the net worth distribution… [the] wealth portfolio is dominated by housing."

In fact, the data shows that, in 2016, 63.7% of people "owned" a house; but only 13.9% of people own stocks and less than 53% of people held a retirement account.[122] And, as mentioned, 50% of people can't come up with $400 overnight.

People are long on houses and not invested in the stock market or other assets.

Finances and the potential of the cash benefit aside, one may find greater "freedom," both financially and emotionally, in never getting attached to a mortgage in the first place.

Secret Shame of America

People do make money on houses – especially ones that are well-bought, but yet: over 60% of America is still broke.

It was reported in the cover story of the May 2016 issue of *The Atlantic*, "The Secret Shame of Middle-Class Americans" is that "nearly half of Americans would have trouble finding $400 to pay for an emergency" (Gabler, 2016).

In 2009, 67% of homes were lived in by the owners. The house represents people's primary and practically only investment/savings tool.

Consider the financial state of Americans in general and then give thought to the financial plan of most Americans – sink money into the house.

Where I'm happy for "Telegram" and all the other people who bought well in the great dip, irrespective of having made money on it or not, I've never found greater psychological or financial liberty than when I closed on the sale of my house and separated myself from the mortgage. It is that experience (separating from ownership and opting to rent) which helps me really appreciate what Dave Ramsey says when he talks about the liberty and pride of being debt-free.

If there is one thing I know for sure, it's that people are very opinionated about housing. They'll fall in love with a house and often pay too much.

My video promoting the merits of renting has had more than 24,170 views. While there are a litany of vocal and opinionated comments of people saying how well they've done on their house (so as to reject the idea of rental), more people "like" the video than "dislike." The "likes" (64%) suggest the silent majority are with the idea and against the conventional wisdom.

While owning a house may be a necessary step on the yellow brick road to financial freedom, renting seems (to me) to be a nice route to personal freedom – if not financial freedom too.

A Lifestyle Choice

The homeownership decision, as opposed to being viewed as an "investment" or "asset," might be better considered in light of lifestyle.

My doctor friend made a good deal of money. Upon finishing his residency, one of his first investments was a condo in Hilton Head – a resort community in South Carolina that experienced massive growth in the 80's and 90's. He liked vacations with his family and had the cash to do it. But, more importantly, he had cash flow.

He used income from his young practice to support an investment in a condo, which both generated rental income and increased in value as popularity of the community grew. He'd go to the condo with the family; but he rented it out more than he stayed in it. It was a cash flow-generating asset for him. Soon, he owned two condos and was compounding wealth.

There are choices in looking at houses – as an investment that generates cash versus living in it as an expense-producing liability. While it is clear one can view second homes as an investment, the primary residences are more likely to be a liability – unless you're running a B&B.

My doctor friend didn't make retirement-level wealth from his primary residence (though it was a nice $1M river view masterpiece), nor from the money made on condo investments. In fact, even if he's wealthy beyond belief, he has not yet retired – though he could – because his practice makes him money and affords his lifestyle.

The fact is the rate of homeownership increases in direct proportion with income. As people make more money, the rate of homeownership tends to increase – as do other investments. Conversely, the underprivileged and lower earners tend to not buy homes nor accumulate investments.

Again, the Mercedes. Is it purchased with income or the reason for the income? Does the house make people rich? Or is the house bought at increasing levels of income?

My doctor friend got rich from his practice (not his house) but made a fortune from other assets he owned.

Chapter 6

The Rat Race

Getting ahead in life remains a very great challenge. Shocking, but 47% of people can't come up with $400 given 24 hours' notice. To do it, they would have to sell something or borrow.[123]

Building a financial future and saving one's soul, these are the two top priorities in life. Though we've got to make sure finances don't take precedence over the spiritual, it is, nonetheless, important to consider financial affairs.

The most remarkable thing in either of these domains is that it doesn't take a massive shift of thinking to change the course of one's future – just application of a perspective and alternative belief system. For example, consider housing as an expense, whether rented or owned.

Many don't deeply consider that one $10,000 investment, plus $100 every month, can grow to over $197,019 in savings in just 25 years' time, at 9% compounded. [124]

Yes, 25 years is a long time and 9% is a high rate, but they're not outrageous figures, as 9% is the proven long-term average of the S&P over the past 90 years.[125]

Comparatively, $200,000 <u>IS</u> a lot of money – especially when you consider the typical American, at 65 years of age, has just $194,226 in total wealth – including about $150,305 in home equity. [126]

So while you'd have a hard time buying a house with a $10,000 down payment, you *<u>can</u>* start saving/investing with $10,000 (or less). It just takes a different viewpoint of what to do with some savings: dump it in a house or place it in an invesment?

How one saves/invests is a choice, a very personal choice!

Everyone's Broke

Of course, $10,000 would be great to be able to set aside as an investment. Many people, however, just can't even imagine having that kind of cash available for discretionary investments. That's understood. Many people, at all levels of income, live paycheck-to-paycheck – often because they spend their earnings on experiences and expensive liabilities, first, rather than applying it to building investment portfolios.

"About half of Americans are not able to come up with $2,000 in 30 days, which means that they stand only one emergency or crisis away from really quite dire circumstances." [127]

People are strapped. Believe me, I know … I've had to sell a car, two times in my life, to pay bills. *Note: one slippery slope and dangerous use of equity in a house is accessing it through a second mortgage for cash to cover shortfalls. That hides and covers critical moments (as I could have done to avoid selling my car …). Not having that backup, I sold cars to pay bills.*

Even if people are broke, it's amazing how when they want to buy a house, they somehow pull together (or borrow) the minimum necessary for a down payment, closing costs, and real estate brokerage fees – fast! Moved in, they then realize how expensive the place really is. Strapped to the house poor train, there's nothing left for a savings/investment plans.

I'd venture to say the guy making $250,000/year is feeling just as broke as the guy making $25,000/year – relatively speaking. In fact, the data shows: "only 25 percent of the people who earn between $100,000 and $150,000 a year could come up with that $2,000 in 30 days."[128]

Even if you have more options with higher income, the truth is people typically increase expenses as earnings grow – to the point that money is always tight. It's incredible: people can't get ahead … but somehow they get strapped to bricks and mortar via a mortgage.

Consumption is killing us financially (and metabolically).

To that end, where the portion of a mortgage going to principal acts as some kind of forced savings, the house (as a commitment device) might be a prudent financial tool. However, the house must be considered for what it is: an expensive luxury – and a large one at that.

Single Largest Expense Item

Throughout recent history, the home proves to be people's single largest investment.

No doubt. People consider: "Well, I have to live somewhere, so I may as well own it [and pay myself]." Right? That line of logic is clear. But the decision has its costs – namely, what economists call "opportunity costs."

Money applied to a down payment gets tied up in the house. Tied up in the house, the down payment can't be used for other things. You can take a second mortgage to access it, which many do, but that is complicated and costs interest.

While borrowing to invest sounds crazy and is crazy according to advice in Dave Ramsey's book *The Total Money Makeover*,[129] hedge funds do it all the time. They borrow money, at low interest rates, and invest it in better-performing assets – they make money on the difference. Many people do something similar and borrow on their house (at a low rate) to place the money in other (higher earning) investments. Some do it with their brokers, while others do it to support entreprenurial dreams.

Today, a lot of people are taking loans or using their credit card to buy Bitcoin, Crytpos, or invest in the Bullish stock market. Before banks put the kibosh on it, America's credit card debt hit record highs, over $1T, in early 2018.

The point is not to endorse the idea of borrowing against one's house to make investments, but rather that money in the house is locked away – somewhat illiquid – you must borrow (or sell the place) to get it back.

Houses are refered to as an "asset" – a "vault" might be a better term. And maybe that is good for most people, because Bitcoin (or other investments) can end badly. By comparision, the house is the archetypal "buy and hold" investment strategy – a safe and conservative approach. Like a ring on a finger is a good "commitment device."

The house ties up money. Make an appointment with the bank if you want to get it out! Or, for starters, just keep money in investments.

Mobility and Freedom

The handcuffs of a mortgage limit personal mobility and financial choices. That may turn out to be a good, or bad, thing depending on investment alternatives. But they are confining ties.

Renting ties up very little – a couple months of deposit, max. If one doesn't like the place or needs to move, getting out of a rental is as simple as sending a termination letter and calling the moving men.

However, getting out of a house, attached to a mortgage, is a whole different story. It can be quick, at times … but, usually, three months at the minimum.

I'm on a prayer chain list at church, and it is for urgent and serious needs. Daily things like a car crash, cancer patient, someone dying, or pregnancy difficulties get posted. People on the list know it is to be used for *only* the most critical matters. Given that, I think the below puts the stress of being stuck with a house in perspective. I received this.

A MAY 30, 2018 NOTE TO THE GROUP ON THE PRAYER CHAIN READ:

I JUST GOT A CALL FROM ONE OF OUR MEMBERS ASKING FOR PRAYERS SO THAT THEY CAN SELL THEIR HOUSE. IT WILL BE A HUGE RELIEF TO THEM IF THIS WORKS OUT; SOMEONE IS COMING TO LOOK AT THEIR PLACE THIS EVENING.

In it all, signing a mortgage is a significantly greater obligation than committing to a rental agreement. It carries not just financial weight, but emotional too.

The parallel to marriage versus living together is, I think, rather fair. There is far more commitment with the wedding, its vows and all the associated emotional and legal obligations. I happen to think marriage is a great comittment device. It's good for socitey and good for me. Buying a house may be good for the economy too but, in my view, buying a house restricts my personal freedom.

In then end it is bit like my friend (who later ended up divorced) would say about marriage: "It's a great institution … but who ever wanted to be institutionalized?"

Personally, I'm in my marriage for life. But the house is a different story.

The "New House Tax"

Outside of obligations attached to a mortgage, consider that, upon buying a house, there's composite of costs I call the "New House Tax." Closing costs and real estate commissions are paid most every time a house is bought and sold. They are a "tax" on buying.

Not to say the agents don't earn it – they do – but commissions consume a nice chunk of change and take a while to pay off. People's nomadic nature, moving once every 4.8 years (on average), cuts directly into the benefit of ownership.

Housing rent vs. buy purchase decisions seem to be made on the assumption of living there "forever." Indeed, most rent vs. buy calculators default to the 30-year time period. But the data suggests that people have a more nomadic nature.

It may be different in every case, and some may move once every 20-30 years, or once every five. But it's kind of like a car, which you can sell too soon (or too long) after it's been bought. Homeownership has a sweet spot too!

Ownership benefit usually has a sweet spot of between 5-20 years – after the New House Tax is paid and before the long-term maintenance and repairs mount up. About the time owning makes better long-term sense (after year five or so), according to statistics, people tend to move!

Personally, I fit the average. In the last 30 years, I've moved about once every five years. We'll see how moving that frequently, excluding appreciation, barely provides time to cover the real estate commissins. Just note that Zillow shows houses appreciated 6.5% in 2017, but projected just 3.0% for 2018.[130]

Appreciation of about 3% per year gets consumed by the 3% real estate commission to be paid on each side of the buy/sell transaction. So, two years of apprecation go straight to the realtor.

Excluding appreciation, it takes takes a long time to pay off the New House Tax. We'll see it is about four years of equity buiding through contributions to principal through a standard mortgage to cover the real estate commissions.

Paying Yourself or the Agent?

It is often said, and people are fast to point out, that owning a house is "paying yourself."

Though paying ourselves might be part of our conditioned thinking and common understanding, it might not be so straightforward.

Mortgage payments include both principal and interest. So in paying the mortage, one builds equity by paying down the principal. Thus the idea of "paying oneself."

But consider the New House Tax on a $300,000 house. For example, real estate commissions of about 6%[131] is about $18,000.

How long does it take to reimburse the commissions and then start "paying yourself"?

The detailed amortization schedule in the Appendix[132] shows that a standard 30-year, 5.28% mortage on $300,000 accumulates about $4,500 in equity in each of the first four years. Per the below table, it would take four years to build $18,335 of equity.

Thus, excluding appreciation, it is in the beginning of year five that the $18,000 of commissions are covered. Only $335 accumulates in principal beyond the $18,000 of commissions.

But there's appreciation to cover the New House Tax, right? Maybe. Or maybe it goes to cover the $64,651 of interest expense …

	Appreciation (a high 5%)	**Interest Paid**		**Principal Paid**	**Real Estate Commissions**
Year 1	$15,000	$15,649		$4,230	$18,000
Year 2	$15,750	$15,422		$4,458	
Year 3	$16,537	$15,182		$4,697	
Year 4	$16,999	$14,929		$4,950	
Total	**$61,182**	**$64,651**		**$18,335**	

With people on average moving about once every five years, it leads one to wonder: are we "paying ourselves" or are we paying the real eastate agents and banks?

Invest (Don't Save) Money

If people could just free up a couple hundred dollars to invest in a different way, the trajectory of their financial strength could change forever, in a massive way.

Most people spend on leisure, new handbags, flat screen TVs, dinners out, and cell phones – while counting on credit cards to cover shortfalls. As the Federal Reserve reported January 8, 2018, outstanding credit card debt hit a record $1.023 trillion.

The savings rate is very low and very few people pay themselves, buying investment, first – perhaps they're too busy paying the bank for their housing every month.

Granted, getting ahead is hard when the expenses keep rolling in – there are just so many shiny objects or "experiences" to buy, and it is hard to avoid "robbing Peter to pay Paul."

One friend told me: "It's not even 'shiny objects.' Summer camp at $375 per kid; adventure course with Dad; $230 for spiritual teen conference; $185 for music lessons; and $100 for soccer" are all necessities of our modern day life. As my friend goes on: "We don't have nice 'stuff? … we throw a lot of money into experiences and spiritual warfare." Life comes at you fast and that is why it is important to start investing early!

In these economic times, many have run out of places to look for additional savings. But they may not be looking at one of the greatest opportunities for savings: their house!

There are certainly many good reasons to spend money on "buying" a house. Building credit and equity in the house might be good reasons. Getting access to a loan, at reasonable rates, to pay down high-interest rate credit cards might be more possible as an owner.

Building up financial strength, for the freedom it provides, is an important key to peace of mind.

If it takes extraordinary investment to build wealth, it might be worth reconsidering (and reducing) housing expense – to build investments more quickly and grow those investments to fund housing and lifestyle.

Life: a Series of Choices

As I told my friend who wanted to buy Bitcoin (with a second mortgage on the house she'd just bought): "You might not want to do that."

The people who do well taking on debt are those generating a bunch of cash to service the debt, comfortably. So, I told her: "Unless you're generating a bunch of cash, to get rich you might just STOP buying useless crap. You'll be surprised by how much a few less items in your shopping cart can save."

She heard that and said, "Yeah, I think I'm going to return that purse I bought yesterday and maybe buy Bitcoin instead." I'll reserve judgment on Bitcoin, but it's similar with housing. Housing is a choice.

That's a basic consideration. Housing might be better categorized as an expense, rather than as an investment.

It is a choice regarding the allocation of funds. Allocate money to a down payment, mortgage interest, tax, and maintenance when you buy. Or, pay (a lower) rent and allocate down payment to other investment plans and use returns from those investments to fund housing.

People locked out of the housing market might initially feel depressed by their inability to buy, but perhaps they shouldn't – they might not be missing out and instead have a great opportunity.

How we choose to spend money has opportunity costs. Money spent on a new handbag is not invested to grow in the market.

When it comes to the choice of housing, one can either: rent or buy. Go big or small. **Buy an "asset" that returns maybe 5% (i.e., a house) and *pay* interest, taxes, and maintenance to hold it; or buy an asset that grows at 9% and *pays you* interest while you hold it.**

Outside of the financial matters there's emotional freedom in living free from mortgage pressure. *Rent Your Way To Freedom!*

Where the propensity and default practice is to pursue home "ownership" as some kind of pinnacle of the American Dream, a look at that decision might be worth a little consideration.

Opportunity Cost

The decision, especially considering all the soft factors involved, is much more complicated and personal than running a bunch of numbers.

For example, I personally prefer freedom from a mortgage (which I can get renting even if I can't and don't want to own a house), but somehow people find security in getting strapped to a house and spending their life working to pay it off. I don't get that.

In the end it's not just the freedom from a mortgage – it is the dollars tied up in the house that could be applied elsewhere. One important consideration in using rent vs. buy calculators is that many do ***not*** allocate for the down payment being invested elsewhere.

That means, comparing renting to buying (with money down) is always going to vote more favorably toward the ownership scenario. Why? Because having equity in the owned house reduces the interest expense – paying less interest means less out of pocket to own. However, this fails to consider the opportunity cost of what the larger down payment could be doing in the market, if not stuck in the house.

At the extreme, with a house that was fully paid off, you'd clearly be free of all mortgage expense. At that point, rent vs. buy a calculator would always point to ownership – it is cheaper on a cash flow basis – if they don't assume you could on the rental side be putting that money in the market.

Paying in-full commits the money to the house, earning a return at the rate of appreciation – generally, something less than 5%.

Borrowing some money or renting leave you with your cash to invest in the market at perhaps 9% or better.

Buying the house with 100% financing (and keeping cash liquid for other investments) might mean paying interest which, if done, would make you little like high-end Margin Traders who use funds borrowed from a broker to access higher returns – a practice Warrren Buffet (and Dave Ramsey, for that matter) would be soundly against, as it "can be ruinous for the average individual investor."[133]

Renting: from the Bank

Where interest-only loans might be extreme, they're not outlandish. Over time, I've grown more favorable to them – perhaps because interest-only loans might be the closest thing to renting, while still owning.

However, once presented with closing papers to get one, I ran and backed out of the house deal altogeher. The broker told me, "Yeah, we use these to get young doctors and lawyers who are going to see a massive increase in wages in houses early." While I qualifed for the loan and house, when I realized the house was too much house and that I'd still be on the hook for the whole amount after 10 years, I ran. I think the broker and agent are still trying to figure out what happened to their "sure deal."

The problem is in the way interest-only loans work. By definiton, you pay "interest only" and don't pay back any principal (or build any equity). That's why monthly payments are lower. That's why I could afford it.

For example, a traditional (principal + interest payment) mortage payment of $1,371 on a $300,000 loan at 4% could be reduced to $1,000 monthly, interest only. That frees up $371 per month, which could be routed to other investments or a matching 401(k). The nice part is (which I didn't realize at the time with my deal) is that the interest-only loans can be converted to a traditional loan after 10 years, for example.

Thing is, since the amount of the loan is never paid down, you're basically renting from the bank and owe the full balance of the loan at maturity – at which point, if you haven't built up other means to pay off the loan or can't get a replacement loan, you're on the street.

The extreme end of using the bank's money would be to put zero percent down and buy with an interest-only loan. I'm not sure they'd let you do it (and I do **NOT** endorse the idea), but that would be paramount to what I call "Renting From the Bank" since the owner would have nothing in it and build no equity.

Renting From the Bank would provide rights to appreciation, but it would also carry all the obligations of homeownership, including maintenance and taxes and, don't forget, the balance of the loan (which could end up "underwater"). Those risks are too big for me and why I've never Rented From the Bank and prefer renting from a landlord.

Ramsey Makeover vs. Kiyosaki Freedom

As noted in his book, *The Total Money Makeover,*[134] Dave Ramsey suggests an end goal for housing is to own it free and clear. A lot of people love that advice. Indeed, Ramsey makes a great point when he talks about the pride and comfort you'll feel walking through a fully paid-off lawn in your bare feet.[135]

Alternatively, a lot of people love the seemingly converse opinion of Robert Kiyosaki's that "your house is not an asset" with the implied suggestion of it having more characteristics of liabaility that you'd seemingly want to put as little money in as possible.

The problem either way is that money committed to the house is locked up and can't be used elsewhere. Perhaps that's why Ramsey's multi-step process suggests maximizing retriement investing and building a college fund BEFORE attacking the house mortgage debt.

I presume Ramsey hates debt and guess Kiyosaki has a different perspective on it. He talks about "good debt" (presumably that used to buy assets) vs. "bad debt" (that used for wasteful doodads).

Outside of debt, I think we'd all agree on one thing: reduce expenses and build your investments *first*, then, once your investments are working for you, use returns from investments to fund your obligations, housing, and lifestyle.

As Dr. Pollack said, "You don't want to rush into buying a home. You want to buy a home in a very sensible way."[136]

Nonetheless, people still want to own. For those who can't heed the call, an interest-only loan may be a way to reduced monthly cashout and straddle both ownership and renting (from the bank).

Personally, I prefer a straight-up rental.

Lago Maggiore

I recently had lunch with an old friend who was in town for business. We've known each other for years; he's been to my house and I've been to his beautiful lakeside home on Lago Maggiore, north of Milan in the Italian Alps.

While telling him about the astounding research and conclusions of this book, he initially retorted as most do: "Yeah, but I've lived for free and, take my older mom for an example. She knows how to buy a house, as an investment, and neither she nor I want to watch and do all the research to trade stocks."

As I explained that I also don't want to trade stocks and just prefer to take the current popular advice of easily buying low-cost ETFs (exchange traded funds) like those available from Vanguard or Schwab, he started to soften.

Gradually, he admitted that he'd lived in his villa 13 years and at 60 +/- was thinking about selling. He reckoned that, after installing the pool and all, he may not have made money. It is nice, but not an investment. He mentioned his wife was reticent to sell because, after all, "they'd just need to buy another house."

My friend explained: "Maybe you're right. Maybe there is a time and point that it is better to buy, about mid-life, now focused on retirement, I'm trying to convince my wife that we do not need another house."

He went on to unravel his vision and line of logic he's using on his wife. As matches up well with the points made herein, he explained: "I told my wife, we don't need another house. I've looked at rental villas in Majorca (a vacation island of Spain) and they are just $2,000 a month. That's $24,000 per year and still only $240,000 or $500,000 after 10 or 20 years, not even what I'd paid on my house in the past."

Then, his eyes brightened a bit as he looked toward a happier retirement and explained, "Even after paying all that rent, I'll still have my money in my bank account growing. And, if I get tired of Majorca, I can move to Florida or wherever."

Ah, he's getting the point. He can have a home, retirement, and money too.

Chapter 7

Building Wealth

Net home equity increased by about 20% or about 6.6% per year in the golden years of the recovery (2013 to 2016). In absolute terms, that was about $107,100 for "those in the bottom half of the income distribution" and "roughly five times larger, at $576,400" for the top 10%.[137]

The data suggests that the rich get richer – the more house you can afford, the more "investment" you control, and the greater absolute benefit to be gained in mean net housing value.

Specifically, at the bottom end, homeowners saw increases in housing value of 13% (4.3% per year) while the top end of owners experienced 25% (8.3% per year).[138] So, where home asset prices increase, the more house you own … the better off you are. Move along, folks. Nothing new here … the rich get richer!

But, improvements in housing is nothing compared impact in wealth coming from increases in business equity. In a sense, the primary residence is chump change.

The average business equity was $1,190,700 in 2016, up 19%, and equity in non-residential property (note: this is NOT the primary residence) was $475,200 **up 72%** – "pooled investments" alone showed growth over 45%.[139]

A house can increase in value and grow wealth; between 13%-25%, in fact, over three years. That's great. But, if the goal is to encourage people toward wealth, the statistics show one might do well to direct people toward business ownership and real estate, as investments, which grew faster over the same period.

Move to the Right

Conventional wisdom would suggest we: go to school, get a good job, and save our money (in our house) to retire rich. Well, Robert Kiyosaki isn't too fond of that plan and I'm not either.

Kiyosaki teaches an alternate path. In his 2011 book, *Rich Dad's CASHFLOW Quadrant: Rich Dad's Guide to Financial Freedom*,[140] Kiyosaki lays out a two-by-two matrix. On the left you have employees and self-employed. This is where it is hard to put a little daylight between expenses (taxes being a big hit) and income. In Kiyosaki's view, people on the left are stuck in the Rat Race. They might be 95% of the population, but they control only 5% of the wealth.

The way out, he suggests, is to move to the right-hand side and become a big Business Owner and, better yet, Investor – where your money makes money. He asserts that his "rich dad" taught him about the right-hand side, where you'll find just 5% of people but 95% of wealth.[141]

Looking at the numbers in the Federal Reserve's Bulletin for September 2017, we see it is indeed true: business owners' wealth far exceeds non-owners by about 6x[142] and it is not just because of their house.

Things which provide cash flow are what Kiyosaki calls "assets." He asserts income-producing "assets" are what make the rich … rich. Owning them is the means to getting out of the Rat Race.

Conversely, things which take money out of your pocket are expenses, better yet: liabilities. Houses, the ones we live in (unless we're running a two-family or B&B), take money out of our pocket. In that sense, they're a liability and not the asset we might hope.

Real estate as an investment is just the kind of thing that *can* provide cash flow and that sector has seen massive growth.

Where we see the growth of real estate investments it causes one to wonder: as a renter, am I on the wrong end of the stick?

If landlords are getting rich, why would I pay them rent and how can renting be better?

The Home as an Investment

Homeownership *may* be an essential stop on the path to personal success; however, it is not a prerequisite requirement to building wealth.

Not only is there plenty that can go wrong in buying a house (you can overpay, you can move too often, you can get a bad mortgage, the neighborhood/market can go south, etc.), but it is just that there are other less expensive, faster-growing investment alternatives.

Nonetheless, the world seems bent on homeownership as the primary "investment" because, after all: everyone needs a place to sleep and no one wants to "throw money away."

Much can be said about the idea of real estate being an asset – when it generates a return for you, as an investment. While some may take Kiyosaki's point to the extreme and question if a home is an "investment" at all, my personal conclusion is: the house we own *IS* a store of value and even an investment, just not a good one in comparison to the other investment options available.

In terms of building wealth, there are different approaches. Another look at the Fed's report, *Changes in U.S. Family Finances* from 2013 to 2016, shows that assets such as bonds and pooled investment funds grew faster, in average value. They grew at 29% and 63%, respectively, in terms of holdings – compared to the mean/average value of houses … which grew 11% (only 3.6% per year, on average) over the same period.[143]

That alone, considering one can get 8%+ in the market and we can get started with just pennies (literally, you can start with just pennies through apps like Acorns.com or Robinhood.com), is enough to convince me.

The primary residence, if considered as an investment, has a massive upfront cost (down payment and the New House Tax), grows slowly, doesn't "rebalance" and reinvest interest to compound in the same way as the market. And, it consumes cash!

In their favor, however, houses DO have: mortgage deductions, leverage, and relative safety. As a part of balanced portfolio, they may make sense. Problem is: the average guy's wealth portfolio (which is like 95% wrapped up in his home) is not so balanced.

The Power of Leverage

Outside of the soft factors, housing, as an investment, benefits from leverage. As leveraged investments go and though people find themselves underwater as a result of the leverage, houses are pretty safe. For some "retail investors" the house may be the only way to access leverage.

Control appreciation of the whole value with just a 10% to 20% down payment is nice. Admittedly, that is a big (very big) advantage which not all simple investments have – based on debt, it might be something Dave Ramsey would hate but Robert Kiyosaki might love. Why?

For example and leaving aside the monthly mortgage payment to maintain the "investment," putting $30,000 down on a $300,000 house would mean you have only 10% in it. Now, let's say it goes up 10% in value.

Oversimplified and leaving aside other factors (like the mortgage, taxes, and maintenance along the way), the way leverage works, the appreciation of 10% to say $330,000 would mean you've doubled the $30,000 of capital originally invested. Where houses generally appreciate close to 5% per year, one can hope that type of Return on Invested Capital (ROIC) *might* be earned in a few short years. On the surface and thanks to leverage, investment in the house seems like a quick path to riches.

With America's primary residence increasing by 11% from 2013-2016, we'd see a 55% return on a 20% down payment. That is nice, really nice! However, as nice as it is, it doesn't match the growth of pooled investments and non-residential property, which increased at 63% and 72%, respectively – not 11% – and may also have been enhanced with leverage.

If leverage is a good thing, staying highly leveraged on your house and not building equity (but rather constantly rebalancing to route free cash to other investments) could be wise financially. What we see, however, is that people want to pay off the house and thereby de-leverage with each mortgage payment they make. Some do a form of "rebalancing" when the house appreciates by pulling money out in the form of a second mortgage – to pay down credit cards or seed other investments.

Both of these behaviors (getting to other, better investments) would seemingly provide evidence to an intuitive understanding that there are other, better places to invest.

The Power of Gross vs. Net

Another thing often overlooked is the big difference between net and gross profit.

Like the Ferrari, it is one thing to buy it but another thing to be able to afford the maintenance. With cars and houses, costs cut at you along the way and reduce the return on the house.

There's a big difference between the gross return and actual net. The death by a thousand cuts is kind of why you can feel house poor as a homeowner, even though the asset is appreciating.

People sing praises of "I made $100,000 on the house. I bought it for $400,000 three years ago and sold it for $500,000 three years later." But, they tend not to include the holding costs and improvement expenses along the way.

Professional real estate investors watch their books more closely, but the average owner tends to see only the gross profit and windfall on payday – the net reality including all the costs in between, not so much.

Frankly, that's understandable. Even billionaire Richard Branson, Founder of The Virgin Group, which employees 60,000 people, is famously known to have difficulty with the difference between net and gross. As the story goes, his accountant had to pull him aside from one meeting and straighten him out.[144]

One major cost of investing is tax. Keeping tax costs low and compound interest are some secrets of the world's wealthiest.

In fact, investor Warren Buffet, who is known for his "buy and hold" strategies, has used low-cost, tax-deferment and rolling over gains to compound earnings and amass fortunes, making him #3 on the Forbes 2018 List of billionaires.[145]

Sure, you can defer taxes with a house, but there are nice 401(k) and Roth IRA plans that do that too.

The Power of Compounding

Appreciation on a house compounds growth from one year to the next. Next year's gains will be made on top of this year's, but it does not reinvest appreciation or not accumulate interest or dividends to be re-invested.

A landlord or property investor can take rent/proceeds from one building and use that to buy the next to maintain leverage and reinvest proceeds.

Houses may grow to a new higher value, based on and including the previous year's increase, but the amount accumulated every year is not "reinvested" to help you own more of that asset.

As we've seen, paying down the mortgage de-leverages the investment. Increases in equity via appreciation or mortgage contributions are not used to buy a larger house or reinvested (until you sell and buy a larger house).

In the market, if you're paid a dividend on a stock, you can set it up to buy more stock. Simplistically, on $1,000 worth of stock, a 10% dividend is easily reinvested to buy $100 more shares – at which point you own $1,100 of that stock. It is not the same or so easily done with the house.

The $300,000 house increasing at a very high rate of 5% per year would take about just two years to arrive at $330,000. That is nice, indeed wonderful. But you have to sell the place (or get a second mortgage) to use the $30,000 increase for a 20% down payment to buy 5x (or $150,000) more house. If the appreciation were reinvested to compounding from there, one would then control a $480,000 ($330,000+$150,000) investment from which to grow.

People do that when they sell and graduate to a new, larger house or refinance to add on, but generally that reinvestment process is not part of the long-term, buy-and-hold housing strategy. I guess that is why we're bent on trying to get a house and fix it up. The sweet equity provides more upside on payday.

Reinvesting dividends (to make money on your money) in the market is as easy as ticking a box in your online account.

Housing Wealth Cap

If one's principal investment is their house, the amount of wealth that can be built is going to be directly related to the house and the amount of equity built over time – as the house increases in value and debt is paid down.

Though houses at the top can increase in absolute prices more significantly, homes increase at a very modest rate – eventually and typically (over the long term and outside of specific market aberrations) in direct proportion and not much over inflation. So, in many senses, the housing investment is capped just over inflation.

As we saw previously, the average increase in net home equity increased more at the top end of houses – in a sense, the bigger the better.

However, the size of house one can afford (and corresponding "investment" one can make in it) is limited by the cash flow available to service the mortgage.

This is true of all investments, but some other investments avail themselves to rebalancing and reinvesting more easily – giving you more bank for your buck over time. Understanding where the long-term benefit of compounding was going to take him is why Warren Buffet says, "I always knew I was going to be rich, so I was never in a hurry."[146]

In the end and until you go through the selling for a profit and scaling up to a bigger investment, the return on the house is capped. Investment in larger houses is limited by the amount of cash available to service the mortgage. Larger houses, with larger mortgages, need more income to support them. Thus, the path to true wealth may be found less in the house and more in moving to the right-hand side of Kiyosaki's Cash Flow Quadrant – where you own businesses and investments that generate cash flow and benefit from reinvestment, rebalancing, and compounding.

With more cash flowing, one can afford more house, more investments, more everything. But houses, the ones we live in, do not increase cash flow – they consume it. So the home might be an investment, but one that is not nearly as liberating as the freedom (emotional and financial) one finds building an investment portfolio.

Blowing the Lid off It

The doctor friend of mine who was making great money from his orthopedic practice in the late 1980's seemingly, with no knowledge of it, mastered the Cash Flow Quadrant theory.

Before the 1986 tax reform, it was the glory days of doctor-hood, and he was making a killing. Making good money from his doctoring (on the left-hand side of Kiyosaki's matrix), he was making a fortune from the medical building, including his MRI business he owned (on the right-hand side.)

I don't think he knows who Robert Kiyosaki is, but my doctor friend would be the archetype example. He made good money from his practice and used that to feed investments in his vacation condos and build his MRI business. His private plane lifestyle was so insane that some joked that he was dealing drugs. In reality, through his doctoring he was "dealing" MRIs – and reinvesting proceeds in stocks to compound wealth.

The true wealth didn't come from his condos or MRI – though they enabled it. His wealth of a lifetime came from the minority stake he held in a bank – shares he was able to buy thanks to income from his businesses.

My doctor friend mastered the three kinds of income: 1) Ordinary Income – from doctoring 2) Passive Income – from condos and MRIs and 3) Portfolio Income – from stocks. He moved quickly through to the enviable bottom right of Kiyosaki's Cash Flow Quadrant.

While his real estate was/is nice (really nice), the return from those was limited. The MRI business was The Goose that Laid the *Silver* Egg. Literally, silver is a by-product of the MRI scanner. He not only got the income from each scan performed, but he also had bars of pure silver in the glove box of his Porsche – literally. Bank shares added wealth.

Interestingly, he eventually sold his medical building to an investor and commenced paying rent as a tenant – for the same bricks, mortar, and square footage he used to "own." He made money, got out, and chose to rent back the bricks and mortar for his medical practice.

Growing Value

It takes time and setting aside funds to build up investments. We can always get more money, but we can't get back time. So, with time being more irreplaceable than money, it pays to take advantage of time and start investing early.

Bigger investment allocations are nonetheless important. That's why, rather than looking under the cushions for a few extra coins, it makes sense to look for bigger savings – perhaps zooming in on the largest family expense, housing!

Lessons from the *Richest Man in Babylon*, a 1926 classic by George Samuel Clauon,[147] tell a great story – I liked the audio version read in an English accent. It is not some arrogant story of "Richie Rich" (as the title may suggest), but rather a story of trials: a man's rough path on the road to building wealth.

Among the many lessons Clauson teaches, principal ideas are: pay yourself first, in the form of contributions to your own wealth account, before anything else; and, do not spend from the wealth account (or interest earned) until interest is being made on the interest earned.

Conventional recommendations often range from suggesting setting aside "whatever you can" to 10%, or even 20% of gross income – before taxes. The more the better! But, even if you can't get to that point, a few hundred can go a long way.

To maintain your lifestyle in retirement, it is recommended to have many times (like 10x or 15x) one's annual expenses built up in an investment account. At that point, one can pull out 4-6% per year, live off the interest, and not worry about spending through the principal.

Using easy numbers, having 15x of a $100,000 income would provide a $1.5M investment account. Pulling off even 5% per year, you'd not even cut into principal and you'd have $75,000 to live on.

Value of Starting Early

Where other financial books touch on housing as a component of the overall financial plan, here we do the inverse.

Other financial analysts and professionals of that field have written plenty on wealth development. If not Clauson's classic, start studying David Bach, Dave Ramsey, and/or Robert Kiyosaki, or, or, or… There are plenty of people. Personally, I found great value in and suggest Tony Robbins' book *Unshakeable: Your Financial Freedom Playbook.*[148] He took a personal mission to help the average guy by compiling advice from the very top of the top financial advisers.

If there is one thing on which advisers universally agree, it is the value of starting early. Among other things, in his book Tony tells a story. From memory and with different numbers, here's the gist:

> Two 18-year-old friends get together and agree to start saving (i.e., investing) $100/month in the market. In both cases, it's assumed they're earning at the long-term average (here stated at 9%), left to compound interest until age 65.

- One guy starts saving immediately, from age 18:
    - He continues until he's 28, just 10 years of saving
    - He never adds another dime after age 28
    - He leaves the balance to compound
    - At age 65 he has an account worth: $463,456
- The other guy starts saving too, but commences at age 28:
    - He contributes every month too
    - He adds $100 month, but for 37 years
    - The balance compounds
    - At age 65 he has $324,967.15

The early bird saves *for just 10 years*; while the other guy delays just 10 years. The late starter saves for 27 *extra* years and ends with less. The guy who starts earlier, finishes richer – though he only put away $12,000 and the late starter puts away $44,400.[149] That's the incredible power of compounded interest and starting early.

Thank you, Tony Robbins, for presenting that information which highlights the value of starting early.

No Money to Save

Life is expensive and, commonly, people can't find any money to save – not even under the sofa cushions.

Thus the need to examine the biggest expense: housing. Some joke about brown bagging it to save money, and Chris Guillebeau suggests the value getting a "side hustle" to make some extra cash and provides his *Side Hustle School* to help people figure it out.[150]

While making more money is a great long-term answer and while controlling expenses on lunch can help in the meantime, controlling the housing expense in the first place might be a bigger source of savings.

Houses are like the Tom Hanks movie suggested: a *Money Pit.*[151] In saving on housing one is the opposite of "penny wise and pound foolish."

Houses, if nothing else, are a great temptation to *spend* money. I need this! Wouldn't that be nice? Money flies out of one's pocket. Building wealth requires *investing/growing* money – not spending or even storing it.

In 2017 people were making over 30% in a simple 401(k). The average return in the S&P over time is 9% – even 18% or 27% might be possible.

The below table shows what a 45-year-old could build, by age 65, at various rates … saving (5%, 10%, or 15%) of a $60,000 salary.

$60,000 Income	Annual Compound Interest Rate		
Amount Saved (from 45 to 65 years)	9%	18%	27%
5% = $250/mo.	$160,864	$421,688	$1,497,699
10% = $500/mo.	$321,728	**$843,377**	$2,995,398
15% = $750/mo.	$482,592	$1,265,065	$4,493,097

(See Appendix: Compound Interest at Various Rates)

The numbers, especially the ones in the bottom right, are astounding.[152] What's even more interesting is the amount of interest being earned. In year 20, the annual interest earned on $500 per month, compounded at 18% (the middle amount in **bold**), is $146,523 per year! Higher rates of interest are critical. Compounding over time grows wealth fast.

What Can $50K Buy?

The price of the average of houses sold in the 3rd quarter of 2017 was $375,700.[153]A 15% down payment on that would be $56,355.

To cover some other price points, roughly speaking, $56,335 is about 20% on a $250,000 house or 10% to access a $500,000 house.

Fifty thousand dollars is a lot of money – like the entry fee to join a very special country club. In this case, however, it's the very special "club" of homeownership, which brings with it the monthly obligation of servicing the loan and paying taxes, maintenance, and repair.

Consider … if not allocated to the down payment on a house, what can $50,000 buy in terms of retirement? Take $50,000 at age 45 and put it to work at 9% (and never save another dime, just compounded the interest) ... it will provide over $280,220 at age 65.

So $50,000, applied to house, buys an average down payment, PLUS the honor of making mortgage payments over the next 20-30 years AND paying property taxes and repairs along the way. But, it's not so sure the $250,000 house will similarly add $280,220 in value over 20 years.

That $50,000 initial investment made at age 45 growing compounded at 9% to $280,220 would be earning about $2,000 in interest per month at age 65. The interest alone could pay for a lot of housing going forward. But the thought naturally leads to: Well, I'll still need a place to live in the meantime and so I may as well pay a mortgage.

The graphic from Zillow shows LESS than $565 per month goes to principal in the first five years, of an average loan for an average house. That means, of the total $2,460/month payment $1,895 per month is going to the combination of: interest, taxes, insurance, and PMI – which seems to provide little value.[154]

For comparison, the December average 2017 median rental home was $1,472/month.[155]

Where Do I Make Even Just 5%?

There are many, many places to make 5%, but it takes a skilled investor.

Trading is not for the faint of heart. Like houses, there's a lot of emotion tied up in it … which is what makes most of us "bad investors." Money can be made from the hip every now and again, but the most successful traders are systematic traders – following a strategy.

Tony Robbins has dedicated his life to making a difference in people's lives. He believes that, even if you manage yourself very well, personally, the whole success package includes financial freedom.

Wanting to help people in total is why Tony took to researching and writing two books on the topic. *Unshakeable: Your Financial Freedom Playbook*,[156] (which is the shorter of the two and might be considered an introduction, even if it was written later) and *Money – Master the Game: 7 Simple Steps to Financial Freedom*[157] – the more detailed blueprint for securing financial freedom.

His books are well worth the read. He suggests, time and again, that buying and holding low-cost index funds (to reduce the negative impact of fees) is a great strategy for the average guy. He might be right – especially considerig the people he interviewed as part of the primary research for his books.

Or, if you love houses, consider real estate as an investment.

Robert Kiyosaki has also dedicated his life to helping people grow their Financial IQ. He offers many great courses and levels of coaching through his Rich Dad company. He shows people how to buy investment properties with little or nothing down and get proper coaching through the process to generate cash flow and value appreciation. He exposes real estate as a true asset.

Either way, reducing expenses (the New House Tax, property taxes, interest, and maintenance) that accompany the luxury called a house might be a great way to scrape together savings that can be invested to make more than 5% per year, growing cash flow and value!

Lego Factor

Kids love playing with them and I am unfortunately constantly stepping on them – Legos. Not only are Legos one of the most popular kids toys, but they're also one of the most expensive. We love to spoil our kids with them.

Indeed, the Toy Industry Association reported in 2016 that parents spent about $6,500 dollars on toys, in general. In 2015, it was similarly about $499 per year.[158] To put that in perspective, $500 per year is $41.50 per month or $1.40 per day.

We've heard about the Latte Factor (the idea that skipping the $5 coffee can be enough to secure a solid retirement), but what about the Lego Factor?

Where we've prevously seen that $50,000 grows to $280,220 over 20 years, we could guess that $5,000 (of toys over ten years), which is about 10% of $50K, would grow to $28,220. If not spent on toys, that's enough to pay for a nice college!

Remember the guys who saved $100 a month (the one does it for 10 years), eventually growing to $463,456 by age 65? Could we perhaps stop the toys and save the $41.50 per month? If so, that is about $5,000 (half of the $12,000 he saved) over 10 years. Might it grow to half ($231,728)?

Delayed gratification and clarity on expenditures (the famous "won't power" – the ability to resist loose spending) is an important measure of what makes the rich, rich. We've all heard about the "stingy millionaires." Are they stingy because they're millionaires or are they millionaires because they're stingy?

I get it. Believe me, I get it. With 8 of them, I get it that kids need toys. We've got to be generous and share. No doubt! But at what price?

Do we want $6,000 worth of spoiled kids and baskets of broken toys or do we want well-educated, disciplined children who graduate college free from debt and with some savings in the bank?

Maybe we could put up to $3,000 after-tax dollars in an ESA (Education Savings Accounts) to grow tax-free for kids' education, up to age 30.

Experience By Association

In a coversation over lunch, talking about my book with the family, I mentioned how people can feel like they really know what they're doing with housing investments just because they live in one.

My kids got the point and started joking around, saying, "Yeah, I eat all the time, so I'll be a great cook." Another jumped in: "I love nice clothes, so I'd make a great designer." And the kicker: "I've lived in houses all my life, so I'd make a great landlord."

While there may be some truth in those examples, in the sense that a passion can become a business, the gap between observational experience and actually doing is wide and deep.

Just because one has observed clothes, investments, or houses does not mean one is going to make it as a great designer, investor, or real estate mogul.

However, that is just what we seem to do. We seem to think that, just because we've lived in houses all our lives or know what we like, that we know how to fix them up or make money on them. Fact is, you can get lucky at something every now and again, but to get good at it takes practice. That's why the average investor does very poorly investing his own money in the market. That's why experts recommed simply buying (and holding) market index funds – which have grown so popular. If you don't know Vanguard, maybe you should!

Houses are something we buy rather irregularly and mostly based on circomstance or need, not investment potential. Yet we want to think we can make money at it.

Some may prove to be very adept with their housing and finances. Personally, for me, the house is bit like nice wine: I know what I like when I taste it, but I could not pick a winner by the variety, region, or year. Heck, not even by the label. I choose based on price. Higher-priced wines must be better, right?

This is one reason why I prefer to leave my investing and housing to professionals. That gives me choice, flexibility and expertise. I like Renting My Way to Freedom.

Home Improvement Doesn't Pay

A little subtlety is the likelihood people have to *overspend* on a house they "own," as compared to conserving and underspending on one they rent! People love to sink money into the bottomless money pit but don't "waste money" on a rental.

The professional house flippers make money in large part because of the good deal they get when they buy and the price for which they sell. But they need to be very well-regulated on how much they spend on improvements in between.

As reported on HGTV, "You're less likely to recoup your investment in a major kitchen or bathroom remodel than you are to get back what you spend on basic home maintenance such as new siding." People who overspend on their house in purchase price or improvements have a hard time making money.

Everyone wants (and often spends on) the granite counters and steam showers. Glitzy kitchens and baths sell – but not all improvements get the return. They sell from an ascetic "curb appeal" perspective, but "the only home improvement likely to return more at resale was a minor (roughly $15,000) kitchen remodel, which returned 92.9 percent." [159]

Big projects take a long time to recover investment-wise. Rich people know this when they make additions and improvements to their house. They make the improvements knowing full-well they'll never getting their money out, but they do it anyway because they want it. That is why, when I rent or (if I) buy, I follow rich people. They spend money in making a house to make it nice for their family and to impress their friends. I ride the coattails of their spending.

The kicker is that most people are novices with real estate investments. Frankly, the reasons I made money on my house was because: a) I bought it from my dad, with a "family discount" and b) I timed the market right when it came time to sell. Were it not for those things, investment from all the improvements in between would have killed me.

They might even be a professor of accounting, but most retail buyers don't time their purchase with the market's investment cycles. Rather, people buy and move based on life events or emotional sprees when they see a house they're dying for – seriously.

Chapter 8

Boiled Frog Syndrome

It is interesting that businesses, in the business of making money, will choose to rent their facility from a professional manager as the logical thing to do. Yet with housing, we tend to buy a little over 60% of the time.

Housing is like the Boiled Frog Syndrome, where a frog goes from taking a bath in a nice warm pot, to then – since they don't jump out – unknowingly boiling to death as the heat of the water rises from the flame underneath.

We too slowly bleed our finances, not realizing how much money we're spending every month on the luxury of homeownership. We've been conditioned to believe that "a house is an asset" and it takes some energy to consider the other side of the story: the house as an expense (or investment), consuming cash.

In analyzing the choice between renting vs. buying, I originally looked at the historic prices with data coming straight from information at the US Census Bureau. [160] They have data on the long-term average (median) home value, 1940-2000. That's what I used. I have not updated it with the more recent Census Data from 2010, because the 60-year period seems fair enough. And the period from 2000 to 2008/2009 was a bubble anomoly – in my opinion.

The recent time may have been the greatest period to be an owner, and perhaps the 2010-2012 period was a great time to buy; however, it's been volitile and it's taken nearly a decade to recover from 2008-2009. Compare that to the stock market, which is "amazingly resilient." For example, "2008 [was] the poorest year for stocks since 1931…. From the March 9 lows to the end of 2009, the S&P 500 soared 64.83%."[161] Then on "March 28, 2013: the S&P 500 ends at 1,569.19, surpassing its previous record closing high set in 2007."[162] It took the housing market an extra three years to recover.

Throwing Your Money Away

Nonetheless, we can't shake the common refrain: you're just throwing your money away when you rent. However, going out to dinner just is also "throwing money away" and we do that.

The subtlety to consider is that housing, like dinner, is an expense. We're "throwing away money" either as rent or a mortgage. Like dinner, we can spend more eating out or less eating at home.

Rent is a more obvious expense: paid, it keeps you in the house another month. A house owned carries the impression of being cheaper.

But consider … houses are expensive and it takes the mortgage being paid to stay in the house another month or two.

In that view, the mortgage (interest – which is the majority of the payment in the first part of loan) is ALSO "throwing your money away." Like eating, which you need to do, there are cheaper and more expensive options. Housing might be considered similarly. In fact, renting might be the cheaper "eat at home" option.

On a standard 30-year mortgage, the interest paid basically doubles the price of the house. A 30-year mortgage on $30,600, at 5.5% interest, would have $31,947 in interest, over and above the principal.

That would be $30,600 for the house itself, plus an additional $31,947 in interest.

What About Mortgage Tax Deductions?

Now, the mortgage is not *exactly* throwing money away because, after all, a mortgage pays down principal and includes a tax deduction on the interest paid.

So, if you have a 30% tax rate and pay mortgage interest, 30% of that interest cost could be deducted from your tax bill.

You're not actually or completely "throwing away money," because some of it comes back in the form of tax savings. Right?

Right!

But not so fast …

Despite the fact that the government is constantly looking to reduce/eliminate that deduction, there is still about 70% of interest being "thrown away" … or about $20,000 in the previous ($31,947) example. You might be getting a discount on taxes, but you're paying a lot to the bank in the meantime.

It reminds me of the joke about the lady who bought the item because it was on sale. Her husband is thinking that it would have been a lot cheaper to have not bought the item at all.

Same here, and as Dave Ramsey says in the Pay Off the Home Mortgage chapter of *The Total Money Makeover*,[163] the mortgage tax deduction is no rationale for keeping a loan, as it is a very expensive way to get a tax discount.

Heck, what it seems is that the government is subsidizing the bank. You pay the bank in full, but the government coughs up the rebate.

Appreciation < Mortgage + Property Tax

In perhaps the simplest terms, if nothing else, owning a house costs at least: mortgage interest + property tax (we'll add in maintenance later).

For most, to hold the house (as an investment) means paying at least the mortgage and the property tax.

We'll get more exact, but as rough estimates, property taxes can be 2% and mortgage interest could average about 5%.

Together that is about 7% per year to hold a house.

Problem is: houses, even in the best markets, appreciate between 4%-6% (call it 5%) per year.

A "back of the paper napkin" calculation would suggest that: in paying 7% and only gaining 5%, it costs about 2% to "own" a house – in addition to the principal, maintenance, and repair.

One might view 2% as "paying yourself" to own a house. Not bad. In fact, 2% is cheap "rent."

On a $300,000 house, 2% is only $6,000 dollars or $500 per month to "own" a house … plus principal (and maintenance).

That's not too bad and understandable. Thus, it feels cheaper to own – as most people don't roll in maintenance and other costs.

It also explains why people who see owning as cheaper can still feel "house poor" at the end of the month – the additional costs take their stealthy toll.

Perhaps it is all just a nominal price to be paid for housing and accumulating appreciation value? Or is it?

Houses *DO* Appreciate!

Since 1940, houses have appreciated in value.

In 1940 the median house value was $2,928. That grew to $119,600 by 2000.

So, it's true: houses *DO* appreciate.

While some periods did better than others, in particular 1970 to 2000, over the long term, houses appreciate at 6.37% (the light blue line).

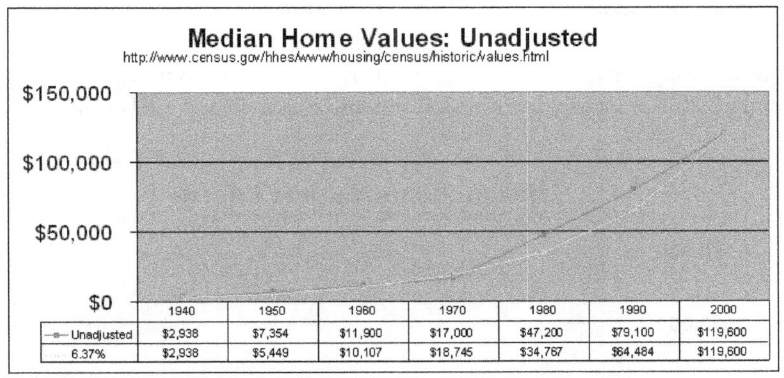

	1940	1950	1960	1970	1980	1990	2000
Unadjusted	$2,938	$7,354	$11,900	$17,000	$47,200	$79,100	$119,600
6.37%	$2,938	$5,449	$10,107	$18,745	$34,767	$64,484	$119,600

(Source Data: US Census Data) [164]

Frankly, that's not bad … at 6.37%. That doubles money every 11 years or so.

Perhaps that's why we're left with the impression that: "houses are a good investment." Heck, after all: "they appreciate in value."

True, they do appreciate in value; in fact: 6.37% *(which is different from the 4.3% previously mentioned because of calculation methods used).*

But wait, there's more … we've got to adjust for inflation.

What About Inflation?

The previous figures, 6.37%, are *un*-adjusted for inflation. They show only the absolute increase in the value of the house, with the current dollar value each year

Take inflation into account and it is interesting to see what happens. Current dollars are the economic term for unadjusted for inflation – it's the actual dollar price. I understand the economic terms "current" and "constant" like this: in Current Dollars we'd still have nickel and dime stores, but in Constant Dollars we now have dollar stores.

Adjusted for inflation, in year 2000 dollars, the house (which was worth $119,600 in 2000) had a real dollar cost of $30,600 back in 1940 constant dollars – not $2,928 stated in 1940 current dollars.

Over the long term, after adjusting for inflation, houses increase in value at only 2.29% annually over and above inflation. That's a BIG difference.

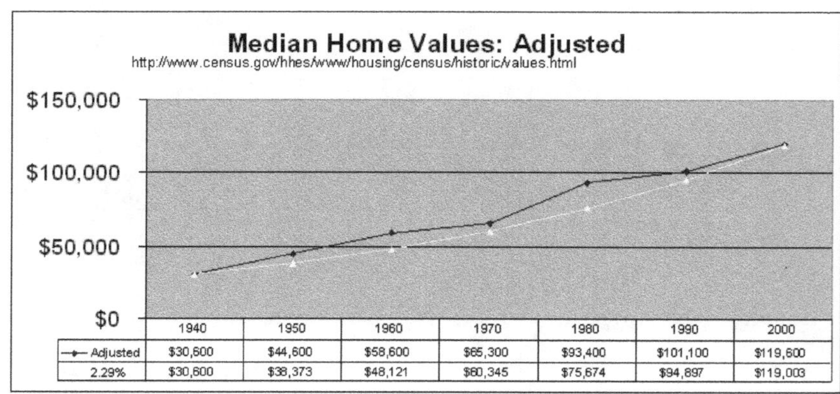

	1940	1950	1960	1970	1980	1990	2000
Adjusted	$30,600	$44,600	$58,600	$65,300	$93,400	$101,100	$119,600
2.29%	$30,600	$38,373	$48,121	$60,345	$75,674	$94,897	$119,003

(Source Data: US Census Data)[165]

2.29% is like an old-school savings account rate – and we have not yet even considered the maintenance upkeep!

Specific markets, locations, or times differ, of course. The blue line shows thus interim periods where short-term gains outpaced the long-term average. Great for flippers. But the long term is more even.

From Bad, to Worse …

Unfortunately, calculations on data from the US Census show that houses appreciate at only 2.29% over inflation.

Assets earning just 2.29% are NOT typically great investments except maybe as a store of value or hedge against inflation.

The weight of the so-called "asset" is even heavier when considered in light of the carrying cost.

One should consider all the other expenses (i.e., liabilities) associated with it, like: maintenance, repairs, and improvements … which are NOT accounted for in and are NOT deducted from the appreciation rates previously shown.

So, from the 2.29% we need to deduct maintenance, repairs, and improvements.

You may still be thinking: "Yeah, but I'll get a tax deduction on the mortgage."

Not so fast; we'll get to that that too ... if new tax plans don't eliminate it first.

Expenses Cut the Return to Just 1.5%

Now, take the maintenance, repairs, and improvements into account (to say nothing about real estate commissions), which also cut into the returns over the period.

Let's say, for example, that the house absorbs a little less than $100/month or about $1,000 per year in improvements. Not saying $100 *every* month, but on average and in constant dollars about $1,000 on maintenance or improvements per year. Not much; a couple trips to Home Depot would take care of that.

Like a mortgage payment, this hypothetical $100 expense is "fixed" in the calculation and is thus overstated at the beginning, in 1940, and understated at the end, 2000. But, as an even number, over 60 years, it adds up to about $60,000.

So, with that assumption, the net on the house is just $29,000 ($89,000-$60,000) over 60 years. That leaves less than $500/year, or about 1.5% of return.

So, all alone and with a "back of the envelope" type of calculation, the improvements consume most of the "appreciation" made on the house.

We feel rich on the day we sell the house (if we have equity) because we don't tend to account for all our "investments" over time; but, we feel "house poor" through the process as we can't even tell from where all the money is sieving out of our wallet.

All this (at least for me) provides a deeper appreciation for the scary fact of what Robert Kiyosaki brought to the forefront in 1997: houses are not assets because they barely appreciate and take money out of your pocket along the way.

Particular situations might be greater or lesser, but the idea remains: renting may not be as expensive as one thinks and buying might be more expensive than one can imagine.

If this house were a business, I'm not sure I'd invest. It needs to generate cash flow income to become interesting.

Money Under the Mattress

The increase from $30,600 to $119,600 netted $89,000 (2.39% annually, adjusted for inflation). Right?

Yes, $89,000 is … nice.

In fact, not bad on what was originally a very small "investment." Nearly three times the money!

But, that is over 60 years. AND it is not like the investment was reinvesting and rebalancing to compound earnings over that time.

As we know, other investments with dividends, rebalancing, and stock repurchasing reinvest proceeds to make "interest on the interest." With the house, the "reinvestment" is in upgrading the house, adding on, or "rebalancing" a new mortgage.

Sure, that is possible. But, the house is more like holding some bars of gold, stuck under your mattress. No reinvesting appreciated value for compounding, or at least not in the same way or as easily done in the market.

The difference in compounded vs. straight line interest is ENORMOUS!

The 8th Wonder of the World

Consider a $10,000 deposit at 9% held for 30 years.

Earning straight interest on the balance provides $37,017 at the end of 30 years. Not bad … it makes nearly three times ($27,017) the money and ends with nearly four times the capital.[166]

But the same $10,000 earning compounding interest annually (reinvesting to have interest on the interest) provides $132,676 at the end of 30 years.[167]

> Straight line interest: $37,017
> Compounded interest: $132,676

Nearly $95,000 difference. That is ENORMOUS. Is there any wonder they call compound interest The 8th Wonder of the World?

So astounding are those numbers, I had to check (and double-check) them, again and again.

But, by basic math, we see that simple interest at 9% on $10,000 earns $900 per year. So the end of 30 years is basically $900 x 30 or $27,000 added to the original $10,000.

Compounding, however, earns $900 the first year. Then $981 the 2nd and then $1,069. And so on … the difference starts really "compounding" (pardon the pun) in later years.

In a sense, the house which grows at 5% from $200,000 to $210,000 in the first year will "compound" as the growth the following year is calculated from $210,000. So, another 5% takes it to $220,500. The extra $500 is growth on growth. That's great! But the extra $500 is not used to buy more house.

Putting your interest to work, so your interest makes interest, is what compounding is all about. A house does not increase the position size or doubling down to "earn interest on the interest." In fact, an investment in the house is "de-leveraging" over time as the principal balance is paid down every year.

Where to Invest?

People are still confounded, not knowing where to invest. So they default to the house.

But, frankly, the hurdle is so low it doesn't matter where you invest. You just have to beat 2.39% or so – the suggested long-term average on houses.

Stop! I take that back. Considering the average individual investor, left to their own devices, makes less than 1.9% … the house might be safer!

So choose wisely.

However, as an example, beat inflation by even just 5% and the savings retirement could be on a totally different trajectory.

As an alternative to sinking $30,600 into a house in 1940, which grows to $119,600 by 2000, invest in something that grows just 5% over inflation.

Doing that would provide $571,583 at the end of the same period – not $119,600 worth of bricks and mortar.

The retirement nest egg is a choice:

- a somewhat illiquid hunk of brick-and-mortar, worth $119,600,
- or $571,583 of liquid cash investments?

I know where I am … how about you?

Millionaire Habits

Fintech has come up with more and more tools lately. Where it used to "take money to make money," people can get started now with literally just pennies.

If you want to invest in the market, broadly: choose Acorns.com. If you want to pick a stock or two, try Robinhood.com. If you want to invest in a basket of the top crypto currencies, try CoinSeed.com. You can start with literally pennies, pulling just the round-ups or small amounts straight from your credit card with each of these.

Acorns has a nice newsletter in which they will often promote people who have become millionaires by saving and squirreling away their money. It is funny how often they site frugality on housing expense as a key determiner of savings.

But where scrimping and savings is not for everyone, tips on building wealth may be more appropriate.

Recently, Jackie Lam gave tips including: "5 Millionarie Habits That Can Help You Build Wealth, Too" summarized here:

- ***Practice perseverance*** *– don't give up; after a set-back, dust yourself off and get up.*
- ***Spend according to your values*** *– forget the fear of missing out (FOMO) or keeping up with The Joneses.*
- ***Save, save, save*** *– 95% of wealthy people save at least 20% of their after-tax income.*
- ***Embrace delayed gratification*** *– save on housing and route to long-term retirement, leverage compound interest.*
- ***Create a not-to-do list*** *– avoid things that aren't worthy of your time and delegate where possible.*

In summary, one key might be to simply know what we're doing and why. Have a strong purpose because building wealth is hard work and the efforts and sacrifices along the way take personal discipline.

Chapter 9

Rent vs. Buy Calculations

It would seem like this whole thing is resolved simply enough by running a few numbers in one of the many rent vs. buy calculators freely available on the web. After all, they generally conclude that buying is usually favorable – which is kind of the problem.

Renting doesn't get a fair shake and people subjected to renting can feel left out, as some kind of second-class citizen. Well, they shouldn't!

As for the calculators, most show results considering a 30-year timeframe. They don't, in general, consider a holistic perspective of life's other considerations, like: a) preference for freedom b) mobility and the fact people move every 4.7 years c) investment alternatives for the down payment and d) timing of purchase with the market factors.

In my research, I ran various scenarios in *The ULTIMATE Rent vs. Buy Calculator* by Micheal Bluejay.[168] Michael's calculator is nice, as it takes into account both the increase in rental price and investment income (made from savings) over the years, and the New Home Tax.

As Michael points out, most all rent vs. buy calculators show that ownership is more favorable. Thus, it's no wonder people are of the mind to buy! But, Michael also does a great job in saying that calculators are only as good as their assumptions.

For me, one major assumption is the fact I could do better with my down payment invested in the market than in brick-and-mortar AND that I'll be moving a few times within the 30 years.

In my opinion, softer factors are major (but often overlooked or under-considered) in the rent vs. buy decision. I've found the calculator on the New York Times interactive[169] does a good job and takes a few more items into account.

A Bias to Buying

Moody's Economy website *had* a rent vs. buy calculator on their site, at least back in 2008/2009.

At that time, I took $119,900 as an example home value and excluded the concept of inflation (from both the rent and buy scenario) and showed a 2% the increase in the home over inflation, as demonstrated in the following charts. A simple rental price, at 1.5 times the estimated mortgage, was used – but, that might have been high and negatively handicapped the rent scenario. The resulting chart has a nice, easy-to-read visual curve.

At first glance, the chart definitely supports the idea and common (mis)conception that it is better to own than rent. After all, it says: "Buying is better than renting after 6 years." Yes, in 24 of the 30 years, it is more favorable to own than rent.

However, a different perspective could rephrase that to say: "*Renting* is *better* than owning <u>*before*</u> year 7."

That's an important factor. How long you plan to stay matters. Stay less than 7 years (many people move frequently) and one is better off renting.

Deeper consideration of the chart would reveal a couple more points in support of the idea of renting versus owning.

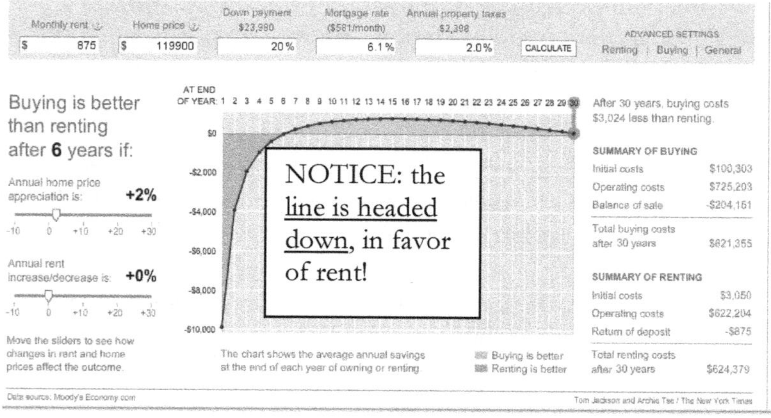

First, the cash flow

What the rent versus own calculations show are annual comparisons. Thus, the chart might say: **"In the 6th year, the annual costs of ownership are less, per year, than renting."** Why is that important?

Look to the right of the chart. It shows that after 30 years, in total, owning the house is only $3,024 cheaper. So, all the risk and money tied up in the house … all for just $3,024 (spread over 30 years) – that's like $30 a month and, actually, that portion is accumulated only in the later years. *Note: that chart has no allocation made for increases of inflation (owned or rented).*

Different calculators, each with different algorithms, provide different results.

As available in the Appendix, *The ULTIMATE Rent vs. Buy Calculator* was run with similar assumptions to the Moody's example. It shows renting is beneficial, until the fourth year, and then, over 30 years, owning is $352,579 better. So, owning is better than renting (financially) over 30 years.[170] Right? Purely speaking, yes!

A quick look at the chart and calculators would suggest one does well to move forward with the impulse and press the BUY button.

Looking at the decision again, however, a few things show up:

- Rather consistently, it works out that, because of closing costs and all the other fees associated with buying (The New House Tax), it is often cheaper to rent during the early years and cheaper to own over the longer term.
- The savings in the near-term years (years 1-6) are orders of magnitude greater than the savings in future years. Renting is $8,406 more favorable in the first year alone, in one calculation.
- The savings on owning accrue in later years, but the annual benefit can diminish as house maintenance increases.

Implications (as I see them): If you want to save money now … rent! If you're going to stay in the same house for 12-24 years, consider buying it. But remember, when building wealth in the market, it pays to start early because the value of compounding kicks in overtime, and that can eventually outpace gains of appreciation or benefit of renting.

Time Value of Money

As any good director of finance will tell you, there is much more value in near-term money than money further off in the future.

For example, if someone were to give you $10,000, would you rather have it today … or next year? Clearly, the sooner you get it the better.

But do rent vs. buy calculators take that into account? Well, yes and no.

The ULTIMATE Rent vs Buy Calculator includes the value of the annual cash flow savings, but it doesn't include the potential alternate use of and value of the down payment earning in the market.

As noted on his site, Michael Bluejay says:

Return on Investment (ROI)

"Some people take the money saved by renting instead of buying and invest it (e.g., into mutual funds). If you're not buying a house, you should certainly invest in something; otherwise, you have no investment.

The Return on Investment listed is just that – the return on the investment. ***That is, it doesn't include the principal of the investment itself.*** *We compare apples to apples for renting vs. buying because on both sides we consider only the return generated [on the amount saved each year] and not the principal." (Emphasis added)*[171]

As I understand that, it would suggest that the calculator there does not take into account the alternate use of the principal (in the market, for example) if not invested in that house.

That is significant and one major reason why I like renting – I have my principal to invest.

How Long Will You Stay?

The analysis, over the long term, shows the "benefit" of owning a house is NOT so cut and dry.

Expensive improvements are made, not only at the beginning of ownership to get the place ready the way you want, but at the end too as the wear and tear of time takes its toll. Today a man is outside repairing the stucco work on my rented home – with no cost to me. The owner needs to do it, or the place falls apart – literally. It's on him, not me.

The "New House Tax" (commissions, early improvements, etc.) can be expensive. Once you get past that initial burden, there are a few years of calm (where it makes sense to own a house) before the long term maintenance starts creeping up.

The sweet spot for owning a house starts to accrue in years 4 to 6 and lasts until years 12 to 15 depending on the particulars of the house and mortgage. It takes few years of those savings, from owning, to cover what you *could have* saved by renting, in the first years.

My conclusion: If you're staying in a house at least "N" years (between 5 and 15 years), it may make sense to own it. And, if you're staying in a house less than 5 or 6 years, it may *not* make sense to own it.

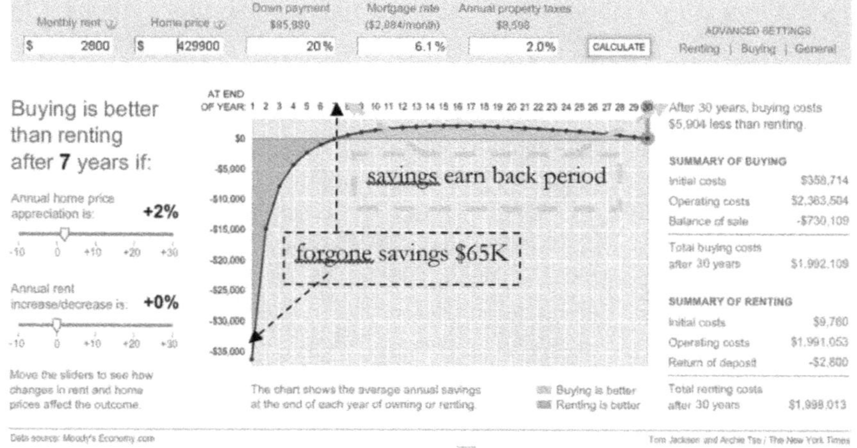

What if its Owned Outright?

While "owning it outright" might reduce interest fees and give an important sense of security and pride, it seems using OPM (other people's money, i.e., the bank's) leaves you with some cash for other investments.

For example, assume buying the house outright – paying no mortgage. As the chart below shows, it is indeed cheaper to own … in fact, $26,177 cheaper over 30 years.

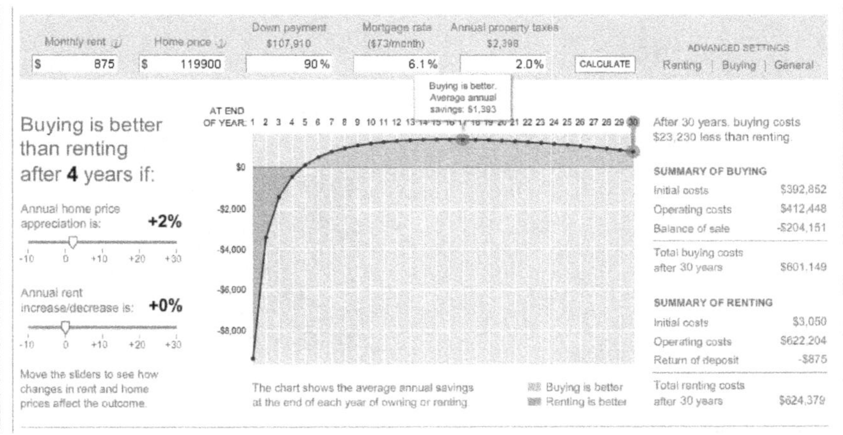

But, once again, in support of renting, consider the following:

You have greater savings (better cash flow) in the near term by renting, which gives you more freedom to invest in other things. Having extra cash buys freedom to invest. Buying a house literally ties up all your money, in the house, making just 2.9%.

The curve rounds over as advantage in favor of owning starts to slide away after year 16.

Most people who are in favor of "owning" feel this way because they believe and want to "own something" … especially over the long term.

Interesting: the numbers suggest, even outright, owning may anyhow round out over time.

Some Examples

In the neighborhood where I grew up in Cincinnati, houses sell for about $250,000 to $450,000 and a rental is between about $950-$2,300.[172]

Specifically, here are some examples of houses that were both for rent and for sale back in 2008/2009. These were nice houses, in nice areas.

Estimated Value ($258,000) **Rental Offer ($1,800)**

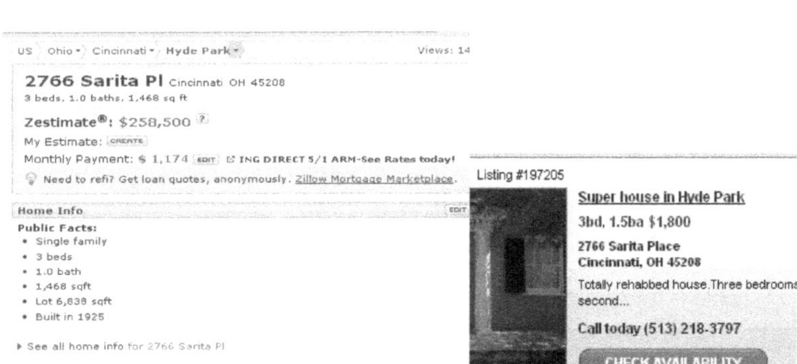

Rent versus Own Calculation *(The Rent vs. Buy calculator says: 'Buy.")*

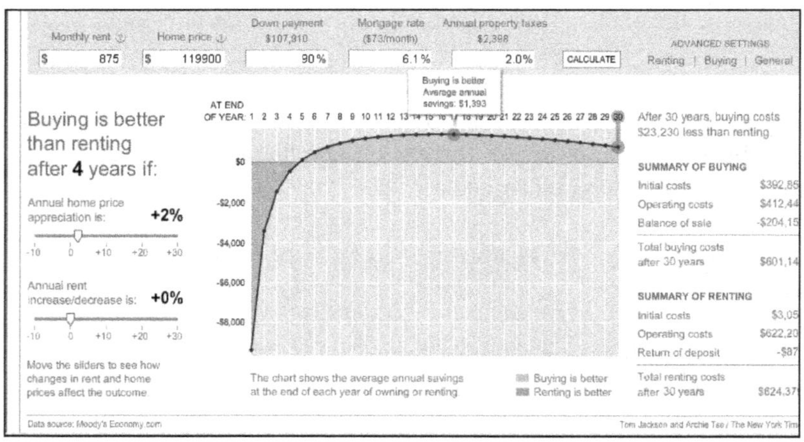

<u>Opinion</u>: Dramatically cheaper to rent, in the near term … and not too great of savings over the long term. Buying is only better by a fraction (about $23,000 better or 1% of the house value), and the poor cash flow upfront doesn't appeal to me.

Another Example

Estimated Value ($429,900) Rental Offer ($2,800)

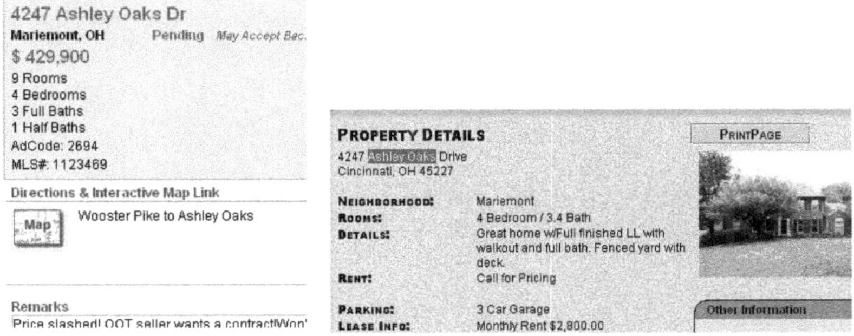

4247 Ashley Oaks Dr
Mariemont, OH
Pending
May Accept Bac.
$ 429,900
9 Rooms
4 Bedrooms
3 Full Baths
1 Half Baths
AdCode: 2694
MLS#: 1123469
Directions & Interactive Map Link
Map
Wooster Pike to Ashley Oaks
Remarks
PROPERTY DETAILS
PRINTPAGE
4247 Ashley Oaks Drive
Cincinnati, OH 45227
NEIGHBORHOOD: Mariemont
ROOMS: 4 Bedroom / 3.4 Bath
DETAILS: Great home w/Full finished LL with walkout and full bath. Fenced yard with deck.
RENT: Call for Pricing
PARKING: 3 Car Garage
LEASE INFO: Monthly Rent $2,800.00
Other Information

Rent versus Own Calculation *(The Rent vs. Buy calculator says: "Buy.")*

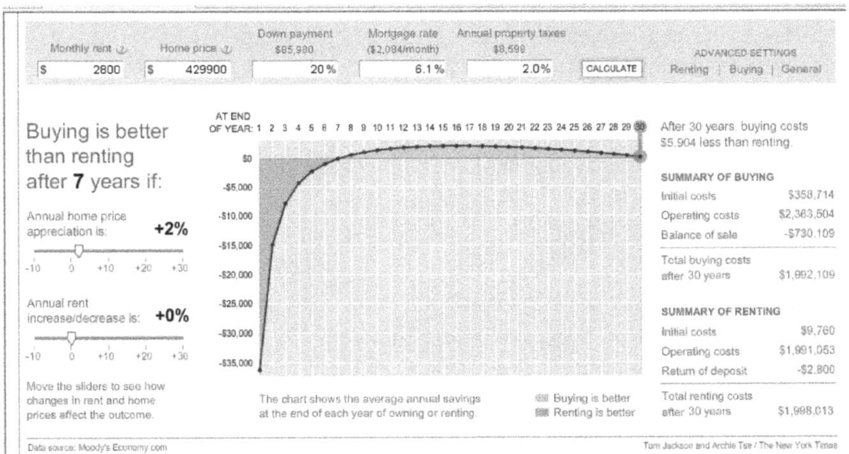

<u>Opinion</u>: The calculator says: "buying is better than rent" (but that is over 30 years). Are you in it for 30 years, or less than 10? And, consider: in just the first two years alone, there's over $50,000 saved by renting. To me, the graph should read: "Better to Rent, before year 7."

Back to the Future

The preceding examples were circa 2009.

In 2017, Zillow listed data on one of those houses showing that it sold in 2015 for $430,000 and was worth just $501,474 in 2017.

4247 Ashley Oaks Dr,
Cincinnati, OH 45227
4 beds · 2.5 baths · 2,708 sqft

SOLD: $430,000
Sold on 07/24/15
Zestimate®:
$501,474
I disagree

So, starting in 2009 and even from 2015 (since it remained flat up to that point), the house has appreciated only: $70,000 or 16% to 2017.

- Bought in 2015 for $430,000 would be 8% per year
- Bought in 2009, for $429,000 would be 2% per year

However, as an investment, if bought in either 2009 or 2015 with a 20% down payment (about $85,000), that house would have made about $71,474 (or 84%) on the down payment.

84% is not bad. Not bad at all. 42% per year since 2015.

Nice! But, if you'd bought in 2009 that is just 10% per year.

And, don't forget … that does NOT take into account holding/carrying costs (mortgage interest and maintenance) or real estate commissions (3% coming and 3% going)! That should all be netted out.

Gosh, I love renting!

The Ultimate Mortgage Calculator

Michael Bluejay gives some great advice on his site and is far more detailed with calculations, available at: www.michaelbluejay.com. *The ULTIMATE Rent vs Buy Calculator* is a great tool.

The calculator on his site, as on most sites, consistently shows that it is almost always more favorable to buy vs. rent. In fact, he says as much in the "Introduction to the Renting vs. Buying Calculator. It's almost always better to buy a home than to rent."[173]

Using the previous example from 2009 ($429,000 value verse $2,800 rental), the calculator shows it is better to own vs. rent, starting in year 3, from a cash flow perspective. [174]

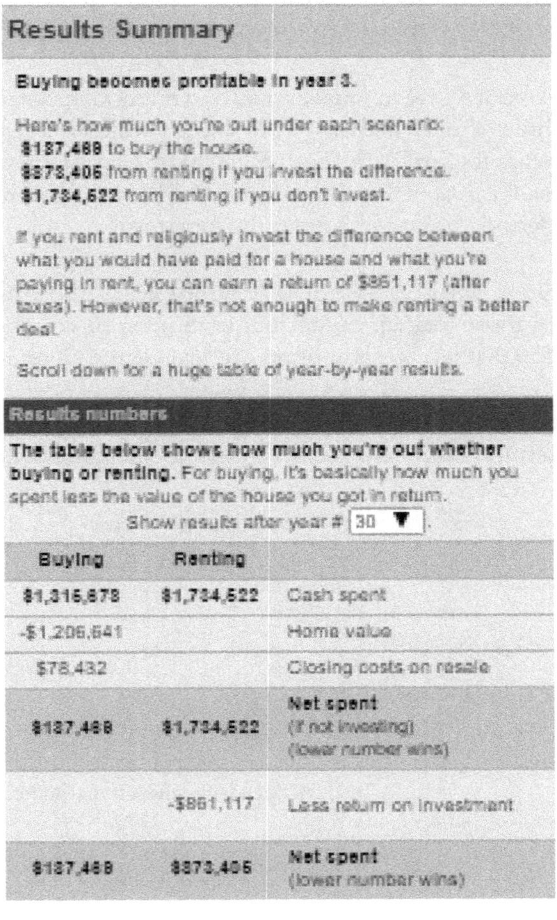

It is even far more favorable to buy, than rent, over the years because it is cheaper every year – from a cash flow perspective (you pay less on the mortgage than you do on the rent).

No doubt!

Based on the way he does his calculation, it is true. And the New York Times calculator also says buying is better, unless renting at $2,585/mo. or less.

However, it would seem the practical, holistic view, including soft factors, might tell a different story in real life.

Results Summary

Buying becomes profitable in year 3.

Here's how much you're out under each scenario:
$187,468 to buy the house.
$873,406 from renting if you invest the difference.
$1,734,522 from renting if you don't invest.

If you rent and religiously invest the difference between what you would have paid for a house and what you're paying in rent, you can earn a return of $861,117 (after taxes). However, that's not enough to make renting a better deal.

Scroll down for a huge table of year-by-year results.

Results numbers

The table below shows how much you're out whether buying or renting. For buying, it's basically how much you spent less the value of the house you got in return.

Show results after year # 30

Buying	Renting	
$1,316,678	$1,734,522	Cash spent
-$1,206,641		Home value
$78,432		Closing costs on resale
$187,468	$1,734,522	**Net spent** (if not investing) (lower number wins)
	-$861,117	Less return on investment
$187,468	$873,406	**Net spent** (lower number wins)

Opportunity Cost of the Down Payment

In economics we talk about "opportunity cost." Choosing to do one thing – spend all your money investing in Yahoo, for example, has not only the loss risk, but also the opportunity cost in that you did NOT invest in FAANG (Facebook, Apple, Amazon, Netflix, and Google).

Some mortgage calculators do *not* take into account this one very important thing: the amount of interest you could be earning if you had your "down payment" routed to the market, rather than a house. Most calculators look at the reinvestment alternatives, for amounts saved annually, but many don't consider the down payment.

So, the question is: what could $50,000 (or even $85,800, if 20% down on a $429,000 house) do for your retirement portfolio?

To put $50K in perspective, one might consider the average 401(k) in June of 2017 had only "$97,700 … which is a big leap from $73,300 five years [before]".[175] That's $25,000 or 34% in a few years on the 401(k). Not bad! Incidentally, that is close to what houses made during the same period.[176] But how about the long term?

So, in essence, the house has done about the same as the 401(k), but both of those lock up capital and both must be continually fed monthly. $50,000 left to compound can grow large all on its own.

$50,000, if not sunk in the house (and with nothing else contributed, just left to compound at 9%), grows to $663,383 over 30 years.

30	$0.00	$54,774.82	$50,000.00	$613,383.92	$663,383.92

Base amount: $50,000.00
Interest Rate: 9%
Effective Annual Rate: 9%
Calculation period: 30 years

Regular Deposit Calculation

« amend figures

Source www.thecalculatorsite.com

When Renting can be Better

Being able to move where you want (when you want) and being able to access more house are things I find to be really, really nice. Not for everyone, but they work for me.

It is with intention that we explore the rationale in so many different ways. The desire to buy is strong, yet the numbers can be bent. Further, even apparent proponents of buying say there are very good reasons to rent.

Michel Bluejay summarizes the point in favor of renting nicely when he says:

"Only when at **least one** (emphasis added) of the following applies is it probably better to rent." [177]

I added emphasis because you need *only one* of the below points he lists, according to his advice, to make renting a better choice.

Many people can tick three or four of them.

- √ **"Your rent is lower than average** – and you expect it to stay that way.
- √ **You plan on moving in a few years.**
- **You're in a super-expensive housing market** (like San Francisco or Honolulu).
- √ **You can get better-than-average returns from whatever you're investing your cash into.**
- √ **The house you would buy is a lot larger than what you would rent."**[178]

On that last point, I've found, that the larger the house … the better deal you can get renting.

It seems rich people somehow find themselves holding houses they don't want to sell, but they are happy to rent. In those situations, "landlords" are less likely to dicker over the small stuff. They just want someone to keep the place warm.

If Michael says it so clearly, why belabor the point?

To OPM or Not OPM …

In addition to providing a good calculator, Michael also provides a good deal of helpful commentary and gets to the heart of the OPM (other people's money) issue too.

He says: "The answer [to the take the banks money or pay in full question] depends on whether [you] can earn more by investing the cash than they'll pay in interest on the mortgage. If your mortgage is 6% and you could earn 10% on your money elsewhere, take the loan. But if the best return you can get on your money is 4%, pay cash."[179] The funny part is, Davey Ramsey speaks against this idea in *The Total Money Makeover.*[180]

A majority of people get themselves strapped to a house through a mortgage. Personally, I believe, since there so many other places to invest, I like to put as little into the house as possible in the first place – keep your money!

Can money tied up in a house do better with other investments? Perhaps yes, especially over the long term, with higher returns, the value of compounding, and avoidance of the New House Tax.

As a simple example, if you have the choice of putting $20,000 in Investment A, which grows at 15% per year, or Investment B, which grows at 4%, all other things equal, you're better off with Investment A. By that logic and where the market has returned 9% over the long term and houses less than 6%, you're better off investing in the market rather than tying up money in a house.

However, that doesn't include the value of leverage – which is big deal. Leverage on the housing investment is the everyday man's way to access "margin trading." It is a major benefit in favor of buying. As long as things appreciate, you're multiplying your returns.

But housing is not just a financial issue alone. It is a lifestyle preference. Renting is a preference for freedom and liquidity. Buying (if not a path to satisfying one's ego) is a preference for laying down roots and/or speculating on the housing market.

Why Go so Deep into this Matter?

Why belabor it then, especially when all the information provided in this book is "use at your own risk"?

Well, because most people don't closely consider the points Michael mentions.

People are led to believe that "renting is throwing your money away" and "a house is an asset." However, people might do well to consider an alternate perspective.

Shelter, i.e. housing, is at the base of Maslow's famous Hierarchy of Needs. People are emotionally attached to houses and it seems a large swath of the middle class can't make much financial headway.

Not to condemn anyone nor to suggest buying is absolutely wrong. There are varying circumstances and many soft factors. It is just that renting is not as bad as one might think (it might even be a way to financial freedom) and the house may not be the asset you think it is.

And, the opportunity cost and interest that could be made on your money in the market … there are many, many good reasons to rent. So, think about it as more than just multiplying by 240 as Michael Bluejuy recommends.

These chapters have hopefully peeled back layers of the onion (it may have made you cry) and exposed in more depth the layers of conventional wisdom in favor of buying.

House Poor or Rental Free

It is not a simple matter of choosing between 9% versus 6%. If only it were. That would be easy.

The "leverage" issue – put up just a portion and accumulate appreciation on the whole – is very appealing as an investment vehicle. But there are soft factors and personal preferences.

Looking into both the financial and softer side of the decision is important because it is ***not*** a scenario where "all other things are equal" in considering renting versus buying. There are extenuating circumstances.

If you're interested and want to reinforce the buy decision, read "Buying a home is an investment"[181] on Michael Bluejay's site. It's a good read. Seriously! I too believe a house ***IS*** an "investment" – I'm just not sure it's a great one. There are a number of points suggesting that, in either case (rent or buy), you can't live for free. You need look at net value – what you get in the end[182]. True! But you also need to look at the lifestyle and freedom along the way. Because, in buying, you might find yourself what he calls "in the hole" or, as we know colloquially, "house poor."

As explained earlier, this book was written as research into my own views – not to challenge Michael Bluejay, David Bach, or anyone else. Those guys are in support of buying and seemingly like putting their money into housing. They may get peace of mind from trading their cash for bricks, mortar, a new kitchen, and roof.

Personally, I get peace of mind from being disconnected from obligations to banks. Some people get into the real estate game, buy properties and rent them out. That can work, well! But, it can also end very badly with debt and tenants to manage. Personally, I find more comfort watching account balances in investment accounts, free from debt obligations, as I rent and enjoy lifestyle freedom. If I were to buy any real estate, it would be through an indx fund in the market.

I documented all this to make sure I was square in my own thinking. But then, seeing that most people don't fully consider the merit of renting … I shared it! I hope it has been enjoyable and valuable.

Chapter 10

Ringing Questions

Detaching from the brick-and-mortar retirement nest egg is hard. It is not something that doesn't come without a few questions. Homeowner diehards (and rental skeptics) will continue to ask:

- But what about buying at the bottom?
- If renting is so good, why does everyone buy?
- But why would I let a landlord make money off me?
- There aren't any good houses for rent. Where do I live?
- What if I'm already in a house and can't get out?
- Where do I invest to get that kind of return?
- Why would I throw my money away (on rent)?

What About Buying at the Bottom?

At the time of originally writing this, in the summer of 2009, following the 2008 crash, people were starting to suspect "a bottom in the housing market." And they were probably right.

No doubt, values had come off greatly in the wake of the Great Recession and there were good deals out there. While hindsight is 20/20, who is to say, at that time, if in late 2009 or 2010 was a good point to jump in?

The experienced and well-financed real estate investors could profit. Since values had come off, there was less downside to risk (and more upside potential to gain on appreciation value).

However, if you'd bought in 2009 there was still plenty left to fall. It wasn't *much* further down from 2009, but the bottom wasn't hit until 2010. If you'd bought in 2009 and sold in 2012, you'd have likely been underwater – losing with leverage can be very damaging.

The Case-Shiller National Home Price Index, as reported in *The Wall Street Journal*, shows the bottom was hit in 2012.

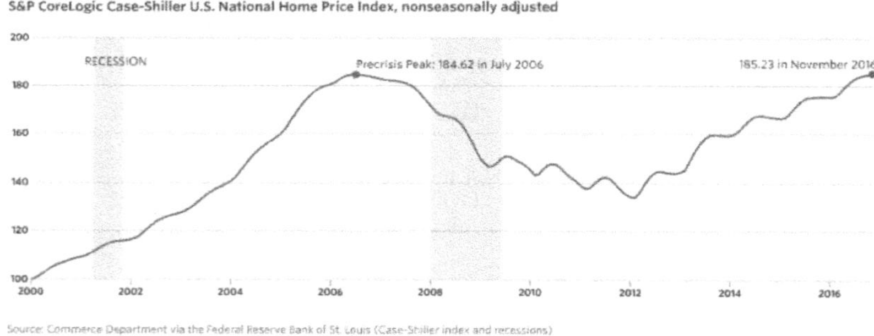

Figure 10 http://graphics.wsj.com/housing-market-recovery/[183]

The interesting part is that it took until 2018, almost a decade later, for the price index to *finally* surpass the July 2006 national non-seasonally adjusted peak. So, if you hadn't sold before 2008 and bought in 2006, you'd have to wait over 10 years to break even. A decade is a long time to wait to recover an investment (and barely make a little).

I'm still shocked with how lucky I was to sell in 2005.

The double-edged sword of leverage

There is the "Perceived Value" of appreciation and "Real Value" of appreciation (after costs) – the difference between the two is significant.

Our mind wants to see the *Perceived* and emotionalize away the *Real* – which includes all the costs we somehow don't see or track on a daily basis. But the costs are more than just the seemingly needless repairs that must be made in preparing a house for sale prior to closing. New windows, painting, HVAC repairs, you name it. The list goes on and on over the years and it all cuts at the return.

Despite the costly reality of houses, the idea of making money on them is appealing.

So appealing is owning a house that we quickly forget the illiquidity. We remember the "good times" – the day we bought and the day we finally sold – we seem to forget all the accounting (and risk) in between.

Leverage is risky. So risky, in fact, is leverage that trading Futures Commodities (a leveraged investment class) is open only to Accredited Investors – people worth $1M or more. But we let just about anyone get highly levered houses, all the time, with 0-20% down. A real chance of loss exists.

Futures commodities are very liquid – you can sell them in a minute, literally. Houses, on the other hand, might take some time to sell … which might not be a bad thing considering trading too frequently often leads to losses.

Leverage is great when it works. The bank is your partner in the deal. The bank's bet is on the promise of repayment. The owner's is on appreciation – over and above holding costs. If it goes up, great! There's leverage on the return. That's nice – very nice!

But besides the fact there are costs along the way to hold the investment, if the house goes down in value, a 5% decline can mean a 50% loss with a 10% down payment. Heck, no wonder banks often require 20% margin and no wonder so many people got "upside down" in 2008/2009.

Carrying Costs

One can get stuck with a house in a downturn – which is ***not*** fun! Beyond the idea of carrying two mortgages, there are costs to holding a house.

In early 2017, the average home inventory was 3 ½ months[184]. One interpretation of that number could mean, from the time of listing, it takes 3 ½ months to sell the house. That's a problem, if you want and need to move right away – especially so when the mortgage is due every month or when the value is declining.

But it happens all the time and that is why some houses sit on the market. Things are changing now. Where realtors used to be appalled at the idea of a rental offer, it is now more common to see a listing include a lease option.

People buy a house on spur of the moment or because they need to move – thinking they'll sell the house they're living in. Soon they wind up carrying two mortgages. Unable to sell the first house, they're pressed to either hold their price (and pay holding costs) or reduce the price. There aren't too many other options.

One family in our old neighborhood, without selling the first, bought a second house (for over $1M). They moved out and listed the first house. The listing started at $1.05M. One year later, through 2017, it is adjusted to $799,000. That's 20% off the original listing.

Clearly, they'd hoped to make money and imagined selling it for more than what they paid. But it doesn't seem to be working out.

It is not a bad house, but it is not the "perfect" one either – as everyone has now come to expect. In the end they'll be lucky to walk with $700,000 after fees, etc. for a house they bought for $899,900 in 2007. So, despite a great recovery of the housing market, they'll lose money on their house.

That kind of story is expensive and hard to recover from. I guess they can afford it, but it just goes to show: not everyone makes money on their house, even with the housing recovery winds at full gale.

Why Does Everyone Buy?

So if renting is so great, then why does everyone buy?

Well, this gets very much into the "conspiracy" of it. Not to say there is a subversive plot or anything, it is just that there are so many people who stand to benefit from the housing and real estate industry.

> Bankers – They make money in the form of interest on a loan, and the economy is dependent on an ever-increasing supply of money. The government and economy want us borrowing (creating) money.
>
> Builders – Clearly, builders make money selling houses; the housing sector is a major employer in America and a big interest group. Heck, New Housing Start-Ups is a major economic indicator.
>
> Government – They make about 2% (+/-) in property taxes. The higher the value of the house, the higher the tax revenue. They have a vested interested in improved lots, worth more, and churning real estate market. *Funny, the appreciating house generates annual cash tax payments (from your wallet) to the government, but you don't get the cash until you liquidate or only in the form a mortgage tax deduction.*
>
> Realtors – They provided good service and deserve a fee. Seriously, the good ones do earn that 6% commission.

Any one of the above is enough, on its own, to drive public policy to push people in favor of homeownership; put all these drivers together and it's no wonder we have an overtone of interest in the homes as the principal means to fulfill the "American Dream."

But what's even bigger is this unspoken way the economy works with the creation of money and how a mortgage holder participates in that. Not only does interest practically double the cost of a house, but where the bank is, literally, in the business of "creating money" (with each loan they issue), there's a national interest in the generation of loans. Loans help "create money." A continuous supply of money keeps the economy liquid.

The housing industry and all that surrounds it is like the flywheel that practically turns the American economy.

Indentured Servitude

The economy runs on debt. The macro economy somehow has mortgage debt at near parity with the whole GDP. Yes, our mortgage debt is near to what America earns.

How is it that every mortgage loan issued creates "new money?"

We've see that writing a "Note" (essentially a promise to the bank) has the borrower part and parcel to the game. Not a bad thing, considering borrowers get new money; but in return for it, borrowers take the obligation to service the debt. That means they go to work to generate income.

In a sense it is one big Ponzi scheme: new money must be generated to pay off old money. While labor is supposed to be the regenerative resource that engages itself every day to create value (and get a wage for it), some people have the habit of taking a second mortgage or using credit cards to fill gaps they can't meet with income to pay for all the things they must have now.

We need new money to keep the fiat currency-based economy afloat. But the whole process can feel a bit like being an indentured servant … just to a mortgage. The house must be sold or loan paid off to "buy freedom" and get out of servitude – to the bank!

Clearly, paying rent, as a renter, is also servitude – to a landlord. But it is easier to walk away. And, you can get out of servitude when your investment income funds the (rental) housing cost. Doing that – building investment income to pay for your expenses – is when one attains true freedom and exits the Rat Race.

The Landlord Makes Money Off Me!

Yes, the landlord does make money. But, that is not a bad thing. After all, the landlord subsidizes the renter's cost of living, as he put's up all the capital and takes on all the risk - and, not all owners are in it to make money.

Of the 16M single-family homes reported for rent, we might classify two kinds of landlords: professional landlords and private owners.

Private Owners. As reported by Rick Palacios Jr. on the New Home Insight's Podcast presented by John Burns Real Estate Consulting, private owners are about "90% of the market." Of that, about 9% own 3-5 units and 81% own just one or two properties. [i] Private owners are trying to make a side income or, for whatever reason, have a house they don't want to sell. This later group will often rent out their house to cover some of the carrying costs – meanwhile they wait (often decades) for the market to rebound and give them the price they want.

This last group of private owners may not be too numerous, but finding one of these situations provides a nice bang for the buck … in my opinion.

For example, the house I live in now is a family estate. The owner doesn't want to live here, now, not just yet. So, I've rented it for up to 9 years … I can leave whenever I want and he'd be left holding the bag. Or, I can accept his standing purchase offer. The ball is in my court.

Professional Landlords. These guys invest in property to make money. For sure, rent is funding them. They're making money off renters - but so too is the restaurant serving dinner. Who cares so long as it's fair!

Actually, it's good … many of these guys have economies of scale. They run rentals, as a business. And, thanks to their experience and resources, they can manage the house cheaper than an individual. So, renters benefit from the landlord's efficiencies. And their monthly profit on a single family is often very low – like just a couple hundred bucks.

Professionals are experienced with finance and good at managing property. That is how they can make money. And they're in it for the long term. Property can be expensive to hold.

Do most owners stay in the same house for 10, 15, 25 years? If not, a couple hundred bucks a month might be worth the flexibility renting provides.

The Business of Renting

Besides volume (managing a large number of units), how does he make money?

Among other things, the landlord places his money in the brick-and-mortar as a hedge against inflation. He's hoping to make a couple percent in Value Appreciation – but that doesn't get him rich, immediately. He's betting long term and, in the meantime, the rental cash flow covers costs and services bank debt. However, he's only making a little on each place. He's bring in cash flow while judging if and when to ever sell the whole thing for a profit.

Let's not forget, landlords benefit from different accounting tax rules and investment strategies.

In fact, well-capitalized and professional run single-family homes built specifically for rental is a growing market. Large companies like American Homes 4 Rent and Tricon American Homes are, thanks to new internet based cloud-computing and mobile apps, able to run single-family homes across large geographic territories with the type of efficiencies formerly reserved to apartment complexes.

As stated on their site, "American Homes 4 Rent…we combine the benefits of a national organization, state-of-the-art leasing platform, experienced in-house property management and maintenance along with brand new homes and amenities to help you feel right at home."

The small-time real estate investors live on the edge of broke because there's not a lot of money made on each unit …

To make real money, they need big volume (10's or 100's of units). That's why private landlords don't make much money with just one house.

However, owning (and living in one unit of) a two-family or duplex might subsidize housing costs or even make money.

For me, the way I look at it, I don't really care if the landlord is making a few hundred bucks off me every month. Like the waiter bringing the food, he's providing a service and so we tip him. We don't have to do the dishes or clean up, so to speak – on my house, lawn care is included.

There is less risk and more convenience, more freedom, and higher quality of ever-improving rental housing. So, even if I lived in a two-family, I might happily take the position as renter – I wouldn't have money tied up in the brick-and-mortar and the owner takes care of repairs!

Still Not Convinced?

Many companies, which are in business to make money, RENT their offices.

Now, these are businessmen. They're in business to make money and realize their wiser decision is to rent versus buy.

Not only do they have greater flexibility to up-scale and downscale as the business fluctuates (remember: family sizes/needs fluctuate too), but they also have better places to invest their capital than in office space. Sure, someone is making money off them, but these (apparently smart) business owners prefer to rent. Why?

Their funds can do much better for them investing in things other than real estate. Yes, some companies do buy their facilities, especially specialized ones and insurance companies – who must manage money over the long term on *conservative*, safe investments (note: "conservative" and "safe" usually equate to low returns).

Many large and small companies prefer to rent – even from a landlord who profits off them.

Why? For freedom (to invest in other things).

Monetary Risk and Objective Emotions

An owner leverages the bank's money with a loan; a renter leverages the owner's capital.

The landlord puts up (and ties up) his assets. Renters use the landlord's financial wherewithal to their benefit.

Investors, as landlords, look at property less emotionally and pay/invest more reasonably. Not so true with homeowners.

A professional landlord, who's in the business to provide a service, needs to provide a nice place – or he won't be in business. To make money, he needs to do that efficiently – or he won't be in business. Thus, renting from a professional increases the chance of getting a good, well-run place.

Professionals who buy and sell all the time know the market – they buy better. They might sell out their position, but a lease can provide the renter a right to stay.

While banks have the upper hand on owners, as borrowers, renters often have leverage over landlords.

The Private Owner

In the end, the private owner, the guy who happens to have an extra house that he can't or doesn't want to sell, for whatever reason, is the one I prefer. Why?

I like these guys because they just want to have the house occupied and want to, with that, make the renter happy. It is in these situations where I have personally found many great deals and found an excellent way to make the house a "home."

I barter for improvements with private owners. I make improvements in exchange for rental credit/reduction. Or, I get owners to pay for new things I want in exchange for slightly higher rent.

Landlords have Depreciation and Expense Deductions

Once a property is dubbed a rental, the landlord has the right to more tax deductions. They may even depreciate the asset along the way and all the expenses associated with it.

These are nice benefits which the landlord experiences annually. By way of accounting, they can build virtual equity more quickly.

Owners don't get the same benefits, annually. Painting the walls or repairing the electricity is coming out of the owner's pocket. Sure, they can keep all the receipts and deduct them from any capital gain at the end, but that is a long time to wait.

For sure, there is money to be made in real estate, if you know what you're doing. And that is just the point: most of us are NOT skilled at property ownership.

Landlords watch the expenses more closely. They keep books and take advantage of financial loopholes and accounting measures (more of which are open to them than to us privately).

As private owners, money runs through our fingers, into the money pit, and we wonder where it all went at the end of the month.

Slumlords, Going by the Wayside

Thankfully, the "slumlord" is becoming a thing of the past. There are too many good rental alternatives to choose from these days.

As real estate agents are quick to point out, these days, the market is demanding. People expect and want perfect. Buyers don't want to have to do anything to a house. There are too many good options to settle for less. The burden is on the seller to make the house nice and very appealing. It is not uncharacteristic for owners to get stuck making many, often expensive, repairs right before selling the house.

Similarly with rentals, they too are expected to be perfect! Landlords must provide nice, competitive housing or they won't have tenants. Or the landlord goes further "down-market."

Unfortunately, that leaves the impoverished with less savory options and that is where the slumlords usually end up. Above that floor, however, it is possible to find a good landlord and have a good relationship with them.

In the last 20 years, I've had 5 of them. We send Christmas cards to each other and are on good terms. Even with children and pets, they like us.

But you may find a bad landlord. If so – just change!

What if I'm Already Stuck (in a House)?

Many people are upside-down, have nearly no equity in their house, or are stuck with houses they'd prefer to have sold. Like gum on a shoe, they can't get rid of it.

Houses are a somewhat illiquid investment. But, even if you're stuck, don't worry …

First, you might not want to step in the same gum twice … that is: once you get out of the house, you might not want to buy back into that same situation – because of some *need* to buy a house. There are other nice places to live. Rent Your Way To Freedom!

Second, get out – even with little or no equity.

In the investment business, there's an expression that says "stop losses short." Something going bad? Get out! Cut your losses and try to make it up somewhere else. Getting to a lower-cost, more affordable situation might facilitate a recovery from a previous (mis)adventure.

Dave Ramsey has a similar recommendation relative to cars. When he finds people in debt, first thing he starts to home in on is the car. What is it? How expensive is it? When he finds people in an expensive situation, his next question is often: how quick can you sell it and get a beater?

However, there are many advisors who would suggest you "hold on for the long term." Stay put. In fact, some people will (or worse … the bank will make them) hold on, and on, and on … to a house – waiting for an offer that makes a profit, or breaks even. The bank has more resources to wait it out.

While holding can make great sense for the bank and be good advice from a stockbroker (especially in the middle of a drawdown), it is less relevant when you *need* to sell a house – but can't. As we've seen, the long term with housing can be really long. And there are costs while carrying it.

Holding a loser stock doesn't cost anything in the meantime. So, it's easier to hold and not "realize the loss" by selling. But, house or stock, there are some times you *need* to sell ... and that "need" is more urgent/painful with an underwater house than with an unrealized stock loss.

Jump Out of the Shadows

National Public Radio (NPR) ran a series on the mortgage crisis.

Their July 7, 2009 episode of *Morning Edition* highlighted "Shadow Inventory" (Noguchi, 2009) – those people waiting in the shadows, wanting, but not ready to sell their houses.

People in the shadows might be at or near negative equity on their house and don't want to sell at the "bottom of the market." They're waiting, hoping the market will rebound. Banks will hold inventory, as they don't want to flood the market all at once.

It raises a question: "Well, who's going to be the first to emerge from the shadows?" In my mind, they'll win!

Sure, one can wait for the market to rebound. A bank, with deeper pockets, can hold longer and refuse a sale that doesn't repay the mortgage. They have a longer investment horizon and less motivation to agree to terms of a short sale. Why should they agree if the owner is anyhow liable, stuck with the carrying costs in the meantime?

But, what if you could step out of the shadows first? Take your losses (before going into negative equity) and get out ahead of any further potential devaluation?

My brother-in-law went through this, rather publicly, with a very prominent house in our hometown. A massive renovation put him in the bad situation to start and then came the unexpected medical bills. Eventually, in about 2015, he had to just walk away from the house.

One still might say, "Fine, I can recover losses and rebuild, I get that. But, I may as well stay in the shadows and hold my (unrealized) loss and wait for the housing market to come back." The logic being: it's going to take just about the same amount of time to hold on or rebuild financially. So I'll stay in my house.

Yes, that is true.

It may take the same amount of time to recover. But emerging from the shadows and getting out sooner helps:

- Reduce the risk associated with a potential further fall
- Get on a lower (rental) cost curve
- Eliminate the maintenance money pit
- Get some equity applied to savings, in better investments
- Solve some problems with the bank

It's worked for my brother in-law. He exited the "shadows," took his lickings, and since went on to rent his way back to freedom. He took a very modest house and rebuilt his financial situation. He has apparently recovered (or relapsed – time will tell), as he recently bought again.

How Long Can You Wait?

In the event we favor the idea of holding, we need to ask the question: just how long can we wait?

For example, and to make the numbers easy, let's say we bought a house for $250,000 with a 10% or $25,000 down payment.

Now, let's say we might have slightly overpaid and the house has dropped in value to $200,000.

First, there's a problem with the "short sell" situation this scenario creates; but let's consider: how long will it take to get back to even?

For a house to go up from $200,000 to $250,000, it requires $50,000 of appreciation. Well, that amounts to a 25% increase ($50,000/$200,000 = 25%) to cover what was originally a 20% loss (($250,000-$200,000)/$200,0000).

Now, how long will it take for the house to appreciate 25%?

During the boom years, a good level of appreciation was 5%/year. So, it may take four or five years to get back even. That's a long time.

If it grows more slowly, it could be 10 years or more. That's a long time to be stuck in a house you don't want, carrying the costs.

Now, how long would it take you to make $25,000 or $50,000 investing?

If you were able to save $500/month, thanks to a cheaper living situation, at the end of the first year you'd have $6,000 saved up. Now, with $6,000 you can start investing in some assets that grow.

Continue the $500/month saving and grow at 15%, it would take:

3 years to save $29,600 **5 years to save $50,527**[185]

You might be renting a cheaper house, but this would be cash in an investment account, not value stuck in a (illiquid) house.

Where do I Live?

One can live virtually anywhere. Back in 2008, I was renting a house that Zillow had listed for $1.5M in value. I was getting it for about $3,500/month. My neighbor at that time was renting a $2.3M house for $5,500/month.

I went on to rent another house valued at $650,000 for $3,500/month … not as good of a deal, but it did the trick for six months. We soon used "location freedom" to move to a chateau in Belgium.

So I've done it for myself and renting is popular now with Millennials. Different from 2008, Zillow now provides both the Zestimate, on the value of the house, and a Rental Zestimate of what you should pay in rent.

From my experience, and especially as you choose to access more house, I've found renting to be cheaper than buying. Besides those exaggerated examples, there are plenty of houses for rent, at more reasonable rates.

Inventory Issues

When I originally wrote this in 2008/2009, Airbnb was just being founded and, though VRBO (Vacation Rental by Owner) had been there for a decade, it was still building up. But now, those sites have far greater inventory and there are far more rental options available these days.

But people still say: there's nothing there to rent! Well, the same thing could be said about buying. I've had people look me up and send "make me move" letters, wanting to buy my house – because there was no inventory. The inventory is limited either way. I guess you could send a letter to see about renting a house that is "for sale" … just ask!

A search on Zillow for 3-bedroom homes in Tampa, FL showed 1,269 For Sale and 397 Rental options. So, there are about 3x more houses, condos, townhomes, etc. for sale than for rent. However, that's still 30% of houses for rent.

Given the right motivation, some For Sales could be turned to rentals. A house on the market with a realtor though may be locked up with a real estate agent, but, keep an eye on it … the listing won't last forever and dual listings with a lease option are growing more common.

A Room with a View (of the Tampa Bay)

As our parents age, we see them go through the dilemma. Beyond taking the car keys away, another big emotional battle is with the house.

According to the defacto plan, by the time people hit retirement they have a fair bit of equity (wealth) in the house. But, just as their wealth peaks, their cash flow starts to decline. Social Security is not enough and people need to start budgeting their retirement spending more carefully. Indeed, one of the fastest growing segments for financial advisers is seniors and retirement planning and one of the biggest assets to manage is the house.

My father-in-law just went through this – he just sold the house which he'd owned free and clear. He arrived to what everyone is (seemingly) geared to do – live "rent free." Still healthy at 83, he continued planning for the future and realized he could not deal with the maintenance and taxes associated with the house, much less fund long-term care insurance.

While he might have continued to afford "living for free" in the house, he chose freedom. He sold the house, moved out, and elected to start paying rent in a condo.

His wife, when she was alive, preferred to have her stuff and house. After she passed, things changed and he'd seen the cost and stress of end stage illness. So he started looking more closely at his situation. He went to the bank to see about getting a reverse mortgage on his house, but the rates were so poor that it didn't work out. He couldn't get money out of his house. So, and with no prompting from me, he decided to sell.

It was a brutal six months of clean-up and de-junking, concurring an endless list of seemingly needless repairs. But, thanks to the help from his oldest daughter and variety of neighbors, he got it done.

He has now moved into a condo that provides him not only long-term care insurance but also: cleaning once a week, laundry service, and three restaurants to choose from if he doesn't want to cook. My father-in-law couldn't have more freedom sitting on his balcony overlooking the Tampa Bay. He's separated from the obligations (physical and mental) of the house, freed up cash, and has one meal per day included in the rent, with a social life to boot!

Closing

I reiterate where it started … there might be good, even great, personal and financial reasons to own.

However, the major message is, in either buying or renting: watch the costs.

Consider the cost of housing (rented or bought) more closely.

Houses are more expensive than one thinks and rental might not be as bad as it's made to seem.

Life is expensive. Money is not necessary for happiness, but it surely helps.

Where the middle class is getting squeezed, people will need all the help they can get.

Start saving/investing money, early. Get investments growing and let interest compound – it's never too late to start!

Freedom, personal and financial, might be more likely renting.

Rent Your Way To Freedom.

The balls and chains of ownership have their weights.

Renting provides great flexibility and freedom.

In it all, rent or buy, beyond finances … it is a choice of lifestyle!

You can, *Live Well Now While You Build Your Freedom.*

Appendix

Robert Frost Poem - 1916[186]

The Road Not Taken

Two roads diverged in a yellow wood,
And sorry I could not travel both
And be one traveller, long I stood
And looked down one as far as I could
To where it bent in the undergrowth;

Then took the other, as just as fair,
And having perhaps the better claim,
Because it was grassy and wanted wear;
Though as for that the passing there
Had worn them really about the same,

And both that morning equally lay
In leaves no step had trodden black.
Oh, I kept the first for another day!
Yet knowing how way leads on to way,
I doubted if I should ever come back.

I shall be telling this with a sigh
Somewhere ages and ages hence:
Two roads diverged in a wood, and I—
I took the one less travelled by,
And that has made all the difference.

Housing Versus Investment Account

Housing Appreciation

Principal Amour	$375,000
Annual Interest	4.50%
Period	30 Years
Compounded	Annual

Year	Yearly Appreciation	Total Appreciati	House Value	Principal Paid	Interest Paid	Net Appreciation after Interest	Prop Tax and Maint	Net Annual Appreciation after interest, Tax, Maint	Net Cumm Appreciation
1	$16,875.00	$16,875.00	$391,875.00	$4,839.73	$13,400.99	$3,474.01	-$7,488.00	-$4,013.99	-$4,013.99
2	$17,634.37	$34,509.37	$409,509.38	$5,062.06	$13,178.66	$4,455.71	-$7,712.64	-$3,256.93	-$7,270.92
3	$18,427.92	$52,937.30	$427,937.30	$5,294.61	$12,946.11	$5,481.81	-$7,944.02	-$2,462.21	-$9,733.13
4	$19,257.18	$72,194.48	$447,194.48	$5,537.85	$12,702.87	$6,554.31	-$8,182.34	-$1,628.03	-$11,361.16
5	$20,123.75	$92,318.23	$467,318.23	$5,792.24	$12,448.48	$7,675.27	-$8,427.81	-$752.54	-$12,113.70
6	$21,029.32	$113,347.55	$488,347.55	$6,058.35	$12,182.37	$8,846.95	-$8,680.64	$166.31	-$11,947.39
7	$21,975.64	$135,323.19	$510,323.19	$6,336.63	$11,904.09	$10,071.65	-$8,941.06	$1,130.49	-$10,816.91
8	$22,964.54	$158,287.73	$533,287.73	$6,627.75	$11,612.97	$11,351.57	-$9,209.30	$2,142.27	-$8,674.63
9	$23,997.95	$182,285.68	$557,285.68	$6,932.24	$11,308.48	$12,689.47	-$9,485.57	$3,203.90	-$5,470.74
10	$25,077.86	$207,363.53	$582,363.53	$7,250.69	$10,990.03	$14,087.83	-$9,770.14	$4,317.69	-$1,153.05
11	$26,206.36	$233,569.89	$608,569.89	$7,583.78	$10,656.94	$15,549.42	-$10,063.26	$5,486.17	$4,333.13
12	$27,385.65	$260,955.54	$635,955.54	$7,932.18	$10,308.54	$17,077.11	-$10,365.14	$6,711.97	$11,045.09
13	$28,618.00	$289,573.54	$664,573.54	$8,296.59	$9,944.13	$18,673.87	-$10,676.10	$7,997.77	$19,042.87
14	$29,905.81	$319,479.35	$694,479.35	$8,677.74	$9,562.98	$20,342.83	-$10,996.38	$9,346.45	$28,389.31
15	$31,251.57	$350,730.92	$725,730.92	$9,076.39	$9,164.33	$22,087.24	-$11,326.27	$10,760.97	$39,150.28
16	$32,657.89	$383,388.81	$758,388.81	$9,493.35	$8,747.37	$23,910.52	-$11,666.06	$12,244.46	$51,394.74
17	$34,127.50	$417,516.30	$792,516.30	$9,929.48	$8,311.24	$25,816.26	-$12,016.04	$13,800.22	$65,194.96
18	$35,663.23	$453,179.54	$828,179.54	$10,385.63	$7,855.09	$27,808.14	-$12,376.52	$15,431.62	$80,626.58
19	$37,268.08	$490,447.62	$865,447.62	$10,862.73	$7,377.99	$29,890.09	-$12,747.82	$17,142.27	$97,768.85
20	$38,945.14	$529,392.76	$904,392.76	$11,361.77	$6,878.95	$32,066.19	-$13,130.25	$18,935.94	$116,704.79
21	$40,697.67	$570,090.43	$945,090.43	$11,883.72	$6,357.00	$34,340.67	-$13,524.16	$20,816.51	$137,521.29
22	$42,529.07	$612,619.50	$987,619.50	$12,429.66	$5,811.06	$36,718.01	-$13,929.89	$22,788.12	$160,309.42
23	$44,442.88	$657,062.38	$1,032,062.38	$13,000.66	$5,240.06	$39,202.82	-$14,347.78	$24,855.04	$185,164.46
24	$46,442.81	$703,505.19	$1,078,505.19	$13,597.92	$4,642.80	$41,800.01	-$14,778.22	$27,021.79	$212,186.25
25	$48,532.73	$752,037.92	$1,127,037.92	$14,222.60	$4,018.12	$44,514.61	-$15,221.56	$29,293.05	$241,479.30
26	$50,716.71	$802,754.63	$1,177,754.63	$14,875.98	$3,364.74	$47,351.97	-$15,678.21	$31,673.76	$273,153.06
27	$52,998.96	$855,753.59	$1,230,753.59	$15,559.38	$2,681.34	$50,317.62	-$16,148.56	$34,169.06	$307,322.12
28	$55,383.91	$911,137.50	$1,286,137.50	$16,274.18	$1,966.54	$53,417.37	-$16,633.01	$36,784.36	$344,106.48
29	$57,876.19	$969,013.68	$1,344,013.68	$17,021.78	$1,218.94	$56,657.25	-$17,132.00	$39,525.25	$383,631.73
30	$60,480.62	$1,029,494.30	$1,404,494.30	$17,803.79	$436.93	$60,043.69	-$17,645.96	$42,397.73	$426,029.46
31	$63,202.24	$1,092,696.54	$1,467,696.54			$63,202.24	-$18,175.34	$45,026.90	$471,056.36
32	$66,046.34	$1,158,742.89	$1,533,742.89			$66,046.34	-$18,720.60	$47,325.74	$518,382.09
33	$69,018.43	$1,227,761.32	$1,602,761.32			$69,018.43	-$19,282.22	$49,736.21	$568,118.30
34	$72,124.26	$1,299,885.58	$1,674,885.58			$72,124.26	-$19,860.69	$52,263.57	$620,381.88
35	$75,369.85	$1,375,255.43	$1,750,255.43			$75,369.85	-$20,456.51	$54,913.34	$675,295.22
36	$78,761.49	$1,454,016.92	$1,829,016.92			$78,761.49	-$21,070.20	$57,691.29	$732,986.51
37	$82,305.76	$1,536,322.68	$1,911,322.68			$82,305.76	-$21,702.31	$60,603.45	$793,589.96
38	$86,009.52	$1,622,332.21	$1,997,332.21			$86,009.52	-$22,353.38	$63,656.14	$857,246.10
39	$89,879.95	$1,712,212.15	$2,087,212.15			$89,879.95	-$23,023.98	$66,855.97	$924,102.08
40	$93,924.55	$1,806,136.70	$2,181,136.70			$93,924.55	-$23,714.70	$70,209.85	$994,311.93
30 Year Totals				$300,001.46	$247,220.14		-$356,244.71		
40 Year Toatls				$300,001.46	$247,220.14		-$564,604.63		

Investment Account Growth

Principal Amoun	$75,000
Annual Interest	9.50%
Period	30 Years
Compounded	Annual

Year	Yearly Interest	Total Interest	Account Balanace	Rent	Cummulative Investment Interest After Rent	Net Balance Investment Account
1	$7,125.00	$7,125.00	$82,125.00	-$17,616.00	-$10,491.00	$64,509.00
2	$7,801.88	$14,926.88	$89,926.88	-$18,144.48	-$20,833.60	$54,166.40
3	$8,543.05	$23,469.93	$98,469.93	-$18,688.81	-$30,979.36	$44,020.64
4	$9,354.64	$32,824.57	$107,824.57	-$19,249.48	-$40,874.20	$34,125.80
5	$10,243.33	$43,067.91	$118,067.91	-$19,826.96	-$50,457.84	$24,542.16
6	$11,216.45	$54,284.36	$129,284.36	-$20,421.77	-$59,663.16	$15,336.84
7	$12,282.01	$66,566.37	$141,566.37	-$21,034.43	-$68,415.57	$6,584.43
8	$13,448.81	$80,015.18	$155,015.18	-$21,665.46	-$76,632.22	-$1,632.22
9	$14,726.44	$94,741.62	$169,741.62	-$22,315.42	-$84,221.20	-$9,221.20
10	$16,125.45	$110,867.07	$185,867.07	-$22,984.88	-$91,080.64	-$16,080.64
11	$17,657.37	$128,524.44	$203,524.44	-$23,674.43	-$97,097.70	-$22,097.70
12	$19,334.82	$147,859.26	$222,859.26	-$24,384.66	-$102,147.54	-$27,147.54
13	$21,171.63	$169,030.89	$244,030.89	-$25,116.20	-$106,092.12	-$31,092.12
14	$23,182.94	$192,213.83	$267,213.83	-$25,869.69	-$108,778.87	-$33,778.87
15	$25,385.31	$217,599.14	$292,599.14	-$26,645.78	-$110,039.34	-$35,039.34
16	$27,796.92	$245,396.06	$320,396.06	-$27,445.15	-$109,687.57	-$34,687.57
17	$30,437.63	$275,833.69	$350,833.69	-$28,268.51	-$107,518.45	-$32,518.45
18	$33,329.20	$309,162.89	$384,162.89	-$29,116.56	-$103,305.81	-$28,305.81
19	$36,495.47	$345,658.36	$420,658.36	-$29,990.06	-$96,800.40	-$21,800.40
20	$39,962.54	$385,620.91	$460,620.91	-$30,889.76	-$87,727.63	-$12,727.63
21	$43,758.99	$429,379.89	$504,379.89	-$31,816.46	-$75,785.09	-$785.09
22	$47,916.09	$477,295.98	$552,295.98	-$32,770.95	-$60,639.95	$14,360.05
23	$52,468.12	$529,764.10	$604,764.10	-$33,754.08	-$41,925.91	$33,074.09
24	$57,452.59	$587,216.69	$662,216.69	-$34,766.70	-$19,240.02	$55,759.98
25	$62,910.59	$650,127.28	$725,127.28	-$35,809.70	$7,860.87	$82,860.87
26	$68,887.09	$719,014.37	$794,014.37	-$36,883.99	$39,863.97	$114,863.97
27	$75,431.37	$794,445.73	$869,445.73	-$37,990.51	$77,304.83	$152,304.83
28	$82,597.34	$877,043.08	$952,043.08	-$39,130.23	$120,771.94	$195,771.94
29	$90,444.09	$967,487.17	$1,042,487.17	-$40,304.13	$170,911.89	$245,911.89
30	$99,036.28	$1,066,523.45	$1,141,523.45	-$41,513.26	$228,434.92	$303,434.92
31	$108,444.73	$1,174,968.18	$1,249,968.18	-$42,758.66	$294,120.99	$369,120.99
32	$118,746.98	$1,293,715.16	$1,368,715.16	-$44,041.42	$368,826.56	$443,826.56
33	$130,027.94	$1,423,743.10	$1,498,743.10	-$45,362.66	$453,491.84	$528,491.84
34	$142,380.59	$1,566,123.69	$1,641,123.69	-$46,723.54	$549,148.89	$624,148.89
35	$155,906.75	$1,722,030.44	$1,797,030.44	-$48,125.24	$656,930.40	$731,930.40
36	$170,717.89	$1,892,748.34	$1,967,748.34	-$49,569.00	$778,079.29	$853,079.29
37	$186,936.09	$2,079,684.43	$2,154,684.43	-$51,056.07	$913,959.30	$988,959.30
38	$204,695.02	$2,284,379.45	$2,359,379.45	-$52,587.75	$1,066,066.57	$1,141,066.57
39	$224,141.05	$2,508,520.50	$2,583,520.50	-$54,165.39	$1,236,042.24	$1,311,042.24
40	$245,434.45	$2,753,954.94	$2,828,954.94	-$55,790.35	$1,425,686.34	$1,500,686.34
30 Year Totals				-$838,088.52		
40 Year Totals				-$863,231.18		

Rent vs. Buy Calculations

$119,900 at 9% compounded annually for 40 years is $3,765,989

40	$0.00	$310,953.26	$119,900.00	$3,646,089.46	$3,765,989.46
41	**$0.00**	**$338,939.05**	**$119,900.00**	**$3,985,028.52**	**$4,104,928.52**

Base amount: $119,900.00
Interest Rate: 9%
Effective Annual Rate: 9%
Calculation period: 41 years

Regular Deposit Calculation

« amend figures

Note: Interest earnings in Year 41 are $338,939

(Source: Compound Interest Calculator on www.thecalculatorsite.com)

$800 of rent over 40 years adds up to $811,683

The total rent adds up to $811,683, including inflation. That's a lot of money "thrown away." But when you consider investing the principal in the market, versus sinking it all into house, compared to buying a $119,900 house outright, renting shows to be more profitable in year 1 and every year after (for a total of $2,226,401 in favor of renting – including $259,153 of investment income in year 40).

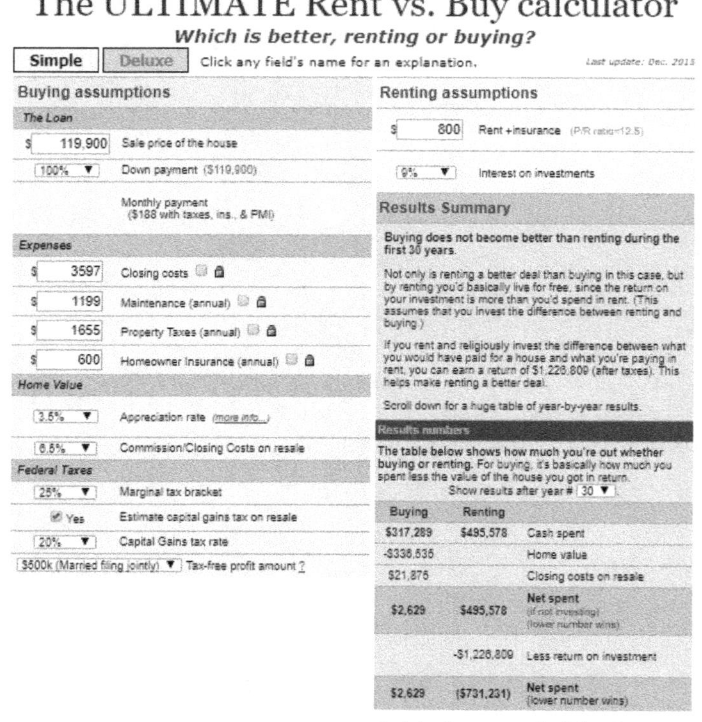

Mega Data Table! (detailed results of Rent vs. Buy)

In pink-row years renting is better. In green-row years buying is better.

Light gray columns are figures for that year. Dark gray columns are running totals.

All fields are explained in detail below the table.

Loan details			Buying (cash out)							House value				Renting				Rent vs. Buy		
Yr.	Interest	Loan Balance	Pmts.	PMI/ FHA fees	Taxes +Ins.	Maint. +Exp. -Rent	Tax Savings	Cash out	Total Cash out	House Value (gross)	Appreciation	Paid Equity	House Value (net)	Rent	Total Rent	Total Principal	Return on invest.	Buying Net	Rent net	Rent vs. Buy
1			119,900		2,265	1,499		127,251	127,251	124,098	4,198	119,900	116,030	9,600	9,600	117,651	9,000	11,221	600	10,621
2					2,334	1,651		3,985	131,136	128,440	8,540	119,900	120,091	9,936	19,536	117,651	18,811	11,045	725	10,320
3					2,416	1,606		4,021	135,158	132,935	13,035	119,900	124,294	10,284	29,820	117,651	29,504	10,863	316	10,547
4					2,500	1,662		4,162	139,320	137,588	17,688	119,900	128,645	10,644	40,463	117,651	41,160	10,675	696	11,371
5					2,588	1,720		4,308	143,628	142,404	22,504	119,900	133,147	11,016	51,480	117,651	53,864	10,480	2,385	12,865
6					2,678	1,780		4,459	148,086	147,388	27,488	119,900	137,808	11,402	62,881	117,651	67,712	10,279	4,831	15,110
7					2,772	1,843		4,615	152,701	152,548	32,648	119,900	142,631	11,801	74,682	117,651	82,807	10,070	8,124	18,194
8					2,869	1,907		4,776	157,477	157,885	37,985	119,900	147,623	12,214	86,896	117,651	99,260	9,854	12,363	22,218
9					2,969	1,974		4,943	162,420	163,411	43,511	119,900	152,790	12,641	99,538	117,651	117,193	9,631	17,656	27,286
10					3,073	2,043		5,116	167,537	169,131	49,231	119,900	158,137	13,084	112,621	117,651	136,741	9,399	24,120	33,519
11					3,181	2,114		5,295	172,832	175,050	55,150	119,900	163,672	13,542	126,163	117,651	158,048	9,160	31,886	41,045
12					3,292	2,188		5,481	178,313	181,177	61,277	119,900	169,401	14,016	140,179	117,651	181,273	8,912	41,094	50,006
13					3,407	2,265		5,673	183,985	187,518	67,618	119,900	175,330	14,506	154,685	117,651	206,587	8,656	51,902	60,558
14					3,527	2,344		5,871	189,856	194,081	74,181	119,900	181,466	15,014	169,699	117,651	234,181	8,390	64,481	72,872
15					3,650	2,426		6,077	195,933	200,874	80,974	119,900	187,817	15,539	185,239	117,651	264,257	8,115	79,019	87,134
16					3,778	2,511		6,289	202,222	207,905	88,005	119,900	194,391	16,083	201,322	117,651	297,041	7,831	95,719	103,550
17					3,910	2,599		6,509	208,732	215,182	95,282	119,900	201,195	16,646	217,968	117,651	332,774	7,537	114,806	122,343
18					4,047	2,690		6,737	215,469	222,713	102,813	119,900	208,237	17,229	235,197	117,651	371,724	7,232	136,527	143,760
19					4,189	2,784		6,973	222,442	230,508	110,608	119,900	215,525	17,832	253,029	117,651	414,160	6,917	161,151	168,068
20					4,335	2,882		7,217	229,659	238,576	118,676	119,900	223,066	18,456	271,485	117,651	460,457	6,591	188,972	195,562
21					4,487	2,983		7,470	237,129	246,926	127,026	119,900	230,876	19,102	290,587	117,651	510,898	6,253	220,311	226,564
22					4,644	3,087		7,731	244,860	255,568	135,668	119,900	238,956	19,771	310,357	117,651	565,579	5,903	255,522	261,425
23					4,807	3,195		8,002	252,861	264,513	144,613	119,900	247,320	20,463	330,820	117,651	625,606	5,542	294,988	300,530
24					4,975	3,307		8,282	261,143	273,771	153,871	119,900	255,976	21,179	351,999	117,651	691,131	5,167	339,133	344,300
25					5,149	3,423		8,572	269,715	283,353	163,453	119,900	264,936	21,920	373,919	117,651	762,334	4,780	388,415	393,195
26					5,329	3,543		8,872	278,586	293,270	173,370	119,900	274,208	22,687	396,606	117,651	839,944	4,379	443,338	447,717
27					5,516	3,666		9,182	287,769	303,535	183,635	119,900	283,805	23,481	420,087	117,651	924,539	3,963	504,452	508,416
28					5,709	3,795		9,504	297,272	314,159	194,259	119,900	293,738	24,303	444,390	117,651	1,018,748	3,534	572,358	575,892
29					5,908	3,928		9,836	307,108	325,154	205,254	119,900	304,019	25,154	469,544	117,651	1,117,256	3,089	647,712	650,801
30					6,115	4,065		10,180	317,289	336,535	216,635	119,900	314,660	26,034	495,578	117,651	1,226,809	2,629	731,231	733,860
31					6,329	4,207		10,537	327,825	348,313	228,413	119,900	325,673	26,945	522,523	117,651	1,346,222	2,152	823,699	825,851
32					6,551	4,356		10,905	338,731	360,504	240,604	119,900	337,071	27,888	550,411	117,651	1,476,382	1,659	925,971	927,630
33					6,780	4,507		11,287	350,018	373,122	253,222	119,900	348,869	28,864	579,275	117,651	1,618,257	1,149	1,038,981	1,040,130
34					7,017	4,665		11,682	361,700	386,181	266,281	119,900	361,079	29,875	609,150	117,651	1,772,900	621	1,163,750	1,164,371
35					7,263	4,828		12,091	373,791	399,697	279,797	119,900	373,717	30,920	640,071	117,651	1,941,462	74	1,301,391	1,301,465
36					7,517	4,997		12,514	386,306	413,687	293,787	119,900	386,797	32,002	672,073	117,651	2,125,194	492	1,453,121	1,452,629
37					7,780	5,172		12,952	399,258	428,166	308,266	119,900	400,335	33,123	705,196	117,651	2,325,461	1,077	1,620,266	1,619,189
38					8,053	5,353		13,406	412,663	443,152	323,252	119,900	414,347	34,282	739,477	117,651	2,543,753	1,683	1,804,276	1,802,592
39					8,335	5,540		13,875	426,538	458,662	338,762	119,900	428,849	35,482	774,959	117,651	2,781,691	2,311	2,006,732	2,004,422
40					8,626	5,734		14,360	440,899	474,715	354,815	119,900	443,859	36,724	811,683	117,651	3,041,044	2,960	2,229,361	2,226,401

(Source: https://michaelbluejay.com/house/rentvsbuy.html)

$1,800 in rent, over 40 years, compared to buying at $119,900

The total rent, including inflation, adds up to $1,826,6286. While the rent vs. buy calculation shows buying is better in year 1, it also shows that over the long run, it flips. In year 31 renting turns out better and in year 40 you've accumulated a $901,622 total advantage, including interest income of $232,900 in year 40.

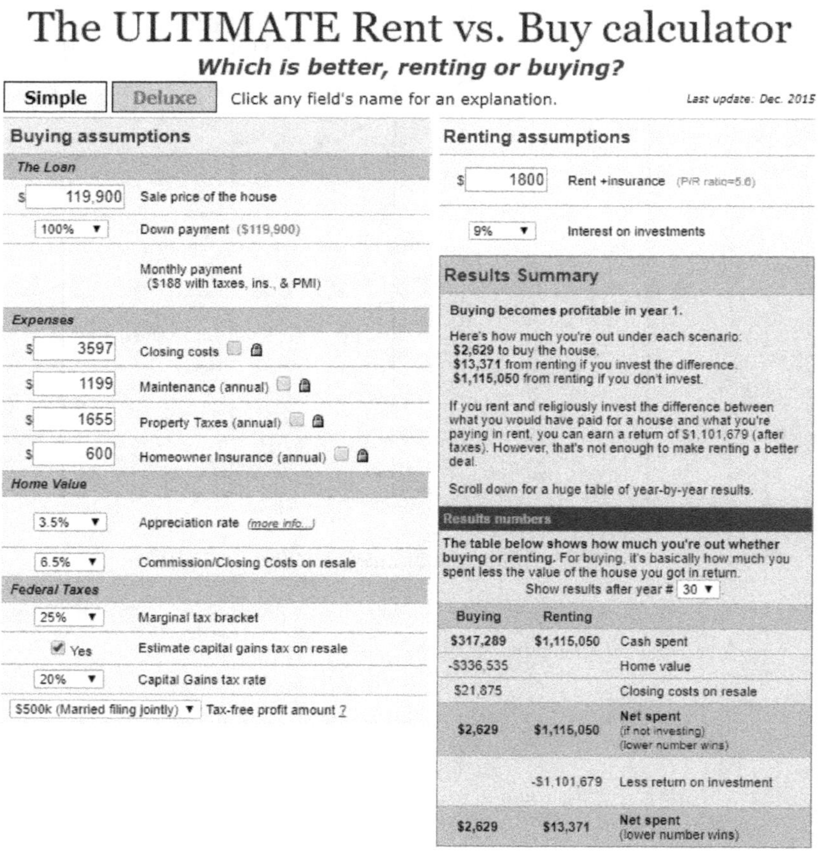

The ULTIMATE Rent vs. Buy calculator

Which is better, renting or buying?

Simple | Deluxe | Click any field's name for an explanation. *Last update: Dec. 2015*

Buying assumptions

The Loan

$ 119,900	Sale price of the house
100% ▼	Down payment ($119,900)
	Monthly payment ($188 with taxes, ins., & PMI)

Expenses

$ 3597	Closing costs
$ 1199	Maintenance (annual)
$ 1655	Property Taxes (annual)
$ 600	Homeowner Insurance (annual)

Home Value

3.5% ▼	Appreciation rate (more info...)
6.5% ▼	Commission/Closing Costs on resale

Federal Taxes

25% ▼	Marginal tax bracket
✔ Yes	Estimate capital gains tax on resale
20% ▼	Capital Gains tax rate
$500k (Married filing jointly) ▼	Tax-free profit amount ?

Renting assumptions

$ 1800	Rent +insurance (P/R ratio=5.6)
9% ▼	Interest on investments

Results Summary

Buying becomes profitable in year 1.

Here's how much you're out under each scenario:
$2,629 to buy the house.
$13,371 from renting if you invest the difference.
$1,115,050 from renting if you don't invest.

If you rent and religiously invest the difference between what you would have paid for a house and what you're paying in rent, you can earn a return of $1,101,679 (after taxes). However, that's not enough to make renting a better deal.

Scroll down for a huge table of year-by-year results.

Results numbers

The table below shows how much you're out whether buying or renting. For buying, it's basically how much you spent less the value of the house you got in return.

Show results after year # 30 ▼

Buying	Renting	
$317,289	$1,115,050	Cash spent
-$336,535		Home value
$21,875		Closing costs on resale
$2,629	**$1,115,050**	**Net spent** (if not investing) (lower number wins)
	-$1,101,679	Less return on investment
$2,629	**$13,371**	**Net spent** (lower number wins)

Mega Data Table! (detailed results of Rent vs. Buy)

In pink-row years renting is better. In green-row years buying is better.

Light gray columns are figures for that year. Dark gray columns are running totals.

All fields are explained in detail below the table.

Loan details			Buying (cash out)							House value				Renting				Rent vs. Buy		
Yr.	Interest	Loan Balance	Pmts.	PMI/ FHA fees	Taxes +Ins.	Maint. +Exp. Rent	Tax Savings	Cash out	Total Cash out	House Value (gross)	Apprec-iation	Paid Equity	House Value (net)	Rent	Total Rent	Total Principal	Return on Invest.	Buying Net	Rent net	Rent vs. Buy
1			119,900		2,255	1,499		127,251	127,251	124,096	4,196	119,900	116,030	21,600	21,600	105,651	8,082	11,221	13,518	2,297
2					2,334	1,551		3,885	131,136	128,440	8,540	119,900	120,091	22,356	43,956	105,651	16,892	11,045	27,064	16,019
3					2,416	1,606		4,021	135,158	132,935	13,035	119,900	124,294	23,138	67,094	105,651	26,495	10,863	40,600	29,737
4					2,500	1,662		4,162	139,320	137,588	17,688	119,900	128,645	23,948	91,043	105,651	36,961	10,675	54,081	43,406
5					2,588	1,720		4,308	143,628	142,404	22,504	119,900	133,147	24,786	115,829	105,651	46,370	10,480	67,459	56,979
6					2,678	1,780		4,459	148,086	147,388	27,488	119,900	137,808	25,654	141,483	105,651	60,806	10,279	80,677	70,399
7					2,772	1,843		4,615	152,701	152,546	32,646	119,900	142,631	26,552	168,035	105,651	74,381	10,070	93,675	83,604
8					2,869	1,907		4,776	157,477	157,885	37,985	119,900	147,623	27,481	195,516	105,651	89,135	9,854	106,381	96,527
9					2,969	1,974		4,943	162,420	163,411	43,511	119,900	152,790	28,443	223,960	105,651	105,240	9,631	118,720	109,089
10					3,073	2,043		5,116	167,537	169,131	49,231	119,900	158,137	29,439	253,398	105,651	122,794	9,399	130,604	121,205
11					3,181	2,114		5,295	172,832	175,050	55,150	119,900	163,672	30,469	283,867	105,651	141,928	9,160	141,939	132,779
12					3,292	2,188		5,481	178,313	181,177	61,277	119,900	169,401	31,536	315,402	105,651	162,783	8,912	152,619	143,707
13					3,407	2,265		5,673	183,985	187,518	67,618	119,900	175,330	32,639	348,041	105,651	185,516	8,656	162,525	153,870
14					3,527	2,344		5,871	189,856	194,081	74,181	119,900	181,466	33,781	381,823	105,651	210,295	8,390	171,528	163,138
15					3,650	2,426		6,077	195,933	200,874	80,974	119,900	187,817	34,964	416,787	105,651	237,304	8,115	179,483	171,367
16					3,778	2,511		6,289	202,222	207,905	88,005	119,900	194,391	36,188	452,974	105,651	266,743	7,831	186,231	178,400
17					3,910	2,599		6,509	208,732	215,182	95,282	119,900	201,195	37,454	490,428	105,651	298,833	7,537	191,596	184,059
18					4,047	2,690		6,737	215,469	222,713	102,813	119,900	208,237	38,765	529,193	105,651	333,610	7,232	195,383	188,151
19					4,189	2,784		6,973	222,442	230,508	110,606	119,900	215,525	40,122	569,315	105,651	371,935	6,917	197,383	190,463
20					4,335	2,882		7,217	229,659	238,576	118,676	119,900	223,068	41,526	610,841	105,651	413,492	6,591	197,350	190,759
21					4,487	2,983		7,470	237,129	246,926	127,026	119,900	230,876	42,979	653,821	105,651	458,788	6,253	195,033	188,780
22					4,644	3,087		7,731	244,860	255,568	135,668	119,900	238,958	44,484	698,304	105,651	508,161	5,903	190,143	184,240
23					4,807	3,195		8,002	252,861	264,513	144,613	119,900	247,320	46,041	744,345	105,651	561,978	5,542	182,367	176,825
24					4,975	3,307		8,282	261,143	273,771	153,871	119,900	255,976	47,652	791,997	105,651	620,638	5,167	171,358	166,191
25					5,149	3,423		8,572	269,715	283,353	163,453	119,900	264,935	49,320	841,317	105,651	684,578	4,780	156,739	151,959
26					5,329	3,543		8,872	278,586	293,270	173,370	119,900	274,208	51,046	892,363	105,651	754,273	4,379	138,090	133,712
27					5,516	3,666		9,182	287,769	303,535	183,635	119,900	283,805	52,833	945,196	105,651	830,239	3,963	114,956	110,993
28					5,709	3,795		9,504	297,272	314,159	194,259	119,900	293,738	54,682	999,878	105,651	913,043	3,534	86,834	83,301
29					5,908	3,928		9,836	307,108	325,154	205,254	119,900	304,019	56,596	1,056,473	105,651	1,003,299	3,089	53,174	50,085
30					6,115	4,065		10,180	317,289	336,535	216,635	119,900	314,660	58,577	1,115,050	105,651	1,101,679	2,629	13,371	10,742
31					6,329	4,207		10,537	327,825	348,313	228,413	119,900	325,673	60,627	1,175,677	105,651	1,208,912	2,152	33,235	35,388
32					6,551	4,355		10,905	338,731	360,504	240,604	119,900	337,071	62,749	1,238,425	105,651	1,325,796	1,659	87,371	89,030
33					6,780	4,507		11,287	350,018	373,122	253,222	119,900	348,869	64,945	1,303,370	105,651	1,453,200	1,149	149,830	150,979
34					7,017	4,665		11,682	361,700	386,181	266,281	119,900	361,079	67,216	1,370,586	105,651	1,592,071	621	221,483	222,103
35					7,263	4,828		12,091	373,791	399,697	279,797	119,900	373,717	69,571	1,440,159	105,651	1,743,439	74	303,281	303,355
36					7,517	4,997		12,514	386,306	413,687	293,787	119,900	386,797	72,006	1,512,164	105,651	1,908,431	492	396,267	395,775
37					7,780	5,172		12,952	399,258	428,168	308,268	119,900	400,335	74,526	1,586,690	105,651	2,088,272	1,077	501,582	500,505
38					8,053	5,353		13,406	412,663	443,152	323,252	119,900	414,347	77,134	1,663,824	105,651	2,284,299	1,683	620,475	618,792
39					8,335	5,540		13,875	426,538	456,662	338,762	119,900	428,849	79,834	1,743,658	105,651	2,497,968	2,311	754,310	752,000
40					8,626	5,734		14,360	440,898	474,715	354,815	119,900	443,859	82,628	1,826,286	105,651	2,730,868	2,960	904,582	901,622

(Source: https://michaelbluejay.com/house/rentvsbuy.html)

$119,900 House (20% down) vs. $800 Rental

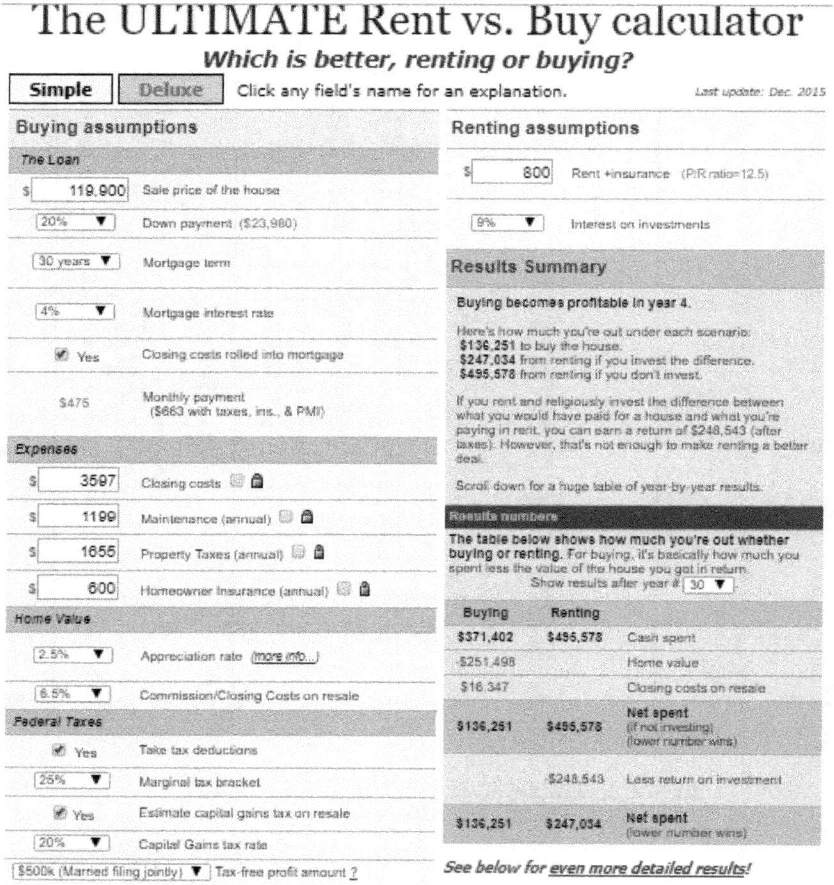

The ULTIMATE Rent vs. Buy calculator

Which is better, renting or buying?

Simple | Deluxe | Click any field's name for an explanation. *Last update: Dec. 2015*

Buying assumptions

The Loan

$ 119,900	Sale price of the house
20% ▼	Down payment ($23,980)
30 years ▼	Mortgage term
4% ▼	Mortgage interest rate
✔ Yes	Closing costs rolled into mortgage
$475	Monthly payment ($663 with taxes, ins., & PMI)

Expenses

$ 3597	Closing costs
$ 1199	Maintenance (annual)
$ 1655	Property Taxes (annual)
$ 600	Homeowner Insurance (annual)

Home Value

2.5% ▼	Appreciation rate (more info...)
6.5% ▼	Commission/Closing Costs on resale

Federal Taxes

✔ Yes	Take tax deductions
25% ▼	Marginal tax bracket
✔ Yes	Estimate capital gains tax on resale
20% ▼	Capital Gains tax rate
$500k (Married filing jointly) ▼	Tax-free profit amount ?

Renting assumptions

$ 800	Rent +insurance (P/R ratio=12.5)
9% ▼	Interest on investments

Results Summary

Buying becomes profitable in year 4.

Here's how much you're out under each scenario:
$136,251 to buy the house.
$247,034 from renting if you invest the difference.
$495,578 from renting if you don't invest.

If you rent and religiously invest the difference between what you would have paid for a house and what you're paying in rent, you can earn a return of $248,543 (after taxes). However, that's not enough to make renting a better deal.

Scroll down for a huge table of year-by-year results.

Results numbers

The table below shows how much you're out whether buying or renting. For buying, it's basically how much you spent less the value of the house you got in return.

Show results after year # 30 ▼

Buying	Renting	
$371,402	$495,578	Cash spent
-$251,498		Home value
$16,347		Closing costs on resale
$136,251	$495,578	**Net spent** (if not investing) (lower number wins)
	-$248,543	Less return on investment
$136,251	$247,034	**Net spent** (lower number wins)

See below for even more detailed results!

Mega Data Table! (detailed results of Rent vs. Buy)

In pink-row years renting is better. In green-row years buying is better.

Light gray columns are figures for that year. Dark gray columns are running totals.

All fields are explained in detail below the table.

	Loan details		Buying (cash out)							House value				Renting				Rent vs. Buy		
Yr.	Interest	Loan Balance	Pmts.	PMI/ FHA fees	Taxes +Ins.	Maint. +Exp. -Rent	Tax Savings	Cash out	Total Cash out	House Value (gross)	Apprec-iation	Paid Equity	House Value (net)	Rent	Total Rent	Total Principal	Return on Princ.	Buying Net	Rent net	Rent vs. Buy
1	3,949	97,764	29,681		2,256	1,499		33,435	33,435	122,897	2,997	25,669	114,908	9,600	9,600	23,836	1,823	16,291	7,777	8,514
2	3,877	95,941	5,701		2,311	1,551		9,064	42,999	125,970	6,070	27,427	117,782	9,936	19,536	23,836	3,811	21,158	16,725	5,433
3	3,803	94,042	5,701		2,369	1,606		9,675	52,676	129,110	9,210	29,257	120,726	10,284	29,820	23,836	5,977	25,992	23,842	2,149
4	3,726	92,067	5,701		2,426	1,662		9,792	62,467	132,347	12,447	31,161	123,746	10,644	40,463	23,836	8,338	30,789	32,125	1,335
5	3,645	90,011	5,701		2,489	1,720		9,911	72,378	135,656	15,756	33,143	126,838	11,016	51,480	23,836	10,513	35,550	40,567	5,017
6	3,561	87,871	5,701		2,551	1,780		10,033	82,411	139,047	19,147	35,205	130,009	11,402	62,881	23,836	13,718	40,273	49,160	8,891
7	3,474	85,644	5,701		2,615	1,843		10,159	92,570	142,523	22,623	37,352	133,259	11,801	74,682	23,836	16,776	44,954	57,906	12,952
8	3,384	83,326	5,701		2,660	1,907		10,289	102,859	146,087	26,187	39,586	136,591	12,214	86,896	23,836	20,109	49,594	66,787	17,193
9	3,289	80,914	5,701		2,747	1,974		10,423	113,282	149,739	29,839	41,911	140,006	12,641	99,538	23,836	23,743	54,190	75,795	21,605
10	3,191	78,403	5,701		2,816	2,043		10,560	123,842	153,482	33,582	44,330	143,506	13,084	112,621	23,836	27,703	58,740	84,919	26,179
11	3,089	75,791	5,701		2,887	2,114		10,702	134,545	157,319	37,419	46,849	147,093	13,542	126,163	23,836	32,019	63,242	94,144	30,902
12	2,982	73,072	5,701		2,959	2,188		10,849	145,393	161,252	41,352	49,470	150,771	14,016	140,179	23,836	36,725	67,694	103,454	35,760
13	2,871	70,242	5,701		3,033	2,265		10,999	156,392	165,283	45,383	52,197	154,540	14,506	154,685	23,836	41,863	72,094	112,832	40,738
14	2,756	67,296	5,701		3,109	2,344		11,154	167,546	169,416	49,516	55,036	158,404	15,014	169,699	23,836	47,443	76,439	122,256	45,816
15	2,636	64,231	5,701		3,186	2,426		11,314	178,860	173,651	53,751	57,991	162,364	15,539	185,239	23,836	53,537	80,728	131,702	50,974
16	2,511	61,041	5,701		3,266	2,511		11,479	190,339	177,992	58,092	61,065	166,423	16,083	201,322	23,836	60,178	84,957	141,143	56,186
17	2,381	57,721	5,701		3,348	2,599		11,648	201,987	182,442	62,542	64,265	170,983	16,646	217,968	23,836	67,418	89,125	150,550	61,425
18	2,246	54,285	5,701		3,431	2,690		11,823	213,810	187,003	67,103	67,596	174,846	17,229	235,197	23,836	75,309	93,227	159,888	66,661
19	2,105	50,689	5,701		3,517	2,784		12,003	225,813	191,678	71,778	71,062	179,219	17,832	253,029	23,836	83,910	97,283	169,119	71,836
20	1,959	46,927	5,701		3,605	2,882		12,188	238,001	196,470	76,570	74,670	183,700	18,456	271,485	23,836	93,285	101,228	178,200	76,972
21	1,806	43,031	5,701		3,695	2,983		12,379	250,380	201,382	81,482	78,424	188,292	19,102	290,587	23,836	103,565	105,119	187,082	81,963
22	1,647	38,978	5,701		3,787	3,087		12,576	262,956	206,416	86,516	82,331	192,929	19,771	310,357	23,836	114,643	108,934	196,714	86,780
23	1,482	34,759	5,701		3,882	3,195		12,779	275,734	211,577	91,677	86,398	197,824	20,463	330,820	23,836	125,785	112,669	204,095	91,367
24	1,310	30,368	5,701		3,979	3,307		12,987	288,722	216,866	96,966	90,630	202,770	21,179	351,999	23,836	140,019	116,320	211,990	95,680
25	1,132	25,798	5,701		4,079	3,423		13,203	301,924	222,288	102,388	95,034	207,839	21,920	373,919	23,836	154,444	119,883	219,475	99,592
26	945	21,042	5,701		4,181	3,543		13,424	315,348	227,845	107,945	99,619	213,036	22,687	396,606	23,836	170,167	123,356	226,439	103,083
27	752	16,092	5,701		4,285	3,668		13,653	329,002	233,541	113,641	104,389	218,361	23,481	420,087	23,836	187,306	126,733	232,781	106,048
28	550	10,941	5,701		4,392	3,795		13,888	342,890	239,380	119,480	109,355	223,820	24,303	444,390	23,836	205,966	130,011	238,404	108,392
29	340	5,580	5,701		4,502	3,928		14,131	357,021	245,364	125,464	114,522	229,416	25,154	469,544	23,836	226,340	133,185	243,195	110,010
30	122	0	5,701		4,615	4,065		14,381	371,402	251,498	131,598	119,900	235,151	26,034	495,578	23,836	248,543	136,251	247,034	110,783
31					4,730	4,207		8,937	380,340	257,786	137,886	119,900	241,030	26,945	522,523	23,836	272,736	139,310	249,787	110,477
32					4,848	4,355		9,203	389,543	264,230	144,330	119,900	247,056	27,888	550,411	23,836	299,105	142,487	251,306	108,819
33					4,969	4,507		9,477	399,019	270,836	150,936	119,900	253,232	28,864	579,275	23,836	327,848	145,787	251,427	105,640
34					5,094	4,665		9,759	408,778	277,607	157,707	119,900	259,563	29,875	609,150	23,836	360,178	149,215	249,972	100,757
35					5,221	4,828		10,049	418,827	284,547	164,647	119,900	266,052	30,920	640,071	23,836	393,327	152,775	246,743	93,968
36					5,352	4,997		10,349	429,175	291,661	171,761	119,900	272,703	32,002	672,073	23,836	430,550	156,472	241,523	85,050
37					5,485	5,172		10,657	439,833	298,953	179,053	119,900	279,521	33,123	705,196	23,836	471,123	160,312	234,072	73,760
38					5,623	5,353		10,975	450,808	306,426	186,526	119,900	286,509	34,282	739,477	23,836	515,348	164,300	224,130	59,830
39					5,763	5,540		11,303	462,112	314,087	194,187	119,900	293,671	35,482	774,959	23,836	563,552	168,440	211,407	42,967
40					5,907	5,734		11,641	473,753	321,939	202,039	119,900	301,012	36,724	811,683	23,836	616,095	172,740	195,587	22,847

(Source: https://michaelbluejay.com/house/rentvsbuy.html)

Buy it Outright: $119,900 house versus $1,800 rent

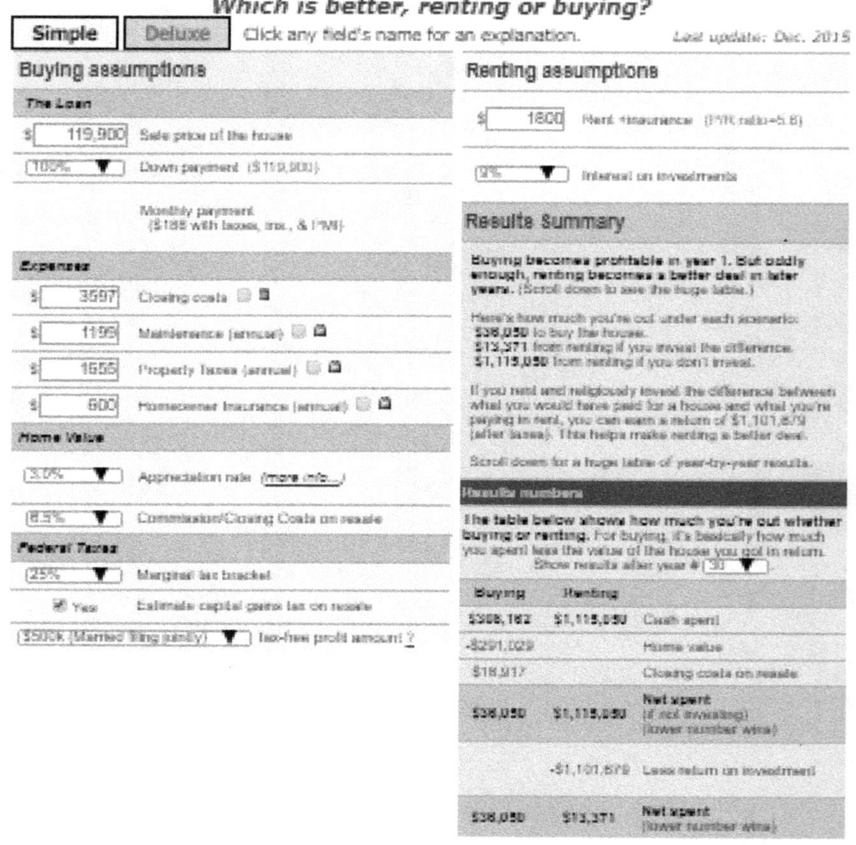
The ULTIMATE Rent vs. Buy calculator
Which is better, renting or buying?
Simple
Deluxe
Click any field's name for an explanation.
Last update: Dec. 2015
Buying assumptions
The Loan
$ 119,900 Sale price of the house
100% Down payment ($119,900)
Monthly payment
Expenses
$ 3597 Closing costs
$ 1199 Maintenance (annual)
$ 1655 Property Taxes (annual)
$ 600 Homeowner Insurance (annual)
Home Value
3.0% Appreciation rate (more info...)
6.5% Commission/Closing Costs on resale
Federal Taxes
25% Marginal tax bracket
Yes Estimate capital gains tax on resale
$500k (Married filing jointly) tax-free profit amount ?
Renting assumptions
$ 1800 Rent +insurance
9% Interest on investments
Results Summary
Buying becomes profitable in year 1. But oddly enough, renting becomes a better deal in later years. (Scroll down to see the huge table.)
Here's how much you're out under each scenario:
$36,050 to buy the house.
$13,371 from renting if you invest the difference.
$1,115,050 from renting if you don't invest.
If you rent and religiously invest the difference between what you would have paid for a house and what you're paying in rent, you can earn a return of $1,101,679 (after taxes). This helps make renting a better deal.
Scroll down for a huge table of year-by-year results.
Results numbers
The table below shows how much you're out whether buying or renting. For buying, it's basically how much you spent less the value of the house you got in return.
Show results after year # 30
Buying Renting
$308,162 $1,115,050 Cash spent
-$291,029 Home value
$18,917 Closing costs on resale
$36,050 $1,115,050 Net spent (if not investing) (lower number wins)
-$1,101,679 Less return on investment
$36,050 $13,371 Net spent (lower number wins)
See below for even more detailed results!

Mega Data Table! (detailed results of Rent vs. Buy)

In pink-row years renting is better. In green-row years buying is better.

Light gray columns are figures for that year. Dark gray columns are running totals.

All fields are explained in detail below the table.

Loan details			Buying (cash out)							House value				Renting				Rent vs. Buy		
Yr.	Interest	Loan balance	Pmts.	PMI/FHA fees	Taxes +Ins.	Maint. +Exp. -Fixed	Tax Savings	Cash out	Total Cash out	House Value (gross)	Apprec-iation	Paid Equity	House Value (net)	Rent	Total Rent	Total Principal	Return on Rental	Buying Net	Rent net	Rent vs. Buy
1			119,900		2,255	1,499		127,251	127,251	123,497	3,597	119,900	115,470	21,600	21,600	105,651	8,082	11,781	13,518	1,738
2					2,323	1,551		3,874	131,125	127,202	7,302	119,900	118,934	22,356	43,956	105,651	16,892	12,191	27,064	14,873
3					2,392	1,606		3,998	135,123	131,018	11,118	119,900	122,502	23,138	67,094	105,651	26,496	12,621	40,600	27,978
4					2,464	1,662		4,126	139,249	134,949	15,049	119,900	126,177	23,948	91,043	105,651	36,987	13,072	54,081	41,009
5					2,538	1,720		4,258	143,507	138,997	19,097	119,900	129,962	24,786	115,829	105,651	48,370	13,546	67,460	53,914
6					2,614	1,780		4,395	147,902	143,167	23,267	119,900	133,861	25,654	141,483	105,651	60,808	14,041	80,677	66,637
7					2,693	1,843		4,535	152,437	147,462	27,562	119,900	137,877	26,552	168,035	105,651	74,381	14,560	93,675	79,114
8					2,773	1,907		4,681	157,118	151,886	31,986	119,900	142,013	27,481	195,516	105,651	89,135	15,105	106,381	91,276
9					2,857	1,974		4,830	161,948	156,442	36,542	119,900	146,274	28,443	223,960	105,651	105,240	15,675	118,720	103,045
10					2,942	2,043		4,985	166,933	161,136	41,236	119,900	150,662	29,439	253,398	105,651	122,794	16,272	130,604	114,333
11					3,031	2,114		5,145	172,078	165,970	46,070	119,900	155,182	30,469	283,867	105,651	141,928	16,897	141,939	125,043
12					3,121	2,188		5,310	177,388	170,949	51,049	119,900	159,837	31,535	315,402	105,651	162,785	17,551	152,819	135,068
13					3,215	2,265		5,480	182,868	176,077	56,177	119,900	164,632	32,639	348,041	105,651	185,518	18,238	162,525	144,288
14					3,312	2,344		5,656	188,524	181,360	61,460	119,900	169,571	33,781	381,823	105,651	210,296	18,953	171,528	152,575
15					3,411	2,426		5,837	194,362	186,800	66,900	119,900	174,658	34,964	416,787	105,651	237,204	19,704	179,483	159,779
16					3,513	2,511		6,025	200,386	192,404	72,504	119,900	179,898	36,188	452,974	105,651	266,743	20,488	186,231	165,743
17					3,619	2,599		6,218	206,604	198,176	78,276	119,900	185,295	37,454	490,428	105,651	298,833	21,309	191,598	170,289
18					3,727	2,690		6,417	213,022	204,122	84,222	119,900	190,854	38,765	529,193	105,651	333,810	22,166	195,383	173,218
19					3,839	2,784		6,623	219,645	210,245	90,345	119,900	196,579	40,122	569,315	105,651	371,935	23,066	197,380	174,315
20					3,954	2,882		6,836	226,481	216,553	96,653	119,900	202,477	41,526	610,841	105,651	413,492	24,004	197,350	173,346
21					4,073	2,983		7,055	233,536	223,049	103,149	119,900	208,551	42,979	653,821	105,651	458,786	24,985	195,033	170,047
22					4,195	3,087		7,282	240,818	229,741	109,841	119,900	214,808	44,484	698,304	105,651	508,161	26,011	190,143	164,132
23					4,321	3,195		7,516	248,334	236,633	116,733	119,900	221,252	46,041	744,345	105,651	561,976	27,083	182,367	155,284
24					4,450	3,307		7,757	256,092	243,732	123,832	119,900	227,889	47,652	791,997	105,651	620,836	28,202	171,369	143,156
25					4,584	3,423		8,007	264,098	251,044	131,144	119,900	234,726	49,320	841,317	105,651	684,578	29,372	156,739	127,368
26					4,721	3,543		8,264	272,362	258,575	138,675	119,900	241,768	51,046	892,363	105,651	754,275	30,595	138,093	107,498
27					4,863	3,666		8,530	280,892	266,333	146,433	119,900	249,021	52,833	945,196	105,651	830,239	31,871	114,956	83,085
28					5,009	3,795		8,804	289,696	274,323	154,423	119,900	256,492	54,682	999,878	105,651	913,043	33,204	86,834	53,630
29					5,159	3,928		9,087	298,783	282,552	162,652	119,900	264,186	56,596	1,056,473	105,651	1,003,258	34,596	53,174	18,577
30					5,314	4,065		9,379	308,162	291,029	171,129	119,900	272,112	58,577	1,115,050	105,651	1,101,679	36,050	13,371	22,679
31					5,473	4,207		9,681	317,843	299,760	179,860	119,900	280,275	60,627	1,175,677	105,651	1,208,912	37,568	33,235	70,803
32					5,638	4,355		9,992	327,835	308,752	188,852	119,900	288,684	62,749	1,238,425	105,651	1,325,798	39,152	87,371	126,523
33					5,807	4,507		10,314	338,149	318,015	198,115	119,900	297,344	64,946	1,303,370	105,651	1,453,200	40,806	149,830	190,635
34					5,981	4,665		10,646	348,795	327,555	207,655	119,900	306,264	67,218	1,370,588	105,651	1,592,071	42,530	221,483	264,013
35					6,160	4,828		10,988	359,783	337,382	217,482	119,900	315,452	69,571	1,440,159	105,651	1,743,438	44,331	303,281	347,612
36					6,345	4,997		11,342	371,126	347,504	227,604	119,900	324,916	72,006	1,512,164	105,651	1,908,431	46,210	396,267	442,477
37					6,536	5,172		11,708	382,833	357,929	238,029	119,900	334,663	74,526	1,586,690	105,651	2,088,272	48,170	501,582	549,752
38					6,732	5,353		12,085	394,918	368,667	248,767	119,900	344,703	77,134	1,663,824	105,651	2,284,299	50,215	620,475	670,690
39					6,934	5,540		12,474	407,392	379,727	259,827	119,900	355,044	79,834	1,743,658	105,651	2,497,968	52,348	754,310	806,658
40					7,142	5,734		12,878	420,268	391,118	271,218	119,900	365,698	82,628	1,826,286	105,651	2,735,868	54,572	904,582	959,154

(Source: https://michaelbluejay.com/house/rentvsbuy.html)

Affodability Calculator

Zillow | Buy | Rent | Sell | Mortgages | Agent finder | Home design | More

Mortgage lenders | Mortgage rates | Mortgage calculator | Lender reviews

Mortgages · Affordability calculator

You can afford $375,142

ANNUAL INCOME	$78,500
DOWN PAYMENT	$65,605
MONTHLY DEBTS	$250
DEBT-TO-INCOME	36%
INTEREST RATE	4.266%
LOAN TERM	360 months
TAXES & INSURANCE INCLUDED?	Yes
PROPERTY TAX	1.2%
HOMEOWNER'S INSURANCE	$800/yr
MORTGAGE INSURANCE	$113/mo
HOA DUES	$0/mo

Monthly Budget

Payment Breakdown

(Source: www.zillow.com Affordability Calculator accessed March 19, 2018)

Median Prices

Home Value (2017/07)

RegionNan	SizeRank	2017-07
Ohio	7	125900
Oklahoma	26	139100
Alabama	21	137400
Arkansas	28	136300
Kentucky	24	146900
West Virgir	32	150500
Pennsylvar	6	161400
Nebraska	33	162600
Missouri	16	160100
Louisiana	23	164400
Wisconsin	18	167100
Georgia	8	1.70E+05
Tennessee	15	1.64E+05
North Carc	9	180200
Illinois	5	190500
New Mexic	31	194400
Florida	4	203100
Texas	2	209200
Idaho	34	206700
North Dak(	39	2.24E+05
Minnesota	19	2.18E+05
Connecticu	27	225300
Arizona	14	229400
Wyoming	41	226700
Nevada	30	245800
Virginia	11	262100
Delaware	37	218200
Maryland	17	259300
Montana	36	255200
Oregon	25	298800
Alaska	38	301500
Washingto	12	321800
Colorado	20	324800
Massachus	13	350200
California	1	456400
District of (	40	5.35E+05
Hawaii	35	527500
New York	3	279400
New Jersey	10	262600
South Carc	22	163600
Utah	29	261600
Average		234561

Home Rental (2018/02)

RegionNan	SizeRank	2018-02
California	1	2650
Texas	2	1495
New York	3	3300
Florida	4	1800
Illinois	5	1550
Pennsylvar	6	1300
Ohio	7	995
Michigan	8	1050
Georgia	9	1300
North Carc	10	1250
New Jersey	11	1850
Virginia	12	1595
Washingto	13	1900
Massachus	14	2550
Indiana	15	1000
Arizona	16	1395
Tennessee	17	1275
Missouri	18	950
Maryland	19	1650
Wisconsin	20	1150
Minnesota	21	1500
Colorado	22	1850
Alabama	23	995
South Carc	24	1300
Louisiana	25	1200
Kentucky	26	1065
Oregon	27	1695
Oklahoma	28	995
Connecticu	29	1700
Iowa	30	1075
Mississippi	31	1100
Arkansas	32	1045
Kansas	33	1080
Utah	34	1400
Nevada	35	1395
New Mexic	36	1200
West Virgir	37	992.5
Nebraska	38	1250
Idaho	39	1250
Hawaii	40	2300
Maine	41	1600
New Hamp	42	1650
Rhode Islar	43	2000
Montana	44	1100
Delaware	45	1300
South Dak(	46	1080
Alaska	47	1550
North Dak(	48	1250
District of (	49	2500
Wyoming	50	1000
Average		1468.45

(Source Zillowhttps://www.zillow.com/research/data/)

Average of Median Rental, All Homes

Median Rental Price		
State	Rank	2017-12
California	1	2600
Texas	2	1495
New York	3	3400
Florida	4	1800
Illinois	5	1550
Pennsylvania	6	1300
Ohio	7	1000
Michigan	8	1050
Georgia	9	1300
North Carolin	10	1275
New Jersey	11	1850
Virginia	12	1600
Washington	13	1900
Massachusett	14	2500
Indiana	15	999
Arizona	16	1350
Tennessee	17	1292.5
Missouri	18	950
Maryland	19	1650
Wisconsin	20	1150
Minnesota	21	1500
Colorado	22	1800
Alabama	23	995
South Carolin	24	1300
Louisiana	25	1225
Kentucky	26	1025
Oregon	27	1695
Oklahoma	28	990
Connecticut	29	1700
Iowa	30	1059.5
Mississippi	31	1100
Arkansas	32	1000
Kansas	33	1050
Utah	34	1400
Nevada	35	1350
New Mexico	36	1200
West Virginia	37	980
Idaho	38	1225
Hawaii	39	2300
Maine	40	1700
New Hampshi	41	1695
Rhode Island	42	1900
Montana	43	1150
Delaware	44	1300
South Dakota	45	1100
Alaska	46	1550
North Dakota	47	1170
District of Col	48	2595
Wyoming	49	1050
	Average	**1,472**

(Source:www.zillow.com Research Data) [187]

NYTimes Rent Vs. Buy

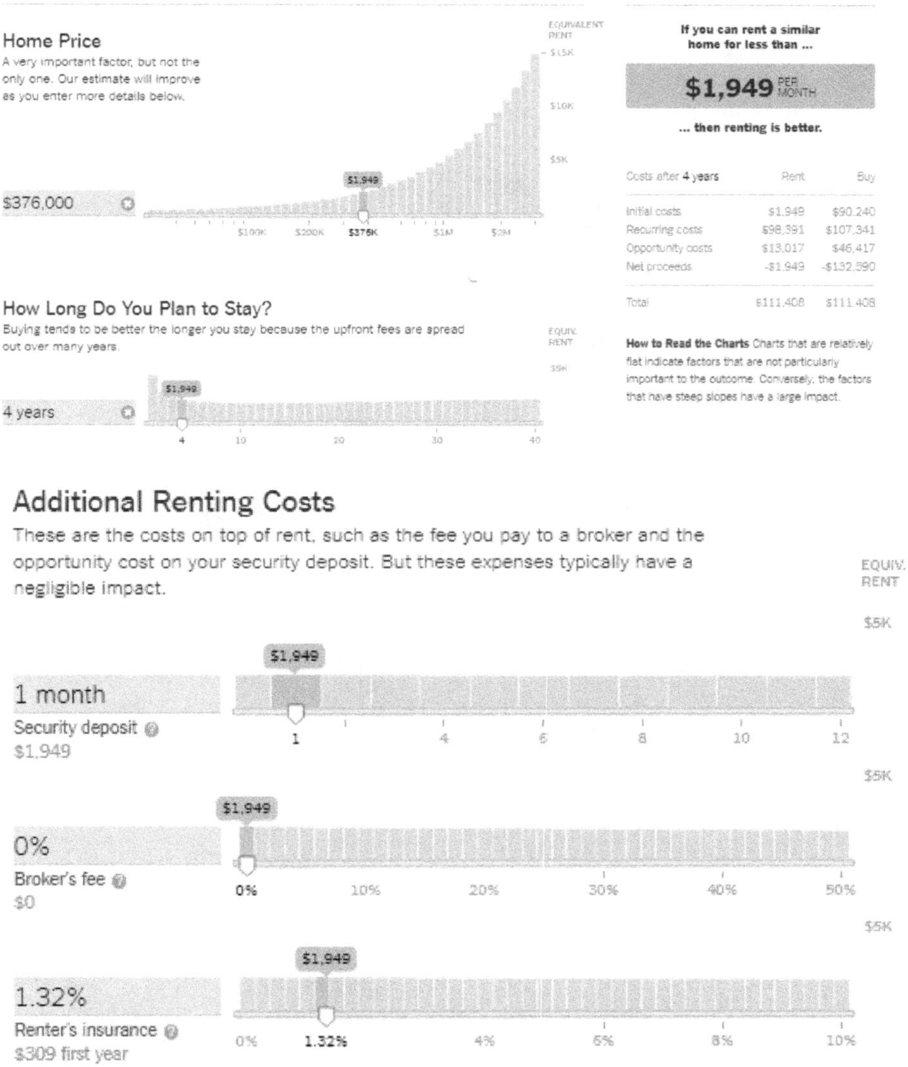

Home Price

A very important factor, but not the only one. Our estimate will improve as you enter more details below.

EQUIVALENT RENT

$15K

$10K

$5K

$1,949

$376,000

$100K $200K $376K $1M $2M

How Long Do You Plan to Stay?

Buying tends to be better the longer you stay because the upfront fees are spread out over many years.

EQUIV. RENT

$5K

$1,949

4 years

4 10 20 30 40

If you can rent a similar home for less than ...

$1,949 PER MONTH

... then renting is better.

Costs after **4 years**	Rent	Buy
Initial costs	$1,949	$90,240
Recurring costs	$98,391	$107,341
Opportunity costs	$13,017	$46,417
Net proceeds	-$1,949	-$132,590
Total	$111,408	$111,408

How to Read the Charts Charts that are relatively flat indicate factors that are not particularly important to the outcome. Conversely, the factors that have steep slopes have a large impact.

Additional Renting Costs

These are the costs on top of rent, such as the fee you pay to a broker and the opportunity cost on your security deposit. But these expenses typically have a negligible impact.

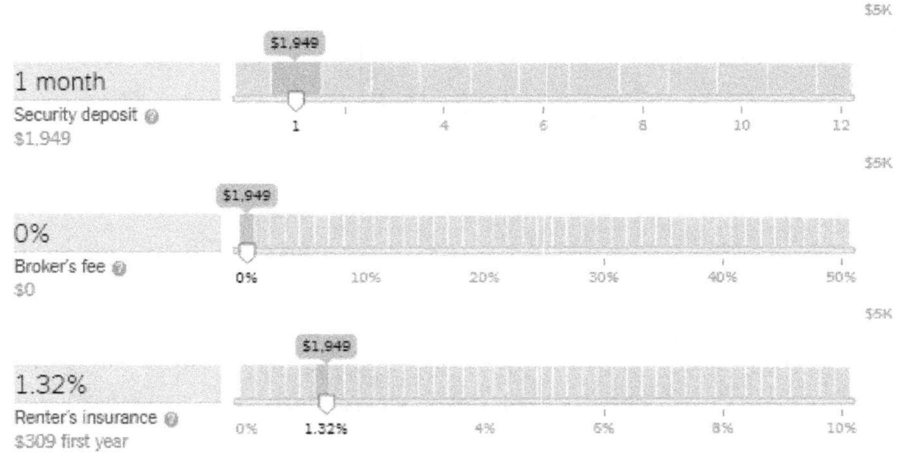

What Are Your Mortgage Details?

In addition to the interest rate and down payment, the calculator takes into account the mortgage-interest tax deduction.

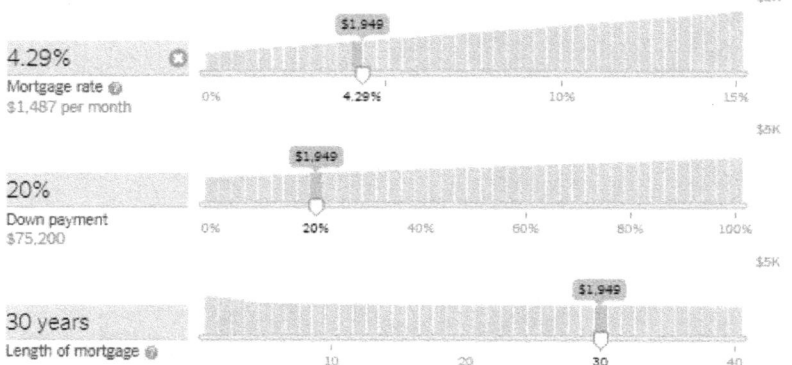

EQUIV. RENT

$5K

$1,949

4.29%

Mortgage rate

$1,487 per month

0% 4.29% 10% 15%

$5K

$1,949

20%

Down payment

$75,200

0% 20% 40% 60% 80% 100%

$5K

$1,949

30 years

Length of mortgage

10 20 30 40

What Does the Future Hold?

How much home prices, rents and stock prices change can have a large impact on your outcome. Unfortunately, these are some of the hardest things to predict. If you choose to rent instead of buying, the calculator assumes that you'll spend your would-be down payment on stocks or another investment.

EQUIV. RENT

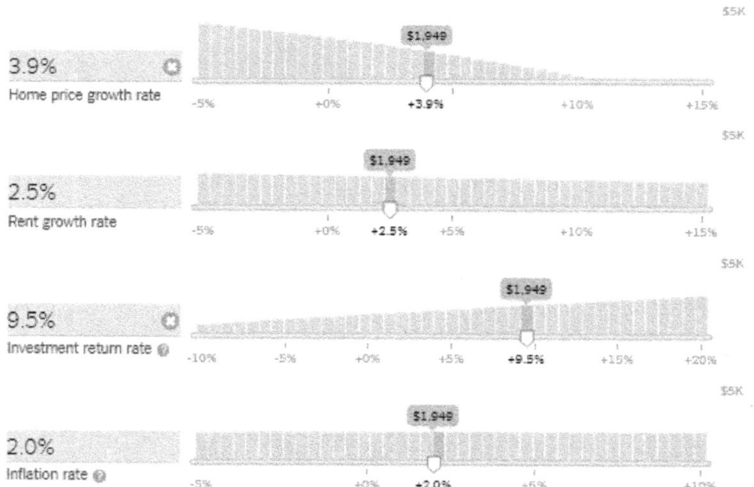

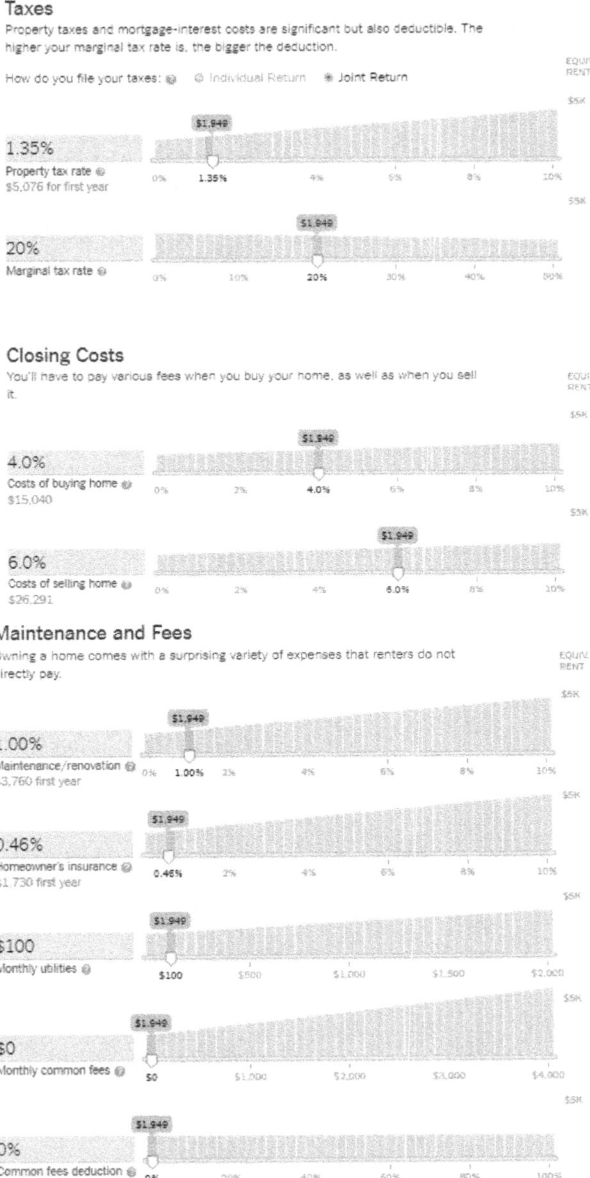
Taxes
Property taxes and mortgage-interest costs are significant but also deductible. The higher your marginal tax rate is, the bigger the deduction.
How do you file your taxes: Individual Return Joint Return
EQUIV. RENT
$5K
$1,949
1.35%
Property tax rate
$5,076 for first year
0% 1.35% 4% 6% 8% 10%
$5K
$1,949
20%
Marginal tax rate
0% 10% 20% 30% 40% 50%
Closing Costs
You'll have to pay various fees when you buy your home, as well as when you sell it.
EQUIV. RENT
$5K
$1,949
4.0%
Costs of buying home
$15,040
0% 2% 4.0% 6% 8% 10%
$5K
$1,949
6.0%
Costs of selling home
$26,291
0% 2% 4% 6.0% 8% 10%
Maintenance and Fees
Owning a home comes with a surprising variety of expenses that renters do not directly pay.
EQUIV. RENT
$5K
$1,949
1.00%
Maintenance/renovation
$3,760 first year
0% 1.00% 2% 4% 6% 8% 10%
$5K
$1,949
0.46%
Homeowner's insurance
$1,730 first year
0.46% 2% 4% 6% 8% 10%
$5K
$1,949
$100
Monthly utilities
$100 $500 $1,000 $1,500 $2,000
$5K
$1,949
$0
Monthly common fees
$0 $1,000 $2,000 $3,000 $4,000
$5K
$1,949
0%
Common fees deduction
0% 20% 40% 60% 80% 100%

(Source: https://www.nytimes.com/interactive/2014/upshot/buy-rent-calculator.html)

Freedom Factor Comps

Address	House Value	Mortgage w/ 20%	Rental				Freedom Factor
			Zestimate	ZIP	Lutz	Breakeven	
1583 Feather Grass Loop,Lutz, FL 3	$ 379,900	$ 1,517	$ 2,295	2086	1684		$ 346.00
17940 Simmons Rd,Lutz, FL 33548	$ 388,236	$ 1,556	$ 2,365	2086	1684	$ 1,949	$ 416.00
1579 Fox Grape Loop,Lutz, FL 3355	$ 376,172	$ 1,654	$ 2,406	2086	1684		$ 457.00

Source: www.Zillow.com

New House Tax Payback

tion Schedule Calculator | $ 300,000 | Term 30 | % 5.25 | Jan | 2018

Date	Interest	Principal	Balance
Jan, 2018	$1,313	$344	$299,656
Feb, 2018	$1,311	$346	$299,310
Mar, 2018	$1,309	$347	$298,963
Apr, 2018	$1,308	$349	$298,614
May, 2018	$1,306	$350	$298,264
Jun, 2018	$1,305	$352	$297,913
Jul, 2018	$1,303	$353	$297,559
Aug, 2018	$1,302	$355	$297,205
Sep, 2018	$1,300	$356	$296,848
Oct, 2018	$1,299	$358	$296,490
Nov, 2018	$1,297	$359	$296,131
Dec, 2018	$1,296	$361	$295,770
2018	**$15,649**	**$4,230**	**$295,770**
Jan, 2019	$1,294	$363	$295,407
Feb, 2019	$1,292	$364	$295,043
Mar, 2019	$1,291	$366	$294,677
Apr, 2019	$1,289	$367	$294,310
May, 2019	$1,288	$369	$293,941
Jun, 2019	$1,286	$371	$293,570
Jul, 2019	$1,284	$372	$293,198
Aug, 2019	$1,283	$374	$292,824
Sep, 2019	$1,281	$376	$292,449
Oct, 2019	$1,279	$377	$292,071
Nov, 2019	$1,278	$379	$291,693
Dec, 2019	$1,276	$380	$291,312
2019	**$15,422**	**$4,458**	**$291,312**
Jan, 2020	$1,274	$382	$290,930
Feb, 2020	$1,273	$384	$290,546
Mar, 2020	$1,271	$385	$290,161
Apr, 2020	$1,269	$387	$289,774
May, 2020	$1,268	$389	$289,385
Jun, 2020	$1,266	$391	$288,994
Jul, 2020	$1,264	$392	$288,602
Aug, 2020	$1,263	$394	$288,208
Sep, 2020	$1,261	$396	$287,812
Oct, 2020	$1,259	$397	$287,415
Nov, 2020	$1,257	$399	$287,016
Dec, 2020	$1,256	$401	$286,615
2020	**$15,182**	**$4,697**	**$286,615**
Jan, 2021	$1,254	$403	$286,212
Feb, 2021	$1,252	$404	$285,808
Mar, 2021	$1,250	$406	$285,401
Apr, 2021	$1,249	$408	$284,993
May, 2021	$1,247	$410	$284,584
Jun, 2021	$1,245	$412	$284,172

Jul, 2021	$1,243	$413	$283,759
Aug, 2021	$1,241	$415	$283,344
Sep, 2021	$1,240	$417	$282,927
Oct, 2021	$1,238	$419	$282,508
Nov, 2021	$1,236	$421	$282,087
Dec, 2021	$1,234	$422	$281,665
2021	**$14,929**	**$4,950**	**$281,665**
Jan, 2022	$1,232	$424	$281,240
Feb, 2022	$1,230	$426	$280,814
Mar, 2022	$1,229	$428	$280,386
Apr, 2022	$1,227	$430	$279,956
May, 2022	$1,225	$432	$279,524
Jun, 2022	$1,223	$434	$279,091
Jul, 2022	$1,221	$436	$278,655
Aug, 2022	$1,219	$437	$278,218
Sep, 2022	$1,217	$439	$277,778
Oct, 2022	$1,215	$441	$277,337
Nov, 2022	$1,213	$443	$276,894
Dec, 2022	$1,211	$445	$276,448
2022	**$14,663**	**$5,216**	**$276,448**
Jan, 2023	$1,209	$447	$276,001
Feb, 2023	$1,208	$449	$275,552
Mar, 2023	$1,206	$451	$275,101

(Source: Amortization Schedule Calculator at www.amortization-calc.com)

Homeownership By County[188] [189]

Country	Ownership		Per Capita Wealth	
	Rank	Rate	Mean	Median
Romania	1	96.4	16,344	8,282
Singapore	2	90.7	268,776	108,850
Slovakia	3	90.3	27,842	20,717
China	4	90	26,872	6,689
Cuba	5	90		
Croatia	6	89.7	26,872	6,689
Lithuania	7	89.4	27,507	17,931
India	8	86.6	8,976	4,295
Hungary	9	86.3	39,813	30,111
Russia	10	84	16,773	3,919
Poland	11	83.5	28,057	10,302
Oman	12	83	34,592	10,461
Norway	13	82.8	320,475	130,543
Bulgaria	14	82.3	17,394	11,782
Estonia	15	81.5	43,158	27,522
Latvia	16	80.2	27,631	17,828
Malta	17	80	22,346	8,737
Mexico	18	80	119,802	67,980
Thailand	19	80	8,311	1,624
Spain	20	78.2	129,578	63,369
Czech Republic	21	78	51,472	23,083
Iceland	22	77.8	587,649	444,999
Slovenia	23	76.2	62,920	42,195
Trinidad and Tobago	24	76	14,028	7,579
Portugal	25	74.9	89,437	38,242

Country	Ownership		Per Capita Wealth	
	Rank	Rate	Mean	Median
Brazil	26	74.4	17,485	4,591
Greece	27	74	111,684	54,665
Cyprus	28	73.1	102,384	20,902
Italy	29	72.9	223,572	124,636
Finland	30	72.7	159,098	57,850
Luxembourg	31	72.5	313,687	167,664
Belgium	32	71.3	278,139	161,589
Sweden	33	70.6	260,667	45,235
Ireland	34	68.6	248,466	84,592
Netherlands	35	67.8	204,045	94,373
Canada	36	67.6	259,271	91,058
Israel	37	67.3	198,406	78,244
Turkey	38	67.3	20,061	5,087
Australia	39	65.5	402,603	195,417
France	40	65	263,399	119,720
New Zealand	41	64.8	337,441	147,593
United States	42	64.5	388,585	55,876
United Kingdom	43	63.5	278,038	102,641
Denmark	44	62.7	281,542	87,231
Japan	45	61.6	225,057	123,724
South Korea	46	56.8	160,609	67,934
Austria	47	55	221,456	57,534
Germany	48	51.9	203,946	47,091
Hong Kong	49	51	193,248	46,079
Switzerland	50	43.4	537,599	229,059

Sale of My House

I sold my house in $530,000 to an incoming professor of accounting, who bought it with zero down.

It was right at the middle of the uptick of the housing boom. It has since never seen that level of a high.

These are the buy/sale records on the house I owned from Zillow.

DATE	EVENT	PRICE
05/07/15	Sold	$430,000
02/07/11	Sold	$350,000
08/07/10	Listing removed	$439,900
10/20/05	Sold	$527,500

(source:www.Zillow.com)

Savings Calculator

Base $10,000 plus $100/mo. 25 yrs at 9% earns $157,019 interest

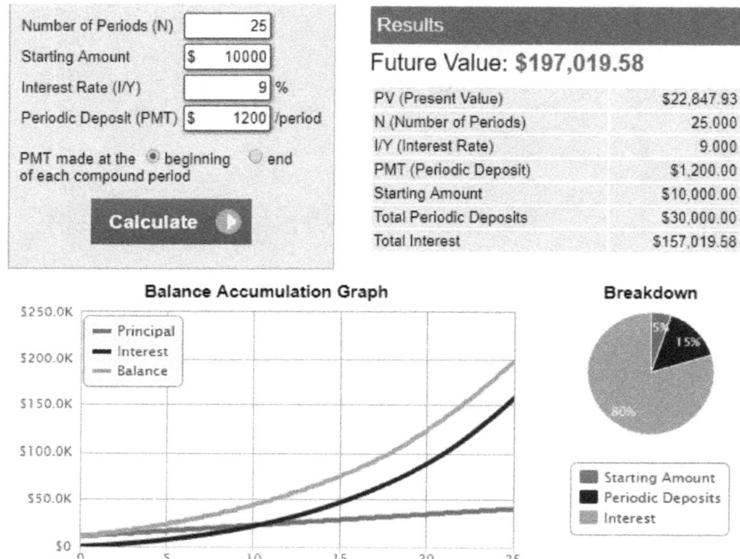

(Source: www.calculator.net/future-value-calculator.html)

Value of Starting Early

$100/mo. for 10 years @ 9%compounding annually

10	$1,200.00	$1,531.66	$12,000.00	$7,108.60	$19,108.60

Base amount: $0.00
Interest Rate: 9%
Effective Annual Rate: 9%
Calculation period: 10 years

Regular Deposit Calculation

« amend figures

37 years of compounding 9% annually from $19,108 = $463,456

37	$38,267.08	$444,348.24	$463,456.84

Base amount: $19,108.60
Interest Rate: 9%
Effective Annual Rate: 9%
Calculation period: 37 years

Standard Calculation

« amend figures

$100/mo. 37 years @ 9% compounding annually = $324,967

37	$1,200.00	$26,786.03	$44,400.00	$280,567.15	$324,967.15

Base amount: $0.00
Interest Rate: 9%
Effective Annual Rate: 9%
Calculation period: 37 years

Regular Deposit Calculation

« amend figures

(Source: Compound Interest Calculator on www.thecalculatorsite.com)

Compound Interest at Various Rates

Invested and Compounded for 20 years.

Year	Year Deposits	Year Interest	Total Deposits	Total Interest	Balance
		$250 per month at 9%			
20	$3,000.00	$13,167.05	$60,000.00	$100,864.03	$160,864.03
		$500 per month at 9%			
20	$6,000.00	$26,334.11	$120,000.00	$201,728.06	$321,728.06
		$750 per month at 9%			
20	$9,000.00	$39,501.16	$180,000.00	$302,592.08	$482,592.08
		$250 per month at 18%			
20	$3,000.00	$73,261.91	$60,000.00	$421,688.57	$481,688.57
		$500 per month at 18%			
20	$6,000.00	$146,523.81	$120,000.00	$843,377.13	$963,377.13
		$750 per month at 18%			
20	$9,000.00	$219,785.72	$180,000.00	$1,265,065.70	$1,445,065.70
		$250 per month at 27%			
20	$3,000.00	$318,103.53	$60,000.00	$1,437,699.04	$1,497,699.04
		$500 per month at 27%			
20	$6,000.00	$636,207.06	$120,000.00	$2,875,398.09	$2,995,398.09
		$750 per month at 27%			
20	$9,000.00	$954,310.60	$180,000.00	$4,313,097.13	$4,493,097.13

(Source: Compound Interest Calculator on www.thecalculatorsite.com)

What Can $50K Buy?

$50,000 compounded at @ 9% for 20 years becomes $230,220

CALCULATION RESULTS GRAPHS OF RESULTS

(interest compounded **yearly** - added at the end of each year)

Year	Year Deposits	Year Interest	Total Deposits	Total Interest	Balance
1	$0.00	$4,500.00	$50,000.00	$4,500.00	$54,500.00
2	$0.00	$4,905.00	$50,000.00	$9,405.00	$59,405.00
3	$0.00	$5,346.45	$50,000.00	$14,751.45	$64,751.45
4	$0.00	$5,827.63	$50,000.00	$20,579.08	$70,579.08
5	$0.00	$6,352.12	$50,000.00	$26,931.20	$76,931.20
6	$0.00	$6,923.81	$50,000.00	$33,855.01	$83,855.01
7	$0.00	$7,546.95	$50,000.00	$41,401.96	$91,401.96
8	$0.00	$8,226.18	$50,000.00	$49,628.13	$99,628.13
9	$0.00	$8,966.53	$50,000.00	$58,594.66	$108,594.66
10	$0.00	$9,773.52	$50,000.00	$68,368.18	$118,368.18
11	$0.00	$10,653.14	$50,000.00	$79,021.32	$129,021.32
12	$0.00	$11,611.92	$50,000.00	$90,633.24	$140,633.24
13	$0.00	$12,656.99	$50,000.00	$103,290.23	$153,290.23
14	$0.00	$13,796.12	$50,000.00	$117,086.35	$167,086.35
15	$0.00	$15,037.77	$50,000.00	$132,124.12	$182,124.12
16	$0.00	$16,391.17	$50,000.00	$148,515.29	$198,515.29
17	$0.00	$17,866.38	$50,000.00	$166,381.67	$216,381.67
18	$0.00	$19,474.35	$50,000.00	$185,856.02	$235,856.02
19	$0.00	$21,227.04	$50,000.00	$207,083.06	$257,083.06
20	**$0.00**	**$23,137.48**	**$50,000.00**	**$230,220.54**	**$280,220.54**

Base amount: $50,000.00
Interest Rate: 9%
Effective Annual Rate: 9%
Calculation period: 20 years

Regular Deposit Calculation

« amend figures

(Source: Compound Interest Calculator on www.thecalculatorsite.com)

Mortgage Interest

Mortgage Calculator

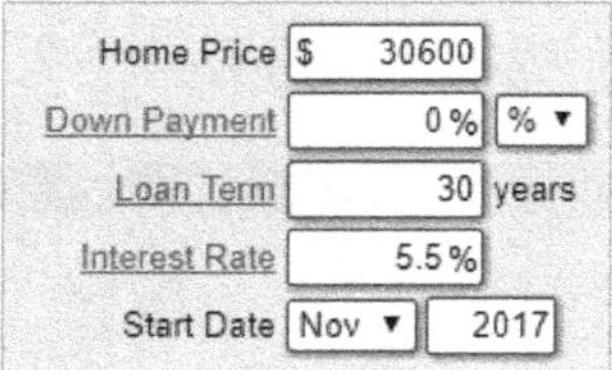

Monthly Pay: $173.74	
Total of 360 Mortgage Payments	$62,547.64
Total Interest	$31,947.64
Mortgage Payoff Date	Nov. 2047

(Source: http://www.calculator.net/mortgage-calculator.htm)

Compound vs Straight Interest Example

Straight Line Interest

($10,000 @ 9% for 30 years is $27,017 earned)

Starting Amount (PV)?:	$10,000.00
Annual Interest Rate?:	9.0000%
Days (-9,999 < # < 47,482)?:	10,957
Start Date (year > 1969)?:	11/16/2016
End Date (year < 2100)?:	11/16/2046
Days In Year?:	365
Interest Earned:	$27,017.26
Future Value (FV):	$37,017.26
Annual Percentage Yield (APY):	4.4563%
Daily Interest Rate:	0.0247%

(Source: https://financial-calculators.com/simple-interest-calculator)

Compounded Interest

($10,000 @ 9% for 30 years is $122,676 earned)

Year	Year Interest	Total Interest	Balance
1	$900.00	$900.00	$10,900.00
2	$981.00	$1,881.00	$11,881.00
3	$1,069.29	$2,950.29	$12,950.29
4	$1,165.53	$4,115.82	$14,115.82
5	$1,270.42	$5,386.24	$15,386.24
6	$1,384.76	$6,771.00	$16,771.00
7	$1,509.39	$8,280.39	$18,280.39
8	$1,645.24	$9,925.63	$19,925.63
9	$1,793.31	$11,718.93	$21,718.93
10	$1,954.70	$13,673.64	$23,673.64
11	$2,130.63	$15,804.26	$25,804.26
12	$2,322.38	$18,126.65	$28,126.65
13	$2,531.40	$20,658.05	$30,658.05
14	$2,759.22	$23,417.27	$33,417.27
15	$3,007.55	$26,424.82	$36,424.82
16	$3,278.23	$29,703.06	$39,703.06
17	$3,573.28	$33,276.33	$43,276.33
18	$3,894.87	$37,171.20	$47,171.20
19	$4,245.41	$41,416.61	$51,416.61
20	$4,627.50	$46,044.11	$56,044.11
21	$5,043.97	$51,088.08	$61,088.08
22	$5,497.93	$56,586.00	$66,586.00
23	$5,992.74	$62,578.74	$72,578.74
24	$6,532.09	$69,110.83	$79,110.83
25	$7,119.97	$76,230.81	$86,230.81
26	$7,760.77	$83,991.58	$93,991.58
27	$8,459.24	$92,450.82	$102,450.82
28	$9,220.57	$101,671.40	$111,671.40
29	$10,050.43	$111,721.82	$121,721.82
30	**$10,954.96**	**$122,676.78**	**$132,676.78**

Base amount: $10,000.00
Interest Rate: 9%
Effective Annual Rate: 9%
Calculation period: 30 years

Standard Calculation

« amend figures

(Source:
http://www.thecalculatorsite.com/finance/calculators/compoundinterestcalculator.php)

How Long Can You Wait?

$6,000 + $500/mo. 5 years (is $19,370) vs. 3 years (is $7,584)

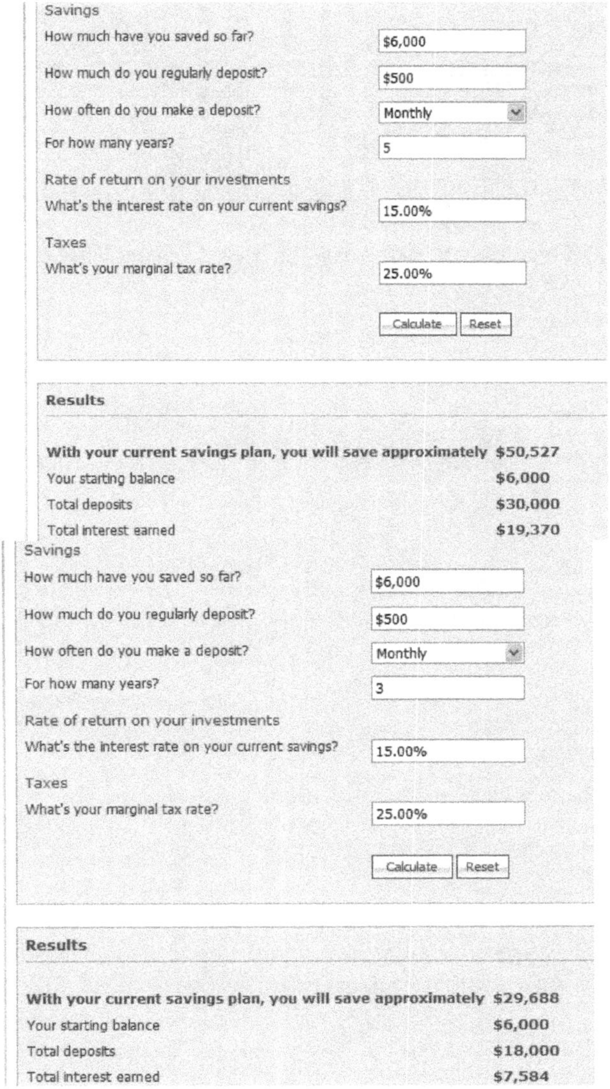

Savings

How much have you saved so far? $6,000

How much do you regularly deposit? $500

How often do you make a deposit? Monthly

For how many years? 5

Rate of return on your investments

What's the interest rate on your current savings? 15.00%

Taxes

What's your marginal tax rate? 25.00%

Calculate Reset

Results

With your current savings plan, you will save approximately	**$50,527**
Your starting balance	**$6,000**
Total deposits	**$30,000**
Total interest earned	**$19,370**

Savings

How much have you saved so far? $6,000

How much do you regularly deposit? $500

How often do you make a deposit? Monthly

For how many years? 3

Rate of return on your investments

What's the interest rate on your current savings? 15.00%

Taxes

What's your marginal tax rate? 25.00%

Calculate Reset

Results

With your current savings plan, you will save approximately	**$29,688**
Your starting balance	**$6,000**
Total deposits	**$18,000**
Total interest earned	**$7,584**

(Source: MSN Money: Personal Finance: http://moneycentral.msn.com/personal-finance/calculators/aim_to_save_calculator/home.aspx#Results)

US Census Data

Analysis of: Historical Census of Housing Tables Home Values

	1940	1950	1960	1970	1980	1990	2000	2009
Perceived Value: Unadjusted	$2,938	$7,354	$11,900	$17,000	$47,200	$79,100	$119,600	$180,100
Perceived Value: Adjusted	$30,600	$44,600	$58,600	$65,300	$93,400	$101,100	$119,600	
2.29%	$30,600	$38,373	$48,121	$60,345	$75,674	$94,897	$119,003	$142,628
Real Value: After $100/mo invest	$30,600	$28,277	$24,111	$18,886	$12,334	$4,117	($6,187)	$0
Real Value after $50/mo invest	$30,600	$31,306	$31,314	$31,324	$31,336	$31,351	$31,370	
5.0%	$30,600	$49,844	$81,191	$132,251	$215,424	$350,902	$571,583	$822,688
6.37%	$2,938	$5,449	$10,107	$18,745	$34,767	$64,484	$119,600	$188,521

Historical Census of Housing Tables Home Values

Median Home Values

2000 1990 1980 1970 1960 1950 1940

Adjusted to 2000 dollars
$119,600 $101,100 $93,400 $65,300 $58,600 $44,600 $30,600

Note: To adjust for inflation, the 1940 to 1990 median home values were adjusted to 2000 dollars using the appropriate CPI-U-RS adjustment factor.

Adjustment factor:
10.4066 6.0579 4.9278 3.8407 1.9794 1.2776

Median Home Values: Unadjusted

$119,600 $79,100 $47,200 $17,000 $11,900 $7,354 $2,938

https://www.census.gov/hhes/www/housing/census/historic/values.html#http://www.census.gov/hhes/www/housing/census/historic/values.html [190]

Some Examples Ultimate Rent vs. Buy

$119,900 house versus $875/month rental

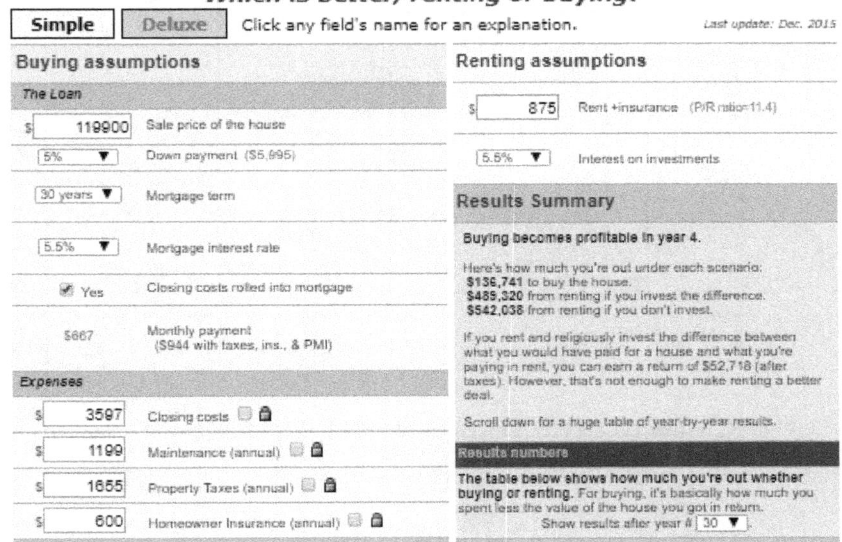

Mega Data Table! (detailed results of Rent vs. Buy)

In pink-row years renting is better. In green-row years buying is better.

Light gray columns are figures for that year. Dark gray columns are running totals.

All fields are explained in detail below the table.

Loan details			Buying (cash out)							House value				Renting				Rent vs. Buy		
Yr.	Interest	Loan Balance	Pmts.	PMI/FHA fees	Taxes +Ins.	Maint. +Exp. -Rent	Tax Savings	Cash out	Total Cash out	House Value (gross)	Appreciation	Paid Equity	House Value (net)	Rent	Total Rent	Total Principal	Return on Invest.	Buying Net	Rent net	Rent vs. Buy
1	6,423	115,919	14,001	1,068	2,255	1,499	($187)	18,636	18,636	124,096	4,196	7,529	116,030	10,500	10,500	8,136	380	18,526	10,120	8,406
2	6,334	114,247	8,006	1,068	2,334	1,561	($105)	12,854	31,491	128,440	8,540	9,150	120,091	10,868	21,368	10,123	875	25,646	20,493	5,153
3	6,239	112,481	8,006	1,068	2,418	1,606	($21)	13,075	44,566	132,935	13,035	10,863	124,294	11,248	32,615	11,950	1,481	32,751	31,134	1,617
4	6,140	110,614	8,006	1,068	2,500	1,662		13,236	57,802	137,588	17,688	12,672	128,645	11,642	44,257	13,545	2,196	39,771	42,061	2,290
5	6,035	108,643	8,006	1,068	2,588	1,720		13,382	71,183	142,404	22,504	14,563	133,147	12,049	56,306	14,677	3,012	46,679	53,294	6,615
6	5,923	106,560	8,006	1,068	2,678	1,780		13,530	84,716	147,388	27,488	16,602	137,808	12,471	68,777	15,909	3,923	53,469	64,853	11,385
7	5,806	104,380	8,006	1,068	2,772	1,843		13,689	98,404	152,546	32,646	18,734	142,631	12,907	81,684	16,721	4,921	60,134	76,763	16,629
8	5,682	102,036	8,006	1,068	2,869	1,907		13,850	112,254	157,885	37,985	20,987	147,823	13,359	95,043	17,212	5,996	66,668	89,047	22,379
9	5,551	99,581	8,006	1,068	2,969	1,974		14,017	126,272	163,411	43,511	23,367	152,790	13,826	108,869	17,403	7,139	73,063	101,730	28,667
10	5,412	96,987	8,006	1,068	3,073	2,043		14,190	140,462	169,131	49,231	25,882	158,137	14,310	123,180	17,403	8,345	79,312	114,834	35,522
11	5,268	94,247	8,006	1,068	3,181	2,114		14,389	154,831	175,050	55,150	28,538	163,672	14,811	137,991	17,403	9,618	86,407	128,373	42,966
12	5,111	91,353	8,006		3,292	2,188		13,487	168,318	181,177	61,277	31,344	169,401	15,330	153,321	17,403	10,961	90,279	142,360	52,090
13	4,948	88,295	8,006		3,407	2,265		13,679	181,997	187,518	67,618	34,308	175,330	15,866	169,187	17,403	12,377	94,962	156,810	61,848
14	4,776	85,084	8,006		3,527	2,344		13,877	195,874	194,081	74,181	37,440	181,466	16,422	185,608	17,403	13,871	99,472	171,737	72,265
15	4,593	81,652	8,006		3,650	2,426		14,083	209,956	200,874	80,974	40,748	187,817	16,996	202,605	17,403	15,448	103,790	187,157	83,366
16	4,401	78,047	8,006		3,778	2,511		14,295	224,251	207,905	88,005	44,242	194,391	17,591	220,196	17,403	17,111	107,907	203,085	95,178
17	4,198	74,238	8,006		3,910	2,599		14,515	238,767	215,182	95,282	47,934	201,195	18,207	238,403	17,403	18,866	111,610	219,537	107,727
18	3,983	70,215	8,006		4,047	2,690		14,743	253,510	222,713	102,813	51,834	208,237	18,844	257,247	17,403	20,717	115,488	236,530	121,042
19	3,756	65,965	8,006		4,189	2,784		14,979	268,489	230,508	110,608	55,955	215,525	19,504	276,750	17,403	22,670	118,929	254,081	135,152
20	3,516	61,475	8,006		4,335	2,882		15,223	283,712	238,576	118,676	60,307	223,088	20,186	296,937	17,403	24,730	122,118	272,206	150,088
21	3,263	56,732	8,006		4,487	2,983		15,476	299,188	246,926	127,026	64,905	230,676	20,893	317,829	17,403	26,904	125,043	290,925	165,882
22	2,995	51,721	8,006		4,644	3,087		15,737	314,925	255,568	135,668	69,762	238,956	21,624	339,453	17,403	29,197	127,889	310,256	182,587
23	2,713	46,427	8,006		4,807	3,196		16,008	330,932	264,513	144,613	74,894	247,320	22,381	361,834	17,403	31,617	130,040	330,218	200,178
24	2,414	40,835	8,006		4,975	3,307		16,288	347,220	273,771	153,871	80,316	255,976	23,164	384,999	17,403	34,169	132,079	350,829	218,750
25	2,099	34,926	8,006		5,149	3,423		16,578	363,798	283,353	163,453	86,041	264,935	23,975	408,973	17,403	36,862	133,790	372,111	238,321
26	1,765	28,687	8,006		5,329	3,543		16,878	380,675	293,270	173,370	92,091	274,208	24,814	433,788	17,403	39,703	135,155	394,085	258,930
27	1,413	22,095	8,006		5,516	3,666		17,188	397,863	303,535	183,635	98,482	283,805	25,683	459,470	17,403	42,700	136,153	416,770	280,617
28	1,041	15,130	8,006		5,709	3,796		17,509	415,373	314,159	194,259	106,233	293,738	26,581	486,052	17,403	45,862	136,764	440,189	303,425
29	649	7,772	8,006		5,908	3,928		17,842	433,215	325,154	205,254	112,365	304,019	27,512	513,563	17,403	49,196	136,968	464,365	327,397
30	233	0	8,006		6,115	4,066		18,186	451,401	336,535	216,635	119,900	314,660	28,475	542,038	17,403	52,716	136,741	489,320	352,579

(Source: **https://michaelbluejay.com/house/rentvsbuy.html)**

Purchase @ $429,900 vs. Rent at 2,800/mo.

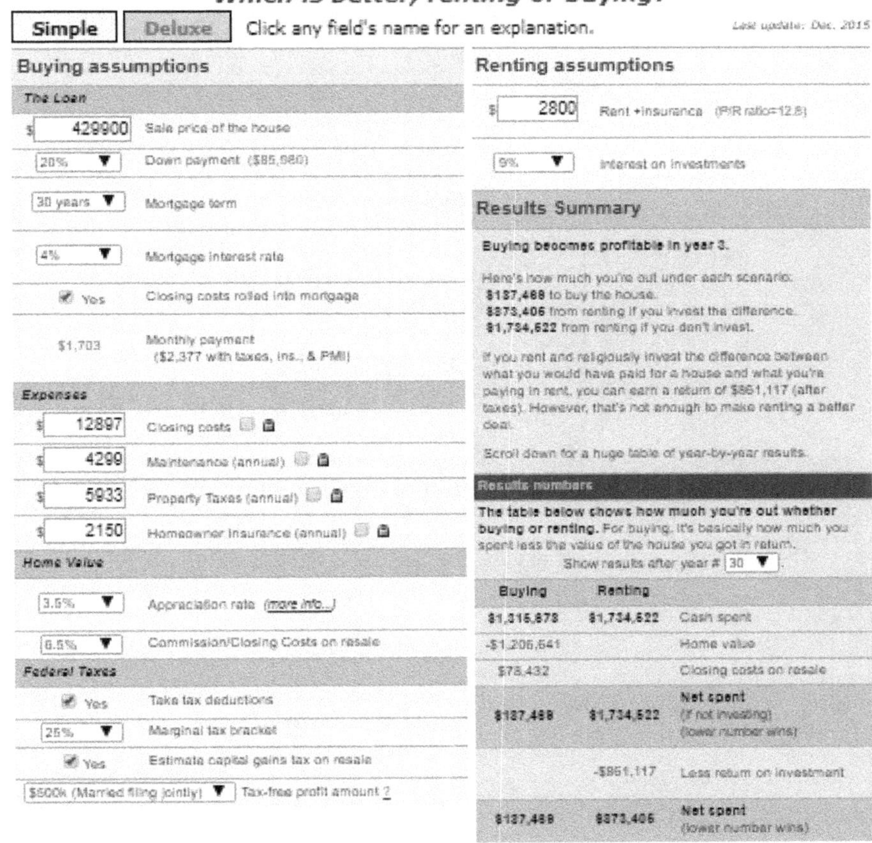

The ULTIMATE Rent vs. Buy calculator

Which is better, renting or buying?

Simple | Deluxe | Click any field's name for an explanation. *Last update: Dec. 2015*

Buying assumptions

The Loan

$ 429900 Sale price of the house

20% ▼ Down payment ($85,980)

30 years ▼ Mortgage term

4% ▼ Mortgage interest rate

Yes Closing costs rolled into mortgage

$1,703 Monthly payment ($2,377 with taxes, ins., & PMI)

Expenses

$ 12897 Closing costs

$ 4299 Maintenance (annual)

$ 5933 Property Taxes (annual)

$ 2150 Homeowner Insurance (annual)

Home Value

3.5% ▼ Appreciation rate (more info...)

6.5% ▼ Commission/Closing Costs on resale

Federal Taxes

Yes Take tax deductions

25% ▼ Marginal tax bracket

Yes Estimate capital gains tax on resale

$500k (Married filing jointly) ▼ Tax-free profit amount ?

Renting assumptions

$ 2800 Rent +insurance (P/R ratio=12.8)

9% ▼ Interest on investments

Results Summary

Buying becomes profitable in year 3.

Here's how much you're out under each scenario:
$187,488 to buy the house.
$873,406 from renting if you invest the difference.
$1,734,522 from renting if you don't invest.

If you rent and religiously invest the difference between what you would have paid for a house and what you're paying in rent, you can earn a return of $861,117 (after taxes). However, that's not enough to make renting a better deal.

Scroll down for a huge table of year-by-year results.

Results numbers

The table below shows how much you're out whether buying or renting. For buying, it's basically how much you spent less the value of the house you got in return.

Show results after year # 30 ▼.

Buying	Renting	
$1,315,673	$1,734,522	Cash spent
-$1,206,641		Home value
$78,432		Closing costs on resale
$187,488	$1,734,522	**Net spent** (if not investing) (lower number wins)
	-$861,117	Less return on investment
$187,489	$873,406	**Net spent** (lower number wins)

Mega Data Table! (detailed results of Rent vs. Buy)

In pink-row years renting is better. In green-row years buying is better.

Light gray columns are figures for that year. Dark gray columns are running totals.

All fields are explained in detail below the table.

Loan details				Buying (cash out)						House value				Renting				Rent vs. Buy		
Yr.	Interest	Loan balance	Pmts.	PMI/FHA fees	Taxes +Ins.	Maint. +Hoa -Rent	Tax Savings	Cash out	Total Cash out	House Value (gross)	Apprec-iation	Paid Equity	House Value (net)	Rent	Total Rent	Total Principal	Return on Invest.	Buying (net)	Rent (net)	Rent vs. Buy
1	14,158	350,533	108,422		8,083	4,599	($2,923)	118,181	118,181	444,948	15,048	92,037	418,325	33,600	33,600	82,581	8,317	50,600	27,283	23,407
2	13,902	343,994	20,442		8,366	4,760	($2,837)	30,731	148,912	460,520	30,620	95,340	432,588	34,776	68,376	82,581	13,203	60,320	55,173	5,147
3	13,636	337,188	20,442		8,659	4,927	($2,748)	31,279	178,191	476,638	46,738	104,900	445,858	35,903	104,389	82,581	20,709	69,722	83,660	13,938
4	13,359	330,104	20,442		8,962	5,099	($2,656)	31,847	210,038	493,320	63,420	111,727	461,264	37,253	141,622	82,581	28,891	78,887	112,732	33,844
5	13,070	322,732	20,442		9,275	5,277	($2,580)	32,435	242,473	510,588	80,896	118,833	477,398	38,557	180,179	82,581	37,808	87,807	142,371	54,564
6	12,770	315,080	20,442		9,600	5,482	($2,480)	33,044	275,517	528,457	98,557	128,226	494,107	39,906	220,085	82,581	47,528	98,470	172,557	76,087
7	12,457	307,075	20,442		9,938	5,853	($2,398)	33,675	309,192	546,953	117,053	133,924	511,401	41,303	261,388	82,581	58,123	104,888	203,285	98,398
8	12,132	298,785	20,442		10,284	5,851	($2,248)	34,329	343,521	566,098	136,198	141,934	529,300	42,749	304,137	82,581	69,672	112,088	234,465	121,479
9	11,793	290,118	20,442		10,644	6,056	($2,138)	35,006	378,527	585,910	156,010	150,270	547,825	44,245	348,381	82,581	82,280	120,817	266,122	146,306
10	11,441	281,115	20,442		11,016	6,268	($2,020)	35,707	414,233	606,418	176,518	158,946	568,909	45,793	394,175	82,581	95,981	128,349	298,194	169,846
11	11,074	271,747	20,442		11,402	6,487	($1,899)	36,433	450,666	627,641	197,741	167,976	586,844	47,396	441,571	82,581	110,936	135,566	330,834	195,068
12	10,692	261,997	20,442		11,801	6,714	($1,773)	37,165	487,851	649,608	219,708	177,373	607,384	49,055	490,626	82,581	127,238	142,464	363,388	220,924
13	10,295	251,890	20,442		12,214	6,949	($1,642)	37,964	525,814	672,346	242,446	187,153	628,842	50,772	541,398	82,581	145,007	149,022	396,391	247,369
14	9,882	241,280	20,442		12,641	7,193	($1,508)	38,770	564,584	695,877	265,977	197,331	650,845	52,549	593,947	82,581	164,375	156,239	429,572	274,342
15	9,452	230,300	20,442		13,084	7,444	($1,365)	39,606	604,190	720,232	290,332	207,924	673,417	54,388	648,335	82,581	185,488	161,072	462,849	301,776
16	9,004	218,881	20,442		13,542	7,705	($1,218)	40,471	644,661	745,441	315,541	218,949	696,987	56,292	704,627	82,581	208,498	166,536	496,129	329,595
17	8,538	206,957	20,442		14,016	7,975	($1,065)	41,367	686,029	771,531	341,631	230,423	721,352	58,262	762,889	82,581	233,580	171,604	529,309	357,704
18	8,053	194,568	20,442		14,506	8,254	($906)	42,296	728,324	798,535	368,635	242,384	748,830	60,301	823,190	82,581	260,919	178,263	582,270	388,008
19	7,548	181,674	20,442		15,014	8,543	($741)	43,257	771,582	826,483	396,583	254,792	772,782	62,412	885,601	82,581	290,720	180,494	594,882	414,388
20	7,023	168,255	20,442		15,540	8,842	($570)	44,253	815,835	855,410	425,510	267,727	799,809	64,596	950,197	82,581	323,202	184,281	626,996	442,714
21	6,478	154,289	20,442		16,083	9,151	($392)	45,285	861,119	885,350	455,450	281,188	827,802	66,857	1,017,054	82,581	358,808	187,606	658,447	470,840
22	5,907	139,754	20,442		16,646	9,471	($207)	46,353	907,473	916,337	486,437	295,197	856,775	69,197	1,086,251	82,581	397,200	190,452	689,051	498,600
23	5,315	124,627	20,442		17,229	9,803	($14)	47,460	954,932	948,408	518,508	309,776	886,782	71,619	1,157,870	82,581	439,265	192,797	718,806	525,808
24	4,699	108,883	20,442		17,832	10,146		48,420	1,003,352	981,603	551,703	324,952	917,789	74,125	1,231,996	82,581	485,118	194,437	746,879	552,442
25	4,057	92,496	20,442		18,498	10,507		49,399	1,052,751	1,015,959	586,059	340,745	949,922	76,720	1,308,715	82,581	535,094	195,326	773,821	578,295
26	3,390	75,448	20,442		19,102	10,869		50,413	1,103,164	1,051,518	621,618	357,181	983,169	79,406	1,388,120	82,581	588,570	195,441	798,550	603,109
27	2,695	57,899	20,442		19,771	11,249		51,462	1,154,626	1,088,321	658,421	374,287	1,017,580	82,184	1,470,304	82,581	646,949	194,745	821,355	626,611
28	1,972	39,229	20,442		20,463	11,643		52,547	1,207,173	1,126,412	696,512	392,080	1,053,195	85,061	1,555,365	82,581	713,872	193,206	841,693	648,487
29	1,219	20,006	20,442		21,179	12,050		53,671	1,260,844	1,165,838	735,938	410,817	1,090,057	88,038	1,643,403	82,581	784,220	190,795	859,183	668,390
30	436	0	20,442		21,920	12,472		54,834	1,315,678	1,208,641	778,741	429,900	1,128,209	91,119	1,734,522	82,581	861,117	187,469	873,405	685,936
31					22,687	12,906		35,596	1,351,274	1,248,873	818,973	429,900	1,167,696	94,308	1,828,830	82,581	944,935	183,577	883,895	700,317
32					23,481	13,360		36,842	1,388,115	1,292,584	862,684	429,900	1,208,566	97,609	1,926,439	82,581	1,036,297	179,550	890,142	710,593
33					24,303	13,828		38,131	1,426,246	1,337,824	907,924	429,900	1,250,865	101,025	2,027,465	82,581	1,135,881	175,361	891,584	716,203
34					25,154	14,312		39,466	1,465,712	1,384,648	954,748	429,900	1,294,646	104,561	2,132,026	82,581	1,244,428	171,088	887,598	716,532
35					26,034	14,813		40,847	1,506,559	1,433,111	1,003,211	429,900	1,339,958	108,221	2,240,247	82,581	1,362,744	166,801	877,503	710,902
36					26,945	15,331		42,277	1,548,836	1,483,269	1,053,369	429,900	1,386,857	112,009	2,352,255	82,581	1,491,708	161,979	860,547	698,569
37					27,889	15,868		43,756	1,592,592	1,535,184	1,105,284	429,900	1,435,397	115,929	2,468,184	82,581	1,632,279	157,195	835,905	678,710
38					28,865	16,423		45,288	1,637,880	1,588,915	1,159,015	429,900	1,485,636	119,986	2,588,171	82,581	1,785,502	152,244	802,669	650,425
39					29,875	16,998		46,873	1,684,752	1,644,527	1,214,627	429,900	1,537,633	124,186	2,712,357	82,581	1,952,515	147,119	759,842	612,723
40					30,920	17,593		48,513	1,733,266	1,702,088	1,272,188	429,900	1,591,450	128,532	2,840,889	82,581	2,134,558	141,816	706,331	564,515

(Source: https://michaelbluejay.com/house/rentvsbuy.html)

$429,000 Rent Vs. Buy New York Times Interactive Results

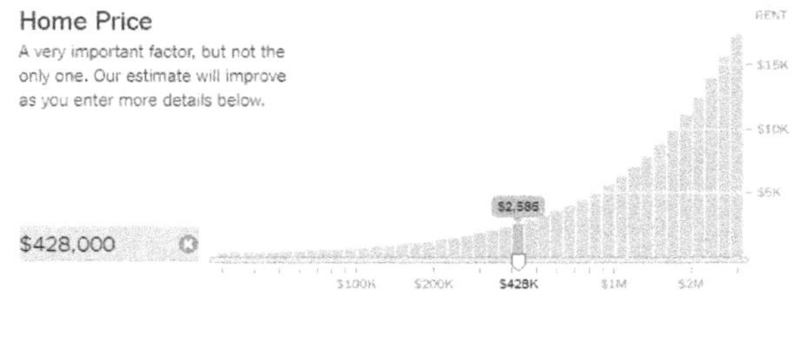

If you can rent a similar home for less than ...

$2,585 PER MONTH

... then renting is better.

Costs after **3 years**	Rent	Buy
Initial costs	$2,585	$102,720
Recurring costs	$96,660	$86,948
Opportunity costs	$8,096	$32,187
Net proceeds	-$2,585	-$117,099
Total	$104,756	$104,756

How to Read the Charts Charts that are relatively flat indicate factors that are not particularly important to the outcome. Conversely, the factors that have steep slopes have a large impact.

How Long Do You Plan to Stay?

Buying tends to be better the longer you stay because the upfront fees are spread out over many years.

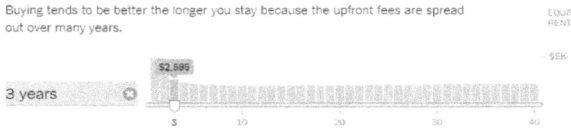

3 years

$2,585

3 10 20 30 40

EQUIV. RENT

$5K

What Are Your Mortgage Details?

In addition to the interest rate and down payment, the calculator takes into account the mortgage-interest tax deduction.

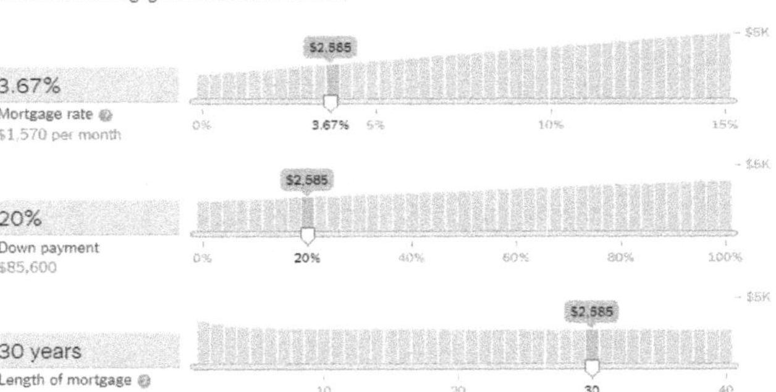

Taxes

Property taxes and mortgage-interest costs are significant but also deductible. The higher your marginal tax rate is, the bigger the deduction.

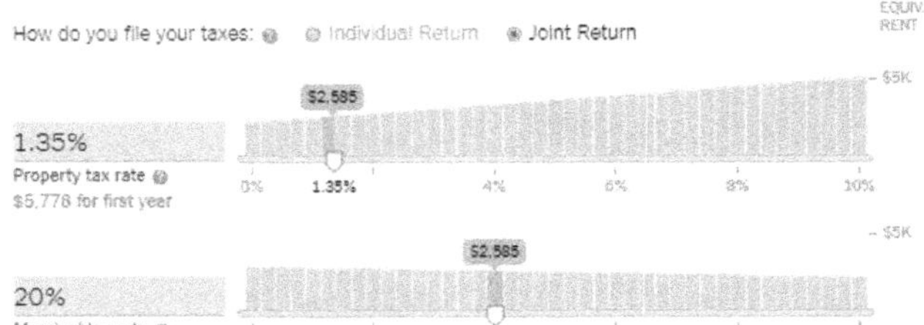

What Does the Future Hold?

How much home prices, rents and stock prices change can have a large impact on your outcome. Unfortunately, these are some of the hardest things to predict. If you choose to rent instead of buying, the calculator assumes that you'll spend your would-be down payment on stocks or another investment.

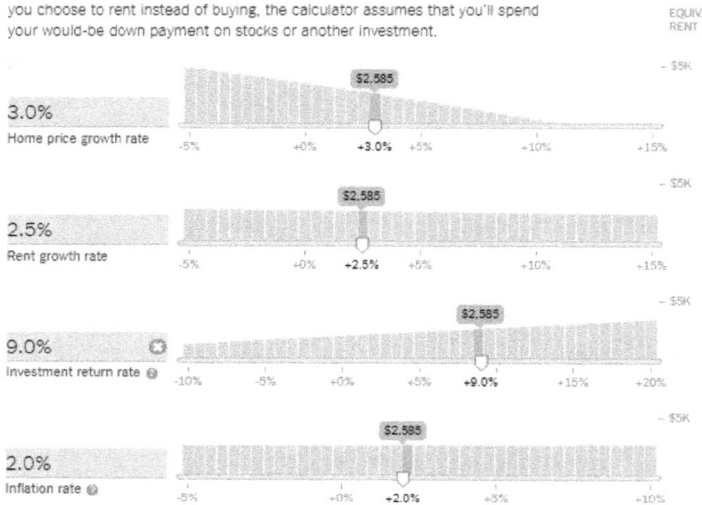

EQUIV. RENT

– $5K

$2,585

3.0%

Home price growth rate

-5% +0% +3.0% +5% +10% +15%

– $5K

$2,585

2.5%

Rent growth rate

-5% +0% +2.5% +5% +10% +15%

– $5K

$2,585

9.0%

Investment return rate

-10% -5% +0% +5% +9.0% +15% +20%

– $5K

$2,585

2.0%

Inflation rate

-5% +0% +2.0% +5% +10%

Closing Costs

You'll have to pay various fees when you buy your home, as well as when you sell it.

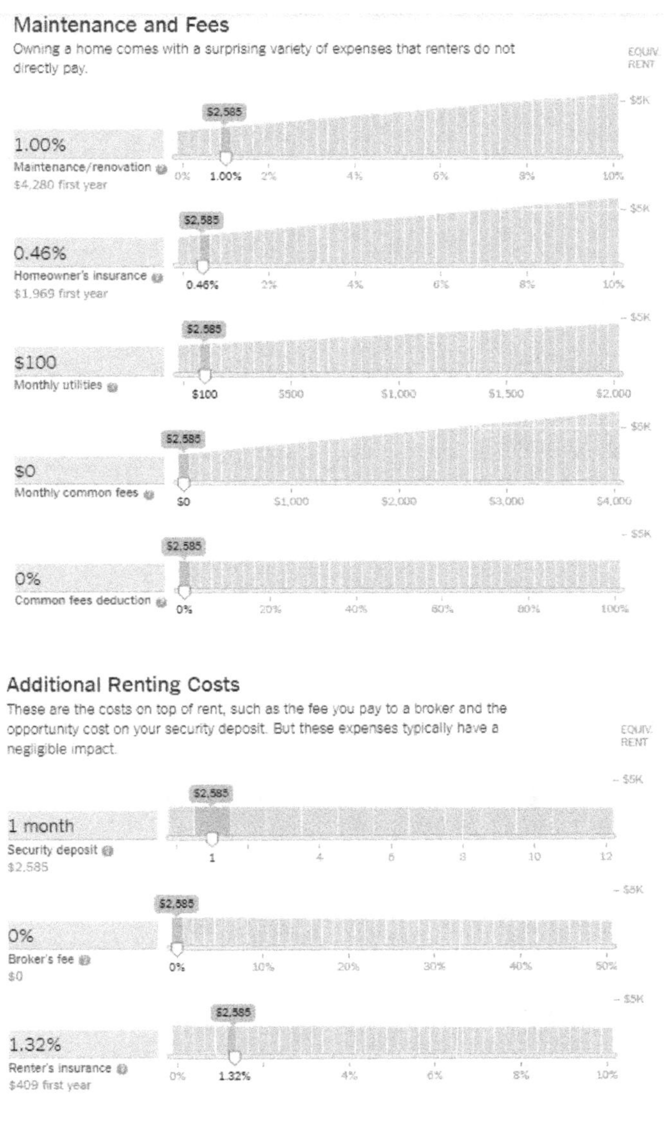

Source https://www.nytimes.com/interactive/2014/upshot/buy-rent-calculator.html

Bibliography

Survey of Consumer Finances. (2017). *Fereral Reserve Bulletin.* Federal Reserve System. Board of Governors of the Federal Reserve System. Retrieved from https://www.federalreserve.gov/publications/files/scf17.pdf

Affordability Calculator. (2018, March 19). Retrieved from www.zillow.com: https://www.zillow.com/mortgage-calculator/house-affordability/

Amortization Schedule Calculator. (2018). Retrieved from amortization-calc.com: http://www.amortization-calc.com/

Average Sales Price of Houses Sold for the United States (ASPUS). (2018, Jan 24). Retrieved from www.fred.org: https://fred.stlouisfed.org/series/ASPUS

Average spend per child on toys worldwide in 2015, by country (in U.S. dollars). (2018). Retrieved from www.statista.com: https://www.statista.com/statistics/750787/global-toy-market-average-spend/

Bach, D. (2001). *Smart Couples Finish Rich: 9 Steps to Creating a Rich Future for You and Your Partner.* Doubleday Canada.

Badal, S. (2018, June 16). Find Out How to Build a Business. *The Rich Dad Radio Show with Robert Kiyosaki.* (K. Kiyosaki, Interviewer)

Benjamin, R. (Director). (1986). *Money Pit* [Motion Picture].

Benjamin, R. (Director). (1986). *Money Pit* [Motion Picture].

Bloomberg. (2017, August 3). *Americans Are Crushing It With Their 401(k) Balances*. Retrieved from www.fortune.com : http://fortune.com/2017/08/03/americans-record-highs-401k-balances/

Bluejay, M. (2015, Dec). *The ULTIMATE Rent vs. Buy calculator.* Retrieved from https://michaelbluejay.com: https://michaelbluejay.com/house/rentvsbuy.html

Bluejay, M. (n.d.). *Buying a home is an investment*. Retrieved from michaelbluejay.com: https://michaelbluejay.com/house/investment.html

Bluejay, M. (n.d.). *Long-term real estate appreciation rate in the U.S.* Retrieved from https://michaelbluejay.com/house/appreciation.html: https://michaelbluejay.com/house/appreciation.html

Bluejay, M. (n.d.). *Paying cash for a home?* Retrieved from michaelbluejay.com: https://michaelbluejay.com/house/payingcash.html

Bob Sullivan. (2015, Jun 14). *Renting: The new American Dream?* Retrieved from USA Today: https://eu.usatoday.com/story/money/personalfinance/2015/06/14/credit-dotcom-renting-american-dream/71053284

Carlson, B. (2016, May 15). *Deconstructing 30 Year Stock Market Returns*. Retrieved from http://awealthofcommonsense.com: http://awealthofcommonsense.com/2016/05/deconstructing-30-year-stock-market-returns/

Casey, D. (2016). Project: FEDcoin. (B. Irish, Interviewer) CaseyResearch. Retrieved from https://secure.caseyresearch.com/chain?cid=MKT336710&eid=MKT337384&snaid=&step=start#AST68199

Chateau Snyers. (n.d.). Hannut. Retrieved from http://gnagna874.skynetblogs.be/archive/2010/06/01/hannut-chateau-de-mr-snyers.html

Clason, G. S. (1926). *The Richest Man in Babylon.* Penguin Books.

Dubner, S. J. (2018, March 28). *Everything You Always Wanted to Know About Money (But Were Afraid to Ask) (Rebroadcast)*. Retrieved from http://freakonomics.com: http://freakonomics.com/podcast/everything-always-wanted-know-money-afraid-ask-rebroadcast/

Dubner, S. J. (November 22, 2017 @ 11:00pm, November 22, 2017 @ 11:00pm November 22, 2017 @ 11:00pm). *Is America Ready for a "No-Lose Lottery"? (Update)*. Retrieved from http://freakonomics.com: http://freakonomics.com/podcast/say-no-no-lose-lottery-rebroadcast/

Easterlin, R. A. (1987). *Birth and Fortune: The Impact of Numbers on Personal Welfare* (2nd Edition ed.). University Of Chicago Press. Retrieved from https://www.amazon.com/Richard-A.-Easterlin/e/B001HCZCLC/ref=ntt_dp_epwbk_0

Elkins, K. (2018, Jan 11). *Self-made millionaire: Use this simple trick to save $44,000 on your mortgage*. Retrieved from www.cnbc.com: https://www.cnbc.com/2018/01/11/millionaire-david-bach-use-this-trick-to-save-44000-on-a-mortgage.html

Frost, R. (1916). The Road Not Taken. *Mountain Interval.*

Gabler, N. (2016, May). The Secret Shame of Middle-Class Americans. *The Atlantic*. Retrieved from https://www.theatlantic.com/magazine/archive/2016/05/my-secret-shame/476415/

Gershon, L. (2014, June 20). *Budgeting Statistics: By the Numbers*. Retrieved from www.creditdonkey.com: https://www.creditdonkey.com/budgeting-statistics.html

Guillebeau, C. (n.d.). *You Need a Side Hustle*. Retrieved from https://sidehustleschool.com: https://sidehustleschool.com/about/

Hanlon, S. (2014, April 24). *Why The Average Investor's Investment Return Is So Low*. Retrieved from www.forbes.com: https://www.forbes.com/sites/advisor/2014/04/24/why-the-average-investors-investment-return-is-so-low/#4aea2dc3111a

Hart Research Associates. (2013). *How Housing Matters: Americans' Attitudes Transformed By The Housing Crisis & Changing Lifestyles.* MacArthur Foundation. Retrieved from https://www.issuelab.org/resource/how-housing-matters-americans-attitudes-transformed-by-the-housing-crisis-changing-lifestyles.html

Historical Census of Housing Tables Home Values. (2002, June 05). Retrieved from www.censs.gov: https://www.census.gov/hhes/www/housing/census/historic/values.html#http://www.census.gov/hhes/www/housing/census/historic/values.html

Historical Census of Housing Tables: Home Values. (2012, June 06). Retrieved from www.census.gov: http://www.census.gov/hhes/www/housing/census/historic/values.html#http://www.census.gov/hhes/www/housing/census/historic/values.html

Homelessness in the United States. (2018, March 26). Retrieved from www.wikipedia.org: https://en.wikipedia.org/wiki/Homelessness_in_the_United_States#Statistics_and_demographics

(2018). *HOUSEHOLD DEBT AND CREDIT REPORT (Q1 2018).* New Yrok: FEDERAL RESERVE BANK of NEW YORK RESEARCH AND S TATISTICS GROUP. Retrieved from www.newyorkfed.org: https://www.newyorkfed.org/medialibrary/interactives/householdcredit/data/pdf/HHDC_2018Q1.pdf

How Fast The Markets Recover. (n.d.). Retrieved from Atlantic Wealth Consulting LLC: http://awc2.com/how-fast-markets-recover/

How Many Times Does the Average Person Move in a Lifetime? (2015, Nov 19). Retrieved from www.a-1firstclass.com: https://news.a1firstclass.com/how-many-times-does-the-average-person-move-in-a-lifetime

Howe, Neil. (2014, July 16). *Are You Born To Be Better Off Than Your Parents? (Part 1 of "Generations in Pursuit of the American Dream").* Retrieved from Fortune.com: https://www.forbes.com/sites/neilhowe/2014/07/16/part-1-generations-in-pursuit-of-the-american-dream/#4dd4ba415db0

Inspired, B. (2017, Nov 2). *A STORY THAT WILL CHANGE YOUR LIFE - One of The Best Speeches Ever by Lisa Nichols (emotional).* Retrieved from www.youtube.com: https://www.youtube.com/watch?v=5NsykK5sAWg

Jo Becker, S. G. (2008, dec 21). *Bush drive for hoe ownership fueled housing bubble*. Retrieved from www.nytimes.com: https://www.nytimes.com/2008/12/21/business/worldbusiness/21iht-admin.4.18853088.html

John Burns. (2016). *Demographic Strategies for Real Estate.* Washington, D.C: John Burns Real Estate Consulting.

Kathy Orton. (2018, May 24). *Mortgage rates have been rising at a pace not seen in almost 50 years*. Retrieved from www.washingtonpost.com: https://www.washingtonpost.com/news/where-we-live/wp/2018/05/24/mortgage-rates-have-been-rising-at-a-pace-not-seen-in-almost-50-years/?noredirect=on&utm_term=.2d9136b199ed

Keri Lumm, B. (2016, Nov 22). *Shocking amount parents spend on toys revealed*. Retrieved from www.aol.com: https://www.aol.com/article/finance/2016/11/22/shocking-amount-parents-spend-on-toys-revealed/21612020/?guccounter=1

Kiyosaki, R. (2011). *Rich Dad's CASHFLOW Quadrant: Rich Dad's Guide to Financial Freedom.* Plata Publishing. doi:1612680054

Kiyosaki, R. (2013, April 5). *Rich Dad Scam #6: Your House is an Asset.* Retrieved from www.richdad.com: http://www.richdad.com/Resources/Rich-Dad-Financial-Education-Blog/april-2013/rich-dad-scam-6-your-house-is-an-asset.aspx

Kiyosaki, R. (2016, December 6). *Repeat After Me: Your House Is Not An Asset.* Retrieved from http://www.richdad.com: http://www.richdad.com/Resources/Rich-Dad-Financial-Education-Blog/August-2010/repeat-after-me-your-house-is-not-an-asset.aspx

Kiyosaki, R. (2018, May 12). How to Find Truth in an Age of Fake News & Fake Teachers - Ryan Holiday. *The Rich Dad Radio Show with Robert Kiyosaki.* Retrieved from http://www.richdad.com/radio: http://www.richdad.com/radio

Kiyosaki, R. a. (1997). *Rich Dad Poor Dad.* Warner Books Ed.

Kulp, K. (2018, Jan 24). *Investing with borrowed money can be a big win — for some.* Retrieved from www.cnbc.com: https://www.cnbc.com/2018/01/24/investing-with-borrowed-money-can-win-big--for-some.html

Lam, J. (018, may 15). *5 Millionaire Habits That Can Help You Build Wealth, Too* . Retrieved from www.grow.acorns.com: https://grow.acorns.com/5-millionaire-habits-that-can-help-you-build-wealth/?utm_source=May30&utm_medium=newsletter/

Lightner, R. (2017, Feb 10). *Home Values Rebound, But Not For Everyone.* Retrieved from www.wsj.com: http://graphics.wsj.com/housing-market-recovery/

List of countries by home ownership rate. (2018, March 10). Retrieved from https://en.wikipedia.org: https://en.wikipedia.org/wiki/List_of_countries_by_home_ownership_rate

List of countries by home ownership rate. (2018, july 13). Retrieved from https://en.wikipedia.org/wiki/List_of_countries_by_home_ownership_rate: https://en.wikipedia.org/wiki/List_of_countries_by_home_ownership_rate

List of Economic Expansions in the United States. (2017, May 29). Retrieved from Wikipedia.org: https://en.wikipedia.org/wiki/List_of_economic_expansions_in_the_United_States

Luisa Kroll and Kerry Dolan. (2018, March 06). *Meet The Members Of The Three-Comma Club.* Retrieved from www.forbes.com: https://www.forbes.com/billionaires/#43b64da4251c

maniaxzero. (2017, Feb 7). *Richard Branson doesn't know Net vs Gross [1m clip].* Retrieved from youtube.com: https://youtu.be/JuVkFjpkhAk

Matthews, C. (2016, Dec 8). *3 Charts That Show the Housing Market Has Finally Recovered.* Retrieved from www.fortune.com: http://fortune.com/2016/12/08/housing-recovery-2/

McCleary, K. (n.d.). *Which Home Improvements Pay Off?* Retrieved from www.hgtv.com: http://www.hgtv.com/design/decorating/clean-and-organize/which-home-improvements-pay-off

Median and Average Sales Prices of New Homes Sold in United States. (2018, Jan). Retrieved from www.census.gov: https://www.census.gov/construction/nrs/pdf/uspricemon.pdf

MIKE BOSTOCK, S. C. (2014). *Is it Better to Rent or Buy?* Retrieved from www.nytimes.com: https://www.nytimes.com/interactive/2014/upshot/buy-rent-calculator.html

Mortgage Calculator - full report. (2018, Jan 24). Retrieved from www.zillow.com: https://www.zillow.com/mortgage/calculator/payment/ModernPaymentCalculatorAdvancedReportPage.htm?{%22homePrice%22:375700,%22downPayment%22:56355,%22rate%22:3.984,%22term%22:%22Fixed30Year%22,%22propertyTaxRate%22:2.41,%22includeTaxesInsurance%22:true,%22s

Mulbrandon, C. (2013, December 5). *100-years-of-family-spending-in-the-us .* Retrieved from Visualizing Economics Blog: http://visualizingeconomics.com/blog/2013/11/18/100-years-of-family-spending-in-the-us

Noguchi, Y. (2009, July 9). *'Shadow' Inventory May Slow Housing Recovery.* Retrieved from www.npr.org: http://www.npr.org/templates/story/story.php?storyId=106113137

Olick, D. (2017, Jan 24). *Why the supply of homes for sale is the lowest since 1999.* Retrieved from www.cnbc.com: https://www.cnbc.com/2017/01/24/why-the-supply-of-homes-for-sale-is-the-lowest-since-1999.html

Pollack, D. H. (2017). *The Index Card: Why Personal Finance Doesn't Have to Be Complicated* (Reprint ed.). Portfolio; Reprint edition. Retrieved from https://www.amazon.com/gp/product/0143130528/ref=as_li_tl?ie=UTF8&tag=freakonomic08-20&camp=1789&creative=9325&linkCode=as2&creativeASIN=0143130528&linkId=fea06c0113b29446aaf3e8927fc625b7

Price-to-Rent Ratio. (n.d.). Retrieved from www.investopedia.com: https://www.investopedia.com/terms/p/price-to-rent-ratio.asp

Ramsey, D. (2013). *The Total Money Makeover: Classic Edition: A Proven Plan for Financial Fitness.* Thomas Nelson.

Ramsey, D. (2016, Oct 20). *Why Is Term Insurance Better Than Whole Life Insurance?* Retrieved from www.youtubce.com: https://www.youtube.com/watch?v=mPRTp6XrScM

Real Estate Investment Trust - REIT. (2018, May 31). Retrieved from investopedia.com: https://www.investopedia.com/terms/r/reit.asp

Reuters. (2018, June 6). *US house prices are going to rise at twice the speed of inflation and pay: Reuters poll.* Retrieved from www.cnbc.com: https://www.cnbc.com/2018/06/06/us-house-prices-are-going-to-rise-at-twice-the-speed-of-inflation-and-pay-reuters-poll.html

Robbins, T. (2014). *Money - Master the Game: 7 Simple Steps to Financial Freedom.* Simon & Schuster, 2014.

Robert Kiyosaki, S. L. (1997). *Rich Dad Poor Dad.* Warner Books Ed.

Santoli, M. (2017, June 19). *The S&P 500 has already met its average return for a full year, but don't expect it to stay here.* Retrieved from www.cnbc.com: https://www.cnbc.com/2017/06/18/the-sp-500-has-already-met-its-average-return-for-a-full-year.html

Sather, A. (2014, April 23). *10 Reasons why Compounding Interest is the 8th Wonder of the World.* Retrieved from www.einvestingforbeginners.com: https://einvestingforbeginners.com/compounding-interest/

Smith, L. (2017, October 24). *The Truth About Real Estate Prices.* Retrieved from www.investopedia.com: https://www.investopedia.com/articles/mortages-real-estate/11/the-truth-about-the-real-estate-market.asp

Stanford marshmallow experiment. (2018, May 28). Retrieved from www.en.wikipedia.org: https://en.wikipedia.org/wiki/Stanford_marshmallow_experiment

Susan Adams. (2014, June 20). *Most Americans Are Unhappy At Work*. Retrieved from Forbes: https://www.forbes.com/sites/susanadams/2014/06/20/most-americans-are-unhappy-at-work/#7e505b5d341a

Tony Robbins, P. M. (2017). *Unshakeable: Your Financial Freedom Playbook*. Simon and Schuster, 2017.

Top countries with the highest average wealth per adult in 2017 (in U.S. dollars). (2017). Retrieved from www.statista.com: https://www.statista.com/statistics/203941/countries-with-the-highest-wealth-per-adult/

United States Home Prices & Values. (2018, Jan 26). Retrieved from www.zillow.com: https://www.zillow.com/home-values/

Valetkevitch, Caroline. (2013, May 6). *Key dates and milestones in the S&P 500's history*. Retrieved from Reuters: https://www.reuters.com/article/us-usa-stocks-sp-timeline-idUSBRE9450WL20130506

Warren Buffett. (2018, May 15). Retrieved from www.en.wikipedia.org: https://en.wikipedia.org/wiki/Warren_Buffett

Whole Life Insurance Policy. (n.d.). Retrieved from /www.investopedia.com: https://www.investopedia.com/terms/w/wholelife.asp

Wong, K. (2016, April 27). *Why the Rent vs. Buy Debate Is Completely Pointless*. Retrieved from www.lifehacker.com: https://twocents.lifehacker.com/why-the-rent-vs-buy-debate-is-completely-pointless-1773179027

Zillow Research- Data. (2018, Jan 24). Retrieved from www.zillow.com: http://files.zillowstatic.com/research/public/State/State_MedianRentalPrice_AllHomes.csv

Endnotes

[1] (Bob Sullivan, 2015)

2 (Elkins, 2018)

3 (John Burns, 2016)

4 (Bob Sullivan, 2015)

[5] (Stanford marshmallow experiment, 2018)

[6] (Bach, 2001)

[7] (Clason, 1926)

[8] (Badal, 2018)

[9] Appendix: Median Prices

[10] (Smith, 2017)

[11] (Average Sales Price of Houses Sold for the United States (ASPUS), 2018)

[12] Appendix Housing Versus Investment Account

[13] Appendix Housing Versus Investment Account

[14] Appendix Housing Versus Investment Account

[15] Appendix Housing Versus Investment Account

[16] Appendix Housing Versus Investment Account

[17] Appendix Housing Versus Investment Account

[18] Appendix Housing Versus Investment Account

[19] Appendix Housing Versus Investment Account

[20] Appendix Housing Versus Investment Account

[21] Appendix Housing Versus Investment Account

[22] Appendix Housing Versus Investment Account

[23] Appendix Housing Versus Investment Account

[24] Appendix Housing Versus Investment Account

[25] Appendix Housing Versus Investment Account

[26] Appendix Housing Versus Investment Account

[27] (RISMedia Staff, n.d.)

[28] (Historical Census of Housing Tables Home Values, 2002)

[29] (Historical Census of Housing Tables Home Values, 2002)

[30] (Ramsey, Why Is Term Insurance Better Than Whole Life Insurance?, 2016)

[31] (Ramsey, Why Is Term Insurance Better Than Whole Life Insurance?, 2016)

[32] (Whole Life Insurance Policy, n.d.)

[33] (Whole Life Insurance Policy, n.d.)

[34] (Ramsey, The Total Money Makeover: Classic Edition: A Proven Plan for Financial Fitness, 2013)

35 (Robert Kiyosaki, Rich Dad Poor Dad, 1997)

[36] (Pollack, 2017)

[37] (Dubner, Everything You Always Wanted to Know About Money (But Were Afraid to Ask) (Rebroadcast), 2018)

[38] (Dubner, Everything You Always Wanted to Know About Money (But Were Afraid to Ask) (Rebroadcast), 2018)

[39] (Dubner, Everything You Always Wanted to Know About Money (But Were Afraid to Ask) (Rebroadcast), 2018)

[40] (Dubner, Everything You Always Wanted to Know About Money (But Were Afraid to Ask) (Rebroadcast), 2018)

[41] (Dubner, Everything You Always Wanted to Know About Money (But Were Afraid to Ask) (Rebroadcast), 2018)

[42] (Kiyosaki R. , Repeat After Me: Your House Is Not An Asset, 2016)

[43] (Kiyosaki R. , Repeat After Me: Your House Is Not An Asset, 2016)

[44] (Dubner, Everything You Always Wanted to Know About Money (But Were Afraid to Ask) (Rebroadcast), 2018)

[45] (Dubner, Everything You Always Wanted to Know About Money (But Were Afraid to Ask) (Rebroadcast), 2018)

[46] (Dubner, Everything You Always Wanted to Know About Money (But Were Afraid to Ask) (Rebroadcast), 2018)

[47] (Dubner, Everything You Always Wanted to Know About Money (But Were Afraid to Ask) (Rebroadcast), 2018)

[48] (Kiyosaki R. , Repeat After Me: Your House Is Not An Asset, 2016)

49 (How Many Times Does the Average Person Move in a Lifetime?, 2015)

50 See section Paying Yourself or the Agent? Showing the 4 years it takes pay down real estate commissions; or, about 18-24 months, at average rates of appreciation.

51 (How Many Times Does the Average Person Move in a Lifetime?, 2015)

52 (List of countries by home ownership rate, 2018)

53 (Top countries with the highest average wealth per adult in 2017 (in U.S. dollars), 2017)

[54] (Kiyosaki R. , How to Find Truth in an Age of Fake News & Fake Teachers - Ryan Holiday, 2018)

[55] (Ramsey, The Total Money Makeover: Classic Edition: A Proven Plan for Financial Fitness, 2013)

56 (Kathy Orton, 2018)

[57] (Reuters, 2018)

58 (John Burns, 2016)

59 Buy it Outright: $119,900 house versus $1,800 rent

60 See appendix:Some Examples Ultimate Rent vs. Buy

61 See appendix:Some Examples Ultimate Rent vs. Buy

62 $1,800 in rent, over 40 years, compared to buying at $119,900

63 $1,800 in rent, over 40 years, compared to buying at $119,900

64Appendix: $119,900 house versus $875/month rental

65 (Warren Buffett, 2018)

66 (Robert Kiyosaki, Rich Dad Poor Dad, 1997)

67 (Kiyosaki R. , Rich Dad Scam #6: Your House is an Asset, 2013)

68 (Bluejay, n.d.).

69 (Carlson, 2016)

70 (Hanlon, 2014)

71 (Tony Robbins, 2017)

72 (Matthews, 2016)

73 (HOUSEHOLD DEBT AND CREDIT REPORT (Q1 2018), 2018)

74 (Bluejay, The ULTIMATE Rent vs. Buy calculator, 2015)

75 (Hart Research Associates, 2013)

76 (Hart Research Associates, 2013)

77 (Hart Research Associates, 2013)

78 (Hart Research Associates, 2013)

[79] (Hart Research Associates, 2013)

[80] Homeownership By County

[81] (John Burns, 2016)

[82] (Hart Research Associates, 2013)

[83] (Homelessness in the United States, 2018)

[84] (Hart Research Associates, 2013)

[85] (Bluejay, The ULTIMATE Rent vs. Buy calculator, 2015)

[86] (Price-to-Rent Ratio, n.d.)

[87] (Price-to-Rent Ratio, n.d.)

[88] (Affordability Calculator, 2018)

[89] (Average Sales Price of Houses Sold for the United States (ASPUS), 2018)

[90] (Wong, 2016)

[91] (MIKE BOSTOCK, 2014)

[92] (Real Estate Investment Trust - REIT, 2018)

[93] (MIKE BOSTOCK, 2014)

94 (Bach, 2001)

95 (Elkins, 2018)

96 (Elkins, 2018)

97 (Survey of Consumer Finances, 2017)

98 (Survey of Consumer Finances, 2017)

99 (Survey of Consumer Finances, 2017)

100 (Survey of Consumer Finances, 2017)

101 (Survey of Consumer Finances, 2017)

102 (Survey of Consumer Finances, 2017)

103 (Elkins, 2018)

104 One must remember that many homeowners are also business owners (which contributes to their overall equity). And many of the top 10% of income earners (91.4% of the time are included as homeowners) will have other investments growing too, at much higher rates. Faster growth of those other investments may just be what is giving them the 7% edge and what skews rate of growth numbers in their favor.

105 (Survey of Consumer Finances, 2017)

106 (Survey of Consumer Finances, 2017)

107 (Gabler, 2016).

108 (Top countries with the highest average wealth per adult in 2017 (in U.S. dollars), 2017)

109 (List of countries by home ownership rate, 2018)

[110] (Jo Becker, 2008)

[111] (Jo Becker, 2008)

[112] (Jo Becker, 2008)

[113] (Jo Becker, 2008)

114 (Gershon, 2014)

115 (Gershon, 2014)

116 (Survey of Consumer Finances, 2017)

117 (Survey of Consumer Finances, 2017)

118 (Survey of Consumer Finances, 2017)

119 pg. 14 (Survey of Consumer Finances, 2017)

120 (Survey of Consumer Finances, 2017)

121 (Survey of Consumer Finances, 2017)

122 Pg. 18 (Survey of Consumer Finances, 2017)

[123] (Gabler, 2016)

124 Appendix: Base $10,000 plus $100/mo. 25 yrs at 9% earns $157,019 interest

125 (Santoli, 2017)

126 Todd Campbell, 2015.

127 (Dubner, 2017)

128 (Dubner, 2017)

[129] (Ramsey, The Total Money Makeover: Classic Edition: A Proven Plan for Financial Fitness, 2013)

130 (United States Home Prices & Values, 2018)

131 While there are two sides to that, seller's (3%) and buyer's (3%), outside of the first house, if you sell one house and buy another, you're going to be paying both sides. Maybe not on the same global value, but the details don't make too significant a difference.

132 New House Tax Payback

[133] (Kulp, 2018)

[134] (Ramsey, The Total Money Makeover: Classic Edition: A Proven Plan for Financial Fitness, 2013)

[135] (Ramsey, The Total Money Makeover: Classic Edition: A Proven Plan for Financial Fitness, 2013)

[136] (Dubner, Everything You Always Wanted to Know About Money (But Were Afraid to Ask) (Rebroadcast), 2018)

137 Page 25 (Survey of Consumer Finances, 2017)

138 Page 25 (Survey of Consumer Finances, 2017)

139 Page 18 (Survey of Consumer Finances, 2017)

140 (Kiyosaki R. , Rich Dad's CASHFLOW Quadrant: Rich Dad's Guide to Financial Freedom, 2011)

141 (Kiyosaki R. , Rich Dad's CASHFLOW Quadrant: Rich Dad's Guide to Financial Freedom, 2011)

142 (Survey of Consumer Finances, 2017)

143 Page 18 (Survey of Consumer Finances, 2017)

144 (maniaxzero, 2017)

[145] (Luisa Kroll and Kerry Dolan, 2018)

[146] (Sather, 2014)

147 (Clauson, 1926)

148 Tony Robbins, 2017

149 See Appendix: Value of Starting Early

[150] (Guillebeau, n.d.)

151 (Benjamin, 1986)

152 Compound Interest at Various Rates

153 (Average Sales Price of Houses Sold for the United States (ASPUS), 2018)

154 (Mortgage Calculator - full report, 2018)

155 Average of Median Rental, All Homes

156 (Tony Robbins, 2017)

157 (Robbins, 2014)

[158] (Average spend per child on toys worldwide in 2015, by country (in U.S. dollars), 2018)

159 (McCleary, n.d.)

160 (Historical Census of Housing Tables: Home Values, 2012)

[161] (How Fast The Markets Recover, n.d.)

[162] (Valetkevitch, Caroline, 2013)

[163] (Ramsey, The Total Money Makeover: Classic Edition: A Proven Plan for Financial Fitness, 2013)

164 (Historical Census of Housing Tables Home Values, 2002)

165 (Historical Census of Housing Tables Home Values, 2002)

166 (See appendix:

Straight Line Interest)

167 (See Appendix: Compounded Interest)

168 (Bluejay, n.d.)

[169] (MIKE BOSTOCK, 2014)

170 (See Appendix

$119,900 house versus $875/month rental)

171 (Bluejay, The ULTIMATE Rent vs. Buy calculator, 2015)

172 Rough Estimates from 2008/2009

173 (Bluejay, n.d.)

174 (See Appendix: Purchase @ $429,900 vs. Rent at 2,800/mo.)

175 (Bloomberg, 2017)

176 $357,700 Average New Home Sale Price Jan. 2017 up from $265,700 in Jan. 2012. (Median and Average Sales Prices of New Homes Sold in United States, 2018)

177 (Bluejay, The ULTIMATE Rent vs. Buy calculator, 2015)

178 (Bluejay, The ULTIMATE Rent vs. Buy calculator, 2015)

179 (Bluejay, Paying cash for a home?, n.d.).

180 (Ramsey, The Total Money Makeover: Classic Edition: A Proven Plan for Financial Fitness, 2013)

181 (Bluejay, Buying a home is an investment, n.d.)

182 (Bluejay, Buying a home is an investment, n.d.)

183 (Lightner, 2017)

184 (Olick, 2017)

185 (See Appendix: How Long Can You Wait?)

186 (Frost, 1916)

187 (Zillow Research- Data, 2018)

188 (List of countries by home ownership rate, 2018)

189 (Top countries with the highest average wealth per adult in 2017 (in U.S. dollars), 2017)

190 (Historical Census of Housing Tables Home Values, 2002)

About the Author

Eric Nies is an economist, author-speaker, and GenX advocate who was heavily influenced by his father's penchant for buying English Tudors. He grew up intending to stay in the solid Midwestern environment but life's path held something different. Over time and through experience, he became a "renter by choice."

Through his work, he exposes undertones of the macro-economy affecting the GenX situation and future, including drivers like secular stagnation and shifts in demographics, finances, and social behaviors.

Eric is the author of two books: *Rent Your Way To Freedom* and the soon-to-be-published *Bypassed: GenX's Vanishing American Dream.* He is recognized internationally for sharing "The BRAVE Principles" – which provide GenXers a path to stave off the brutal reality of the vanishing American Dream and reclaim the life they envisioned.

After earning an Economics degree, he found himself in the "rental only" housing market of Monte Carlo, Monaco – where he rented housing from the late billionaire Hélène Pallanca-Pastor.

Eric grew favorable to the freedom and flexibility afforded by renting. There was, however, an anchor: he was still chained (by the desire, indeed social conditioning) to own. So, he bought a house in his hometown, in fact, the house in which he was born – an English Tudor – from his father!

Growing concerned with the logic (or illogic) of his rental preference amid the litany of typical objections he'd hear from friends and family, he leaned on his Economics training and took to research – to better understand the issue, originally just for himself.

Is the American Dream inextricably linked to homeownership? And are people who are locked out of the housing market doomed? Eric's viewpoint, with data to back up the argument, suggests not. You can: *Rent Your Way to Freedom.*

www.ingramcontent.com/pod-product-compliance
Lightning Source LLC
Chambersburg PA
CBHW031923190326
41519CB00007B/393

* 9 7 8 1 7 3 2 1 0 5 7 1 3 *